A Year with Timothy Keller

Also by Timothy Keller

A Year with Timothy Keller

Daily devotions from his best-loved books

Timothy Keller

HODDER

This devotional collection first published in Great
Britain in 2023 by Hodder & Stoughton
An Hachette UK Company

Published in association with Abner Stein and McCormick Literary
This paperback edition published 2024

I

A CIP catalogue record for this title is available from the British Library

Paperback ISBN 978 1 399 81454 6
Hardback ISBN 978 1 399 81452 2
ebook ISBN 978 1 399 81455 3

Typeset in Bembo by Hewer Text UK Ltd, Edinburgh
Printed and bound in Great Britain by Clays Ltd, Elcograf S.p.A.

Hodder & Stoughton policy is to use papers that are natural, renewable
and recyclable products and made from wood grown in sustainable
forests. The logging and manufacturing processes are expected to
conform to the environmental regulations of the country of origin.

Hodder & Stoughton Ltd
Carmelite House
50 Victoria Embankment
London EC4Y 0DZ

www.hodderfaith.com

Acknowledging, with deep gratitude, all we have learned from our British fathers in the faith: C. S. Lewis, J. R. R. Tolkien, Martyn Lloyd-Jones, Charles Spurgeon, George Whitefield, Robert Murray M'Cheyne, John Owen, Samuel Rutherford, Thomas Brooks, J. I. Packer, John Stott, Dick Lucas, and others I have forgotten to name.

Kathy Keller

Creation and Shalom

God saw all that he had made, and it was very good.

Genesis 1:31

In most ancient creation accounts, creation is the by-product of some kind of warfare or other act of violence. Virtually never is the creation deliberate and planned. Secular scientific accounts of the origin of things are, interestingly, almost identical to the older pagan ones. The physical shape of the world as well as the biological life is the product of violent forces.

Unique among the creation accounts, the Bible depicts a world that is brimming with dynamic, abundant forms of life that are perfectly interwoven, interdependent and mutually enhancing and enriching. The Creator's response to this is delight. He keeps repeating that it is all *good*. When he creates human beings, he instructs them to continue to cultivate and draw out the vast resources of creation like a gardener does in a garden. 'Go keep this going,' the Creator seems to be saying in Genesis 1:28, 'Have a ball!'[1]

The Hebrew word for this perfect, harmonious interdependence among all parts of creation is called *shalom*. We translate it as 'peace,' but the English word is basically negative, referring to the absence of trouble or hostility. The Hebrew word means much more than that. It means absolute wholeness—full, harmonious, joyful, flourishing life.

The Reason for God

The fall and loss of Shalom

[. . .] sin entered the world through one man, and death through sin, and in this way death came to all people, because all sinned.

Romans 5:12

The devastating loss of *shalom* through sin is described in Genesis 3. We are told that as soon as we determined to serve ourselves instead of God—as soon as we abandoned living for and enjoying God as our highest good—the entire created world became broken. Human beings are so integral to the fabric of things that when human beings turned from God the entire warp and woof of the world unraveled. Disease, genetic disorders, famine, natural disasters, ageing and death itself are as much the result of sin as are oppression, war, crime and violence. We have lost God's *shalom*—physically, spiritually, socially, psychologically, culturally. Things now fall apart. In Romans 8, Paul says that the entire world is now 'in bondage to decay' and 'subjected to frustration' and will not be put right until we are put right.

[. . .] Sin is not simply doing bad things; it is putting good things in the place of God. So the only solution is not simply to change our behavior, but to reorient and center the entire heart and life on God.

The Reason for God

Jesus died for you

*But God demonstrates his own love for us in this: while we were still
sinners, Christ died for us.*

Romans 5:8

Remember this—if you don't live for Jesus you will live for
something else. If you live for your career and you don't do
well it may punish you all of your life, and you will feel like a
failure. If you live for your children and they don't turn out all
right you could be absolutely in torment because you feel worth-
less as a person.

If Jesus is your center and Lord and you fail him, he will forgive
you. Your career can't die for your sins. You might say, 'If I were a
Christian I'd be going around pursued by guilt all the time!' But
we *all* are being pursued by guilt because we must have an identity
and there must be *some* standard to live up to by which we get that
identity. Whatever you base your life on—you have to live up to
that. Jesus is the one Lord you can live for who died for you—who
breathed his last breath for you.

The Reason for God

Avoiding Jesus through religion

Therefore no one will be declared righteous in God's sight by the works of the law; rather, through the law we become conscious of our sin.

Romans 3:20

Sin and evil are self-centeredness and pride that lead to oppression against others, but there are two forms of this. One form is being very bad and breaking all the rules, and the other form is being very good and keeping all the rules and becoming self-righteous. There are two ways to be your own Savior and Lord. The first is by saying, 'I am going to live my life the way *I* want.' The second is described by Flannery O'Connor, who wrote about one of her characters, Hazel Motes, that 'he knew that the best way to avoid Jesus was to avoid sin'.[2] If you are avoiding sin and living morally so that God will have to bless and save you, then, ironically, you may be looking to Jesus as a teacher, model and helper but you are avoiding him as Savior. You are trusting in your own goodness rather than in Jesus for your standing with God. You are trying to save yourself by following Jesus.

That, ironically, is a rejection of the gospel of Jesus. It is a Christianised form of religion. It is possible to avoid Jesus as Savior as much by keeping all the biblical rules as by breaking them. [...] You need a complete transformation of the very motives of your heart.

The Reason for God

The difference of Grace

For it is by grace you have been saved, through faith—and this is not from yourselves, it is the gift of God—not by works, so that no one can boast.

Ephesians 2:8–9

There is, then, a great gulf between the understanding that God accepts us because of our efforts and the understanding that God accepts us because of what Jesus has done. Religion operates on the principle 'I obey—therefore I am accepted by God.' But the operating principle of the gospel is 'I am accepted by God through what Christ has done—therefore I obey.' Two people living their lives on the basis of these two different principles may sit next to each other in the church pew. They both pray, give money generously and are loyal and faithful to their family and church, trying to live decent lives. However, they do so out of two radically different motivations, in two radically different spiritual identities, and the result is two radically different kinds of lives.

The primary difference is that of motivation. In religion, we try to obey the divine standards out of fear. We believe that if we don't obey we are going to lose God's blessing in this world and the next. In the gospel, the motivation is one of gratitude for the blessing we have already received because of Christ. While the moralist is forced into obedience, motivated by fear of rejection, a Christian rushes into obedience, motivated by a desire to please and resemble the one who gave his life for us.

The Reason for God

The freedom of self-forgetfulness

I have been crucified with Christ and I no longer live, but Christ lives in me. The life I now live in the body, I live by faith in the Son of God, who loved me and gave himself for me.

Galatians 2:20

When my own personal grasp of the gospel was very weak, my self-view swung wildly between two poles. When I was performing up to my standards—in academic work, professional achievement or relationships—I felt confident but not humble. I was likely to be proud and unsympathetic to failing people. When I was not living up to standards, I felt humble but not confident, a failure. I discovered, however, that the gospel contained the resources to build a unique identity. In Christ I could know I was accepted by grace not only despite my flaws, but because I was willing to admit them.

The Christian gospel is that I am so flawed that Jesus had to die for me, yet I am so loved and valued that Jesus was glad to die for me. This leads to deep humility and deep confidence at the same time. It undermines both swaggering and snivelling. I cannot feel superior to anyone, and yet I have nothing to prove to anyone. I do not think more of myself nor less of myself. Instead, I think of myself less. I don't need to notice myself—how I'm doing, how I'm being regarded—so often.

The Reason for God

The forgiveness of God

The law requires that nearly everything be cleansed with blood, and without the shedding of blood there is no forgiveness.

Hebrews 9:22

'Why did Jesus have to die? Couldn't God just forgive us?' This is what many ask, but [...] no one 'just' forgives, if the evil is serious. Forgiveness means bearing the cost instead of making the wrongdoer do it, so you can reach out in love to seek your enemy's renewal and change. Forgiveness means absorbing the debt of the sin yourself. Everyone who forgives great evil goes through a death into resurrection, and experiences nails, blood, sweat and tears.

Should it surprise us, then, that when God determined to forgive us rather than punish us for all the ways we have wronged him and one another, that he went to the cross in the person of Jesus Christ and died there? As Bonhoeffer says, everyone who forgives someone bears the other's sins. On the cross we see God doing visibly and cosmically what every human being must do to forgive someone, though on an infinitely greater scale. I would argue, of course, that human forgiveness works this way because we unavoidably reflect the image of our Creator. That is why we should not be surprised that if *we* sense that the only way to triumph over evil is to go through the suffering of forgiveness, that this would be far more true of God, whose just passion to defeat evil and loving desire to forgive others are both infinitely greater than ours.

The Reason for God

The divine dance

After Jesus said this, he looked toward heaven and prayed: 'Father, the hour has come. Glorify your Son, that your Son may glorify you.'

John 17:1

Christianity, alone among the world faiths, teaches that God is triune. The doctrine of the Trinity is that God is one being who exists eternally in three persons: Father, Son and Holy Spirit. The Trinity means that God is, in essence, relational.

The Gospel writer John describes the Son as living from all eternity in the 'bosom of the Father' (John 1:18, NKJV), an ancient metaphor for love and intimacy. Later in John's Gospel, Jesus, the Son, describes the Spirit as living to 'glorify' him (John 16:14). In turn, the Son glorifies the Father (17:4) and the Father, the Son (17:5). This has been going on for all eternity (17:5b).

[...] What does it mean, then, that the Father, Son and Holy Spirit glorify one another? If we think of it graphically, we could say that self-centeredness is to be stationary, static. In self-centeredness we demand that others orbit around us. We will do things and give affection to others, as long as it helps us meet our personal goals and fulfills us.

The inner life of the triune God, however, is utterly different. The life of the Trinity is characterized not by self-centeredness but by mutually self-giving love.

The Reason for God

Joining creation's dance

'What no eye has seen, what no ear has heard, and what no human mind has conceived'—the things God has prepared for those who love him—these are the things God has revealed to us by his Spirit.

1 Corinthians 2:9–10

God did not create us to get the cosmic, infinite joy of mutual love and glorification, but to share it. We were made to join in the dance. If we will center our lives on him, serving him not out of self-interest, but just for the sake of who he is, for the sake of his beauty and glory, we will enter the dance and share in the joy and love he lives in. We were designed, then, not just for belief in God in some general way, nor for a vague kind of inspiration or spirituality. We were made to center our lives upon him, to make the purpose and passion of our lives knowing, serving, delighting and resembling him. This growth in happiness will go on eternally, increasing unimaginably (1 Cor. 2:7–10).

This leads to a uniquely positive view of the material world. The world is not, as other creation accounts would have it, an illusion, the result of a battle among the gods, nor the accidental outcome of natural forces. It was made in joy and therefore is good in and of itself. The universe is understood as a dance of beings united by energies binding yet distinct, like planets orbiting stars, like tides and seasons, 'like atoms in a molecule, like the tones in a chord, like the living organisms on this earth, like the mother with the baby stirring in her body.'³ The love of the inner life of the Trinity is written all through it. Creation is a dance!

The Reason for God

Deeds of justice and service

Learn to do right; seek justice. Defend the oppressed. Take up the cause of the fatherless; plead the case of the widow.

Isaiah 1:17

The story of the gospel makes sense of moral obligation and our belief in the reality of justice, so Christians do restorative and redistributive justice wherever they can. The story of the gospel makes sense of our indelible religiousness, so Christians do evangelism, pointing the way to forgiveness and reconciliation with God through Jesus. The gospel makes sense of our profoundly relational character, so Christians work sacrificially to strengthen human communities around them as well as the Christian community, the church. The gospel story also makes sense of our delight in the presence of beauty, so Christians become stewards of the material world, from those who cultivate the natural creation through science and gardening to those who give themselves to artistic endeavours, all knowing why these things are necessary for human flourishing. The skies and trees 'sing' of the glory of God, and by caring for them and celebrating them we free their voices to praise him and delight us. In short, the Christian life means not only building up the Christian community through encouraging people to faith in Christ, but building up the human community through deeds of justice and service.

Christians, then, are the true 'revolutionaries' who work for justice and truth, and we labor in expectation of a perfect world in which:

He will wipe every tear from their eyes. There will be no more death or mourning or crying or pain, for the old order of things has passed away.

Revelation 21:4

The Reason for God

Grace makes us servants

'Whoever wants to become great among you must be your servant, and whoever wants to be first must be slave of all.'

Mark 10:43–4

Jesus conducts a major critique of religion. His famous Sermon on the Mount (Matthew chapters 5, 6 and 7) does not criticize irreligious people, but rather religious ones. In his famous discourse the people he criticizes pray, give to the poor, and seek to live according to the Bible, but they do so in order to get acclaim and power for themselves. They believe they will get leverage over others and even over God because of their spiritual performance ('They think they will be heard because of their many words'—Matt. 6:7). This makes them judgmental and condemning, quick to give criticism, and unwilling to take it. They are fanatics.

[. . .] The God of Jesus and the prophets, however, saves completely by grace. He cannot be manipulated by religious and moral performance—he can only be reached through repentance, through the *giving up* of power. If we are saved by sheer grace we can only become grateful, willing servants of God and of everyone around us.

The Reason for God

God of love and justice

The LORD is righteous in all his ways and faithful in all he does . . . The
LORD watches over all who love him, but all the wicked he will destroy.

Psalm 145:17, 20

In Christianity God is both a God of love and of justice. Many people struggle with this. They believe that a loving God can't be a judging God. Like most other Christian ministers in our society, I have been asked literally thousands of times, 'How can a God of love be also a God filled with wrath and anger? If he is loving and perfect, he should forgive and accept everyone. He shouldn't get angry.'

I always start my response by pointing out that all loving people are sometimes filled with wrath, not just despite of but because of their love. If you love a person and you see someone ruining them—even they themselves—you get angry. As Becky Pippert puts it in her book *Hope Has Its Reasons*:

Think how we feel when we see someone we love ravaged by unwise actions or
relationships. Do we respond with benign tolerance as we might toward stran-
gers? Far from it . . . Anger isn't the opposite of love. Hate is, and the final form
of hate is indifference . . . God's wrath is not a cranky explosion, but his settled
opposition to the cancer . . . which is eating out the insides of the human race he
loves with his whole being.[4]

The Bible says that God's wrath flows from his love and delight in his creation. He is angry at evil and injustice because it is destroying its peace and integrity.

The Reason for God

Miracles lead to worship

You are the God who performs miracles; you display your power among the peoples.

Psalm 77:14

Miracles are hard to believe in, and they should be. In Matthew 28 we are told that the apostles met the risen Jesus on a mountainside in Galilee. 'When they saw him, they worshipped him; but some doubted' (verse 17). That is a remarkable admission. Here is the author of an early Christian document telling us that some of the founders of Christianity couldn't believe the miracle of the resurrection, even when they were looking straight at him with their eyes and touching him with their hands. There is no other reason for this to be in the account unless it really happened.

The passage shows us several things. It is a warning not to think that only we modern, scientific people have to struggle with the idea of the miraculous, while ancient, more primitive people did not. The apostles responded like any group of modern people—some believed their eyes and some didn't. It is also an encouragement to patience. All the apostles ended up as great leaders in the church, but some had a lot more trouble believing than others.

The most instructive thing about this text is, however, what it says about the purpose of biblical miracles. They lead not simply to cognitive belief, but to *worship*, to awe and wonder.

The Reason for God

Two sons

Now the tax collectors and sinners were all gathering round to hear Jesus. But the Pharisees and the teachers of the law muttered, 'This man welcomes sinners, and eats with them.' Then Jesus told them this parable . . .

Luke 15:1–3

Jesus' story might best be named the Parable of the Two Lost Sons. It is a drama in two acts, with Act 1 entitled 'The Lost Younger Brother' and Act 2 'The Lost Elder Brother.'

Act 1 begins with a short but shocking request. The younger son comes to the father and says, 'Give me my share of the estate.' The original listeners would have been amazed by such a request. [. . .] Here the younger son asks for his inheritance *now*, which was a sign of deep disrespect. To ask this while the father still lived was the same as to wish him dead. [. . .]

This younger brother, then, is asking his father to tear his life apart. And the father does so, for the love of his son. Most of Jesus' listeners would have never seen a Middle Eastern patriarch respond like this. The father patiently endures a tremendous loss of honor as well as the pain of rejected love. Ordinarily when our love is rejected we get angry, retaliate, and do what we can to diminish our affection for the rejecting person, so we won't hurt so much. But this father maintains his affection for his son and bears the agony.

The Prodigal God

Two kinds of people

Jesus continued, 'There was a man who had two sons . . .'

Luke 15:11

Most readings of this parable have concentrated on the flight and return of the younger brother—the 'Prodigal Son.' That misses the real message of the story, however, because there are two brothers, each of whom represents a different way to be alienated from God, and a different way to seek acceptance into the kingdom of heaven.

[...] The targets of this story are not 'wayward sinners' but religious people who do everything the Bible requires. Jesus is pleading not so much with immoral outsiders as with moral insiders. He wants to show them their blindness, narrowness, and self-righteousness, and how these things are destroying both their own souls and the lives of the people around them. It is a mistake, then, to think that Jesus tells this story primarily to assure younger brothers of his unconditional love.

No, the original listeners were not melted into tears by this story but rather they were thunderstruck, offended, and infuriated. Jesus' purpose is not to warm our hearts but to shatter our categories. Through this parable Jesus challenges what nearly everyone has ever thought about God, sin, and salvation. His story reveals the destructive self-centeredness of the younger brother, but it also condemns the elder brother's moralistic life in the strongest terms. Jesus is saying that both the irreligious and the religious are spiritually lost, both life-paths are dead ends, and that every thought the human race has had about how to connect to God has been wrong.

The Prodigal God

The younger brother's plan

Not long after that, the younger son got together all he had, set off for a distant country and there squandered his wealth in wild living. After he had spent everything, there was a severe famine in that whole country, and he began to be in need. So he went and hired himself out to a citizen of that country, who sent him to his fields to feed pigs.

Luke 15:13–15

The son goes off to 'a distant country' and squanders everything he has through an out-of-control lifestyle. When he is literally down in the mud with the pigs, he 'comes to his senses' and devises a plan. First, he says to himself, he will return to his father and admit that he was wrong and that he has forfeited the right to be his son. But second, he intends to ask his father to 'make me like one of your hired servants'.

[. . .] The younger son comes within sight of the house. His father sees him and runs—*runs* to him! As a general rule, distinguished Middle Eastern patriarchs did not run. Children might run; women might run; young men might run. But not the paterfamilias, the dignified pillar of the community, the owner of the great estate. He would not pick up his robes and bare his legs like some boy. But this father does. He runs to his son and, showing his emotions openly, falls upon him and kisses him.

The Prodigal God

The father's welcome

'But the father said to his servants, "Quick! Bring the best robe and put it on him. Put a ring on his finger and sandals on his feet. Bring the fattened calf and kill it. Let's have a feast and celebrate. For this son of mine was dead and is alive again; he was lost and is found." So they began to celebrate.'

Luke 15:22–3

What a scene! The father has yet to deal with the much more complicated and poisonous spiritual condition of the elder brother in Act 2. But Act 1 already challenges the mindset of elder brothers with a startling message: God's love and forgiveness can pardon and restore any and every kind of sin or wrongdoing. It doesn't matter who you are or what you've done. It doesn't matter if you've deliberately oppressed or even murdered people, or how much you've abused yourself. The younger brother knew that in his father's house there was abundant 'food to spare,' but he also discovered that there was grace to spare. There is no evil that the father's love cannot pardon and cover, there is no sin that is a match for his grace.

Act 1, then, demonstrates the lavish prodigality of God's grace. Jesus shows the father pouncing on his son in love not only before he has a chance to clean up his life and evidence a change of heart, but even before he can recite his repentance speech. Nothing, not even abject contrition, merits the favor of God. The Father's love and acceptance are absolutely free.

The Prodigal God

The elder brother's anger

'Meanwhile, the elder son was in the field. When he came near the house, he heard music and dancing. So he called one of the servants and asked him what was going on . . . The older brother became angry and refused to go in. So his father went out and pleaded with him.'

Luke 15:25–6, 28

Finally we come to the denouement. How will the father respond to his older son's open rebellion? What will he do? A man of his time and place might have disowned his son on the spot. Instead, he responds again with amazing tenderness. 'My son,' he begins, 'despite how you've insulted me publicly, I still want you in the feast. I am not going to disown your brother, but I don't want to disown you, either. I challenge you to swallow your pride and come into the feast. The choice is yours. Will you, or will you not?' It is an unexpectedly gracious, dramatic appeal.

The listeners are on the edge of their seats. Will the family finally be reunited in unity and love? Will the brothers be reconciled? Will the elder brother be softened by this remarkable offer and be reconciled to the father?

Just as all these thoughts pass through our mind, the story ends! Why doesn't Jesus finish the story and tell us what happened?! It is because the real audience for this story is the Pharisees, the elder brothers. Jesus is pleading with his enemies to respond to his message. What is that message? The answer to that question will emerge as we take time [. . .] to understand the main points Jesus is seeking to drive home here. In short, Jesus is redefining everything we thought we knew about connecting to God. He is redefining sin, what it means to be lost, and what it means to be saved.

The Prodigal God

Two ways to rebel

'But he answered his father, "Look! All these years I've been slaving for you and never disobeyed your orders. Yet you never gave me even a young goat so I could celebrate with my friends."'

Luke 15:29

What did the older son most want? If we think about it we realize that he wanted the same thing as his brother. He was just as resentful of the father as was the younger son. He, too, wanted the father's goods rather than the father himself. However, while the younger brother went far away, the elder brother stayed close and 'never disobeyed.' That was his way to get control. His unspoken demand is, 'I have never disobeyed you! Now you have to do things in my life the way I want them to be done.'

The hearts of the two brothers were the same. Both sons resented their father's authority and sought ways of getting out from under it. They each wanted to get into a position in which they could tell the father what to do. Each one, in other words, rebelled—but one did so by being very bad and the other by being extremely good. Both were alienated from the father's heart; both were lost sons.

[...] It's a shocking message: Careful obedience to God's law may serve as a strategy for rebelling against God.

The Prodigal God

Insecurity or joy?

'"My son," the father said, "you are always with me, and everything I have is yours."'

Luke 15:31

[A] sign of the elder-brother spirit is a lack of assurance of the father's love. The older son says, 'You never threw *me* a party.' There is no dancing or festiveness about the elder brother's relationship with his father. As long as you are trying to earn your salvation by controlling God through goodness, you will never be sure you have been good enough for him. You simply aren't sure God loves and delights in you.

[...] perhaps the clearest symptom of this lack of assurance is a dry prayer life. Though elder brothers may be diligent in prayer, there is no wonder, awe, intimacy, or delight in their conversations with God. Think of three kinds of people—a business associate you don't really like, a friend you enjoy doing things with, and someone you are in love with, and who is in love with you. Your conversations with the business associate will be quite goal-oriented. You won't be interested in chitchat. With your friend you may open your heart about some of the problems you are having. But with your lover you will sense a strong impulse to speak about what you find beautiful about him or her.

The Prodigal God

God's initiating love

There is no fear in love. But perfect love drives out fear, because fear has to do with punishment. The one who fears is not made perfect in love. We love because he first loved us.

1 John 4:18–19

What do we need to escape the shackles of our particular brand of lostness, whether it be younger-brother or elder-brother? How can the inner dynamic of the heart be changed from one of fear and anger to one of joy, love, and gratitude?

The first thing we need is God's initiating love. Notice how the father comes out to each son and expresses love to him, in order to bring him in. He does not wait for his younger son on the porch of his home, impatiently tapping his foot, murmuring, 'Here comes that son of mine. After all he's done, there had better be some real groveling!' There's not a hint of such an attitude. No, he runs and kisses him before his son can confess. It's not the repentance that causes the father's love, but rather the reverse. The father's lavish affection makes the son's expression of remorse far easier.

The father also goes out to the angry, resentful elder brother, begging him to come into the feast. This picture is like a double-edged sword. It shows that even the most religious and moral people need the initiating grace of God, that they are just as lost; and it shows there is hope, yes, even for Pharisees.

The Prodigal God

The true elder brother

In him we have redemption through his blood, the forgiveness of sins, in accordance with the riches of God's grace.

Ephesians 1:7

By putting a flawed elder brother in the story, Jesus is inviting us to imagine and yearn for a true one.

And we have him. Think of the kind of brother we need. We need one who does not just go to the next country to find us but who will come all the way from heaven to earth. We need one who is willing to pay not just a finite amount of money, but, at the infinite cost of his own life to bring us into God's family, for our debt is so much greater. Either as elder brothers or as younger brothers we have rebelled against the father. We deserve alienation, isolation, and rejection. The point of the parable is that forgiveness always involves a price—someone has to pay. There was no way for the younger brother to return to the family unless the older brother bore the cost himself. Our true elder brother paid our debt, on the cross, in our place.

There Jesus was stripped naked of his robe and dignity so that we could be clothed with a dignity and standing we don't deserve. On the cross Jesus was treated as an outcast so that we could be brought into God's family freely by grace. There Jesus drank the cup of eternal justice so that we might have the cup of the Father's joy. There was no other way for the heavenly Father to bring us in, except at the expense of our true elder brother.

The Prodigal God

Our longing for home

So the LORD God banished him from the Garden of Eden to work the ground from which he had been taken.

Genesis 3:23

It is important to read Jesus' parable of the lost son in the context of the whole of Luke, chapter 15, but the story has an even larger context. If we read the narrative in light of the Bible's sweeping theme of exile and homecoming we will understand that Jesus has given us more than a moving account of individual redemption. He has retold the story of the whole human race, and promised nothing less than hope for the world.

In Jesus' parable the younger brother goes off into a distant country expecting a better life but is disappointed. He begins to long for home, remembering the food in his father's house. So do we all.

[...] In the beginning of the book of Genesis we learn the reason why all people feel like exiles, like we aren't really home. We are told there that we were created to live in the garden of God.

However, the Bible teaches that, as in Jesus' parable, God was the 'father' of that home and we chafed under his authority. We wanted to live without God's interference, and so we turned away, and became alienated from him, and lost our home for the same reason the younger brother lost his. The result was exile.

The Bible says that we have been wandering as spiritual exiles ever since. That is, we have been living in a world that no longer fits our deepest longings.

The Prodigal God

The feast at the end of history

Be strong, do not fear; your God will come [. . .] he will come to save you. Then will the eyes of the blind be opened and the ears of the deaf unstopped. Then will the lame leap like a deer, and the mute tongue shout for joy. Water will gush forth in the wilderness and streams in the desert.

Isaiah 35:4–6

At the end of the story of the prodigal sons, there is a feast of homecoming. So too at the end of the book of Revelation, at the end of history, there is a feast, the 'wedding supper of the Lamb' (Rev. 19). The Lamb is Jesus, who was sacrificed for the sins of the world so that we could be pardoned and brought home. This feast happens in the New Jerusalem, the City of God that comes down out of heaven to fill the earth (Rev. 21). We are told that the very presence of God is in this city, and so is, remarkably, the tree of life, whose leaves now effect 'the healing of the nations' (Rev. 22:2). The tree of life, of course, was in the Garden of Eden. At the end of history the whole earth has become the Garden of God again. Death and decay and suffering are gone. The nations are no longer at war.

[. . .] Jesus will make the world our perfect home again. We will no longer be living 'east of Eden,' always wandering and never arriving. We will come, and the father will meet us and embrace us, and we will be brought into the feast.

The Prodigal God

Experiencing the feast

You make known to me the path of life; you will fill me with joy in your presence, with eternal pleasures at your right hand.

Psalm 16:11

Jesus' salvation is a feast, and therefore when we believe in and rest in his work for us, through the Holy Spirit he becomes real to our hearts. His love is like honey, or like wine. Rather than only believing that he is loving, we can come to sense the reality, the beauty, and the power of his love. His love can become more real to you than the love of anyone else. It can delight, galvanize, and console you. That will lift you up and free you from fear like nothing else.

This makes all the difference. If you are filled with shame and guilt, you do not merely need to believe in the abstract concept of God's mercy. You must sense, on the palate of the heart, as it were, the sweetness of his mercy. Then you will know you are accepted. If you are filled with worry and anxiety, you do not only need to believe that God is in control of history. You must see, with eyes of the heart, his dazzling majesty. Then you will know he has things in hand.

Is it really possible to have this kind of experience? [... Jesus offers us] access to the presence of the Father. It is only a foretaste now, and it waxes and wanes over the years as we pray and seek his face with the help of the Spirit. But it is available. The hymn writer Isaac Watts speaks of it in these lines: 'The hill of Zion yields a thousand sacred sweets *before* we reach the heavenly fields or walk the golden streets.'

The Prodigal God

Not just the ABCs, but the A to Z

What shall we say, then? Shall we go on sinning so that grace may increase? By no means! We are those who have died to sin; how can we live in it any longer?

Romans 6:1–2

The gospel is therefore not just the ABCs of the Christian life, but the A to Z of the Christian life. Our problems arise largely because we don't continually return to the gospel to work it in and live it out. That is why Martin Luther wrote, 'The truth of the Gospel is the principal article of all Christian doctrine ... Most necessary is it that we know this article well, teach it to others, and beat it into their heads continually.'[5]

'Wait,' I have heard people object. 'You mean that in order to grow in Christ, you keep telling yourself how graciously loved and accepted you are? That doesn't seem to be the best way to make progress. Maybe the motivation of religion was negative, but at least it was effective! You knew you had to obey God because if you didn't, he wouldn't answer your prayers or take you to heaven. But if you remove this fear and talk so much about free grace and unmerited acceptance—what incentive will you have to live a good life? It seems like this gospel way of living won't produce people who are as faithful and diligent to obey God's will without question.'

But if, when you have lost all fear of punishment you also have lost incentive to live an obedient life, then what was your motivation in the first place? It could only have been fear. What other incentive is there? Awed, grateful love.

The Prodigal God

You are not your own

You are not your own; you were bought at a price.

1 Corinthians 6:19–20

Some years ago I met a woman who began coming to Redeemer, the church where I am a minister. She said that she had gone to a church growing up and she had always heard that God accepts us only if we are sufficiently good and ethical. She had never heard the message she was now hearing, that we can be accepted by God by sheer grace through the work of Christ regardless of anything we do or have done. She said, 'That is a scary idea! Oh, it's good scary, but still scary.'

I was intrigued. I asked her what was so scary about unmerited free grace? She replied something like this: 'If I was saved by my good works—then there would be a limit to what God could ask of me or put me through. I would be like a taxpayer with rights. I would have done my duty and now I would deserve a certain quality of life. But if it is really true that I am a sinner saved by sheer grace—at God's infinite cost—then there's nothing he cannot ask of me.' She could see immediately that the wonderful-beyond-belief teaching of salvation by sheer grace had two edges to it. On the one hand it cut away slavish fear. God loves us freely, despite our flaws and failures. Yet she also knew that if Jesus really had done this for her—she was not her own. She was bought with a price.

The Prodigal God

Why justice matters

The scroll of the prophet Isaiah was handed to him. Unrolling it, he found the place where it is written: 'The Spirit of the Lord is on me, because he has anointed me to proclaim good news to the poor. He has sent me to proclaim freedom for the prisoners and recovery of sight for the blind, to set the oppressed free, to proclaim the year of the Lord's favour.'

Luke 4:17–19

These are the words Jesus read in the synagogue in Nazareth when he announced the beginning of his ministry. He identified himself as the 'Servant of the Lord,' prophesied by Isaiah, who would 'bring justice' to the world (Isa. 42:1–7). Most people know that Jesus came to bring forgiveness and grace. Less well known is the biblical teaching that a true experience of the grace of Jesus Christ inevitably motivates a man or woman to seek justice in the world.

[. . . T]here is a direct relationship between a person's grasp and experience of God's grace, and his or her heart for justice and the poor. [. . .] as I preached the classic message that God does *not* give us justice but saves us by free grace, I discovered that those most affected by the message became the most sensitive to the social inequities around them. One man in my church [. . .] went through a profound transformation. He moved out of a sterile, moralistic understanding of life and began to understand that his salvation was based on the free, unmerited grace of Jesus. It gave him a new warmth, joy, and confidence that everyone could see. But it had another surprising effect. 'You know,' he said to me one day, 'I've been a racist all my life.' I was startled, because I had not yet preached to him or to the congregation on that subject. He had put it together for himself. When he lost his Phariseeism, his spiritual self-righteousness, he said, he lost his racism.

Generous Justice

Justice is care for the vulnerable

And what does the LORD require of you? To act justly and to love mercy and to walk humbly with your God.

Micah 6:8

Micah 6:8 is a summary of how God wants us to live. To walk humbly with God is to know him intimately and to be attentive to what he desires and loves. And what does that consist of? The text says to 'do justice and love mercy,' which seem at first glance to be two different things, but they are not. The term for 'mercy' is the Hebrew word *chesedh*, God's unconditional grace and compassion. The word for 'justice' is the Hebrew term *mishpat*. In Micah 6:8, '*mishpat* puts the emphasis on the action, *chesedh* puts it on the attitude [or motive] behind the action.'[6] To walk with God, then, we must do justice, out of merciful love.

The word *mishpat* in its various forms occurs more than two hundred times in the Hebrew Old Testament. Its most basic meaning is to treat people equitably. So Leviticus 24:22 warns Israel to 'have the same *mishpat* ['rule of law'] for the foreigner and the native-born.' *Mishpat* means acquitting or punishing every person on the merits of the case, regardless of race or social status. Anyone who does the same wrong should be given the same penalty. But *mishpat* means more than just the punishment of wrongdoing. It also means to give people their rights. [...] So we read, 'Defend the rights of the poor and needy' (Prov. 31:9). *Mishpat,* then, is giving people what they are due, whether punishment or protection or care.

Generous Justice

Justice reflects the character of God

The LORD your God ... defends the cause [mishpat] of the fatherless and the widow, and loves the foreigner [immigrant], giving them food and clothing.

Deuteronomy 10:17–18

It is striking to see how often God is introduced as the defender of these vulnerable groups. Don't miss the significance of this. When people ask me, 'How do you want to be introduced?' I usually propose they say, 'This is Tim Keller, minister at Redeemer Presbyterian Church in New York City.' Of course I am many other things, but that is the main thing I spend my time doing in public life. Realize, then, how significant it is that the biblical writers introduce God as 'a father to the fatherless, a defender of widows' (Ps. 68:4–5). This is one of the main things he does in the world. He identifies with the powerless, he takes up their cause.

It is hard for us to understand how revolutionary this was in the ancient world. Sri Lankan scholar Vinoth Ramachandra calls this 'scandalous justice'. He writes that in virtually all the ancient cultures of the world, the power of the gods was channeled through and identified with the elites of society, the kings, priests, and military captains, not the outcasts. To oppose the leaders of society, then, was to oppose the gods. 'But here, in Israel's rival vision,' it is not high-ranking males but 'the orphan, the widow, and the stranger' with whom Yahweh takes his stand. His power is exercised in history for their empowerment.'[7] So, from ancient times, the God of the Bible stood out from the gods of all other religions as a God on the side of the powerless, and of justice for the poor.

Generous Justice

Justice is right relationships

I rescued the poor who cried for help, and the fatherless who had none to assist them. The one who was dying blessed me; I made the widow's heart sing. I put on righteousness [tzadeqah] as my clothing; justice [mishpat] was my robe and my turban. I was eyes to the blind and feet to the lame. I was a father to the needy; I took up the case of the stranger [immigrant]. I broke the fangs of the wicked and snatched the victims from their teeth.

Job 29:12–17

We must have a strong concern for the poor, but there is more to the biblical idea of justice than that. We get more insight when we consider a second Hebrew word that can be translated as 'being just,' though it usually translated as 'being righteous.' The word is *tzadeqah*, and it refers to a life of right relationships. Bible scholar Alec Motyer defines 'righteous' as those 'right with God and therefore committed to putting right all other relationships in life.'

This means, then, that biblical righteousness is inevitably 'social,' because it is about relationships. When most modern people see the word 'righteousness' in the Bible, they tend to think of it in terms of private morality, such as sexual chastity or diligence in prayer and Bible study. But in the Bible *tzadeqah* refers to day-to-day living in which a person conducts *all* relationships in family and society with fairness, generosity, and equity. It is not surprising, then, to discover that *tzadeqah* and *mishpat* are brought together scores of times in the Bible. [. . .] When these two words, *tzadeqah* and *mishpat*, are tied together, as they are over three dozen times, the English expression that best conveys the meaning is 'social justice.'

Generous Justice

Jesus and the vulnerable

Jesus replied, 'Go back and report to John what you hear and see: the blind receive sight, the lame walk, those who have leprosy are cleansed, the deaf hear, the dead are raised, and the good news is proclaimed to the poor.'

Matthew 11:4–5

Here is the same care for the vulnerable that characterizes the heart of God. While clearly Jesus was preaching the good news to all, he showed throughout his ministry the particular interest in the poor and the downtrodden that God has always had.

Jesus, in his incarnation, 'moved in' with the poor. He lived with, ate with, and associated with the socially ostracized (Matt. 9:13). He raised the son of the poor widow (Luke 7:11–16) and showed the greatest respect to the immoral woman who was a social outcast (Luke 7:36ff). Indeed, Jesus spoke with women in public, something that a man with any standing in society would not have done, but Jesus resisted the sexism of his day (John 4:27).[8] Jesus also refused to go along with the racism of his culture, making a hated Samaritan the hero of one of his most famous parables (Luke 10:26ff) and touching off a riot when he claimed that God loved Gentiles like the widow of Zarephath and Naaman the Syrian as much as Jews (Luke 4:25–7). Jesus showed special concern for children, despite his apostles' belief that they were not worth Jesus' time (Luke 18:15).

Generous Justice

Generous hospitality

Then Jesus said to his host, 'When you give a luncheon or dinner, do not invite your friends, your brothers or sisters, your relatives, or your rich neighbours; if you do, they may invite you back and so you will be repaid. But when you give a banquet, invite the poor, the crippled, the lame, the blind . . .

Luke 14:12–13

What was Jesus saying here? Later in this same chapter, Jesus tells his disciples that they must 'hate' their fathers and mothers if they are going to follow him (Luke 14:26). This sounds shocking to us, but it is a Semitic idiomatic expression. Jesus did not mean literally that we should hate our parents, since this would contradict his own teaching (Mark 7:9–13) and the Ten Commandments. Rather, the expression meant that your love and loyalty for Jesus should so exceed all other loyalties that they look like 'hate' by comparison. This way of speaking sheds light on Jesus' statement about banquets.

When Jesus said, 'don't invite your friends for dinner', he should not be taken literally, any more than when he said we should hate our father and our mother. Indeed, Jesus often ate meals in homes with his friends and peers. Rather—to put this in a more modern context—he is saying that we should spend *far* more of our money and wealth on the poor than we do on our own entertainment, or on vacations, or on eating out and socializing with important peers.

Generous Justice

33

Jesus' new community

*All the believers were together and had everything in common. They
sold property and possessions to give to anyone who had need.*

Acts 2:44–5

The early church responded to Jesus' calls for justice and mercy.
The apostle Paul viewed ministry to the poor as so important
that it was one of the last things he admonished the Ephesian
church to do before he left them for the last time. In his farewell
address, Paul was able to ground this duty in the teaching of Jesus.
'We must help the weak,' he said, 'remembering the words the
Lord Jesus himself said: "It is more blessed to give than to receive"'
(Acts 20:35). You don't use your 'last words' without saying something that is all-important to you. For Paul it was: 'Don't only
preach—help the poor.'

Though the church was no longer a nation-state like Israel, the
New Testament writers recognized the concern for justice and
mercy in the Mosaic legislation and applied it to the church
community in a variety of ways. Many Mosaic laws worked
toward diminishing the great gap that tends to grow between rich
and poor. From the law of 'Jubilee' (Lev. 25) to the rules for gathering manna in Exodus 16, the principle was to increase 'equality.'
When Paul wrote to the Corinthian church to ask for an offering
to relieve starving Christians in Palestine, he quoted Exodus 16:18
and then said, 'At the present time your plenty will supply what
they need, so that in turn their plenty will supply what you need.
The goal is equality' (2 Cor. 8:14).

Generous Justice

The secret of marriage

'A man shall leave his father and mother and be united to his wife, and the two will become one flesh.' This is a profound mystery . . .

Ephesians 5:31–2

I'm tired of listening to sentimental talks on marriage. At weddings, in church, and in Sunday school, much of what I've heard on the subject has as much depth as a Hallmark card. While marriage is many things, it is anything *but* sentimental. Marriage is glorious but hard. It's a burning joy and strength, and yet it is also blood, sweat, and tears, humbling defeats and exhausting victories. No marriage I know more than a few weeks old could be described as a fairy tale come true. Therefore, it is not surprising that the only phrase in Paul's famous discourse on marriage in Ephesians 5 that many couples can relate to is verse 32, printed above. Sometimes you fall into bed, after a long, hard day of trying to understand each other, and you can only sigh: 'This is all a profound mystery!' At times, your marriage seems to be an unsolvable puzzle, a maze in which you feel lost.

I believe all this, and yet there's no relationship between human beings that is greater or more important than marriage. In the Bible's account, God himself officiates at the first wedding (Gen. 2:22–5). And when the man sees the woman, he breaks into poetry and exclaims, 'At last!' Everything in the text proclaims that marriage, next to our relationship to God, is the most profound relationship there is. And that is why, like knowing God himself, coming to know and love your spouse is difficult and painful yet rewarding and wondrous.

The most painful, the most wonderful—this is the biblical understanding of marriage, and there has never been a more important time to lift it up and give it prominence in our culture.

The Meaning of Marriage

You never marry the right person

And over all these virtues put on love, which binds them all together in perfect unity.

Colossians 3:14

As a pastor I have spoken to thousands of couples, some working on marriage-seeking, some working on marriage-sustaining, and some working on marriage-saving. I've heard them say over and over, 'Love *shouldn't* be this hard; it should come naturally.' [...] The Christian answer to this is that *no* two people are compatible. Duke University ethics professor Stanley Hauerwas has famously made this point:

Destructive to marriage is the self-fulfillment ethic that assumes marriage and the family are primarily institutions of personal fulfillment, necessary for us to become 'whole' and happy. The assumption is that there is someone just right for us to marry and that if we look closely enough we will find the right person. This moral assumption overlooks a crucial aspect to marriage. It fails to appreciate the fact that we always marry the wrong person.

We never know whom we marry; we just think we do. Or even if we first marry the right person, just give it a while and he or she will change. For marriage, being [the enormous thing it is] means we are not the same person after we have entered it. The primary problem is ... learning how to love and care for the stranger to whom you find yourself married.[9]

[...] Marriage brings you into more intense proximity to another human being than any other relationship can. Therefore, the moment you marry someone, you and your spouse begin to change in profound ways, and you can't know ahead of time what those changes will be. So you don't know, you can't know, who your spouse will actually be in the future until you get there.

The Meaning of Marriage

Two sinners under one roof

*Bear with each other and forgive one another if any of you has a griev-
ance against someone. Forgive as the Lord forgave you.*

Colossians 3:13

Hauerwas gives us the first reason that no two people are
compatible for marriage—namely, that marriage profoundly
changes us. But there is another reason. Any two people who
enter into marriage are spiritually broken by sin, which among
other things means to be self-centered—living life *incurvatus in
se*.[10] As author Denis de Rougemont said, 'Why should neurotic,
selfish, immature people suddenly become angels when they fall
in love . . .?'[11]

That is why a good marriage is *more* painfully hard to achieve
than athletic or artistic prowess. Raw, natural talent does not
enable you to play baseball as a pro or write great literature without enduring discipline and enormous work. Why would it be
easy to live lovingly and well with another human being in light
of what is profoundly wrong within our human nature? Indeed,
many people who have mastered athletics and art have failed
miserably at marriage. So the biblical doctrine of sin explains why
marriage—more than anything else that is good and important in
this fallen world—is so painful and hard.

The Meaning of Marriage

The goodness of singleness

Are you unmarried? Do not look for a wife. But if you do marry, you have not sinned, and if a virgin marries, she has not sinned. But those who marry will face many troubles in this life, and I want to spare you this. What I mean . . . is that the time is short.

1 Corinthians 7:27–8 (NIV 1984)

Single people cannot live their lives well as singles without a balanced, informed view of marriage. If they do not have that, they will either over-desire or under-desire marriage, and either of those ways of thinking will distort their lives. [. . .]

This passage is very confusing on its surface. This view of marriage seems at profound variance with the exalted picture of marriage in Ephesians 5:21ff. Was Paul just having a bad day when he wrote this chapter? [. . .]

But Christianity's founder, Jesus Christ, and leading theologian, St. Paul, were both single their entire lives. Single adults cannot be seen as somehow less fully formed or realized human beings than married persons because Jesus Christ, a single man, was the perfect man (Heb. 4:15; 1 Pet. 2:22). Paul's assessment in 1 Corinthians 7 is that singleness is a good condition blessed by God, and in many circumstances, it is actually better than marriage. As a result of this revolutionary attitude, the early church did not pressure people to marry (as we see in Paul's letter) and institutionally supported poor widows so they did not have to remarry. [. . .]

Why did the early church have this attitude? The Christian gospel and hope of the future kingdom de-idolized marriage.

The Meaning of Marriage

Jacob's longing

Now Laban had two daughters; the name of the older was Leah, and the name of the younger was Rachel. Leah had weak eyes, but Rachel had a lovely figure and was beautiful. Jacob was in love with Rachel and said, 'I'll work for you seven years in return for your younger daughter Rachel.'

Genesis 29:16–18

The human longing for true love has always been celebrated in song and story, but in our contemporary culture it has been magnified to an astonishing degree. [...]

There is a story in the Bible that illustrates how the quest for love can become a form of slavery. It is the story of Jacob and Leah in Genesis 29, and while very ancient it has never been more relevant. It has always been possible to make romantic love and marriage into a counterfeit god, but we live in a culture that makes it even easier to mistake love for God, to be swept up by it, and to rest all our hopes for happiness upon it.

[...] Jacob's life was empty. He never had his father's love, he had lost his beloved mother's love, and he certainly had no sense of God's love and care. Then he beheld the most beautiful woman he had ever seen, and he must have said to himself, 'If I had her, finally, something would be right in my miserable life. If I had her, it would fix things.' All the longings of his heart for meaning and affirmation were fixed on Rachel.

Counterfeit Gods

The devastation of idolatry

When morning came, there was Leah! So Jacob said to Laban, 'What is this you have done to me? I served you for Rachel, didn't I? Why have you deceived me?'

Genesis 29:25

We may wonder how Jacob could have been so gullible, but Jacob's behavior was that of an addict. There are many ways that romantic love can function as a kind of drug to help us escape the reality of our lives. Sally, [a] beautiful woman who was trapped in abusive relationships, once said to me that 'men were my alcohol. Only if I was on a man's arm could I face life and feel good about myself.' Another example is the older man who abandons his spouse for a far younger woman, in a desperate effort to hide the reality that he is aging. Then there is the young man who finds a woman desirable only until she sleeps with him a couple of times, after which he loses interest in her. For him, women are simply a necessary commodity to help him feel desirable and powerful. Our fears and inner barrenness make love a narcotic, a way to medicate ourselves, and addicts always make foolish, destructive choices.

That is what had happened to Jacob. Rachel was not just his wife, but his 'savior.' He wanted and needed Rachel so profoundly that he heard and saw only the things he wanted to hear and see. That is why he became vulnerable to Laban's deception. Later, Jacob's idolatry of Rachel created decades of misery in his family. He adored and favored Rachel's sons over Leah's, spoiling and embittering the hearts of all his children, and poisoning the family system. We have a phrase to describe someone who has fallen in love: 'He worships the ground she walks on.' How destructive this can be when it is literally the case.

Counterfeit Gods

Leah's breakthrough

*When the LORD saw that Leah was not loved, he enabled her to
conceive [. . .] She conceived again, and when she gave birth to a son
she said, 'This time I will praise the LORD.'*

Genesis 29:31–5

L eah is the one person in this sad story to make some spiritual
progress, though this happens only at its very end. Look first
at what God does in her. One of the things Hebrew scholars
notice is that in all of Leah's statements, she was calling on *the Lord*.
She used the name *Yahweh*. 'The Lord [Yahweh] has seen my
misery,' she says in verse 32. How did she know about Yahweh?

Elohim was the generic Hebrew word for God. All cultures at
that time had some general idea of God or gods, but Yahweh was
the name of the God who had revealed himself to Abraham, and
later to Moses. He was the one who told Abraham that he would
bless the earth through his line. The only way Leah could have
known about *Yahweh* was if Jacob had told her about the promise
to his grandfather. So even though she was struggling and confused,
she was nonetheless reaching out to a personal God of grace.

After years of childbearing, however, there's a breakthrough.
When Leah gave birth to her last son, Judah, she said, '*This* time, I
will praise the LORD.' There was a defiance in that claim. It was a
different declaration from the ones she had made after the other
births. There was no mention of husband or child. It appears that
finally, she had taken her heart's deepest hopes off of her husband
and her children, and had put them on the Lord. Jacob and Laban
had stolen Leah's life, but when she gave her heart finally to the
Lord, she got her life back.

Counterfeit Gods

41

The true bridegroom

I am jealous for you with a godly jealousy. I promised you to one husband, to Christ, so that I might present you as a pure virgin to him.

2 Corinthians 11:2

We shouldn't just look at what God did in [Leah]. We have to also look at what God did *for* her. [... Her last] child was Judah, and in Genesis 49 we are told that it is through him that the true King, the Messiah, will someday come. God had come to the girl that nobody wanted, the unloved, and made *her* the ancestral mother of Jesus. Salvation came into the world, not through beautiful Rachel, but through the unwanted one, the unloved one. [...]

And here is the power to overcome our idolatries. There are many people in the world who have not found a romantic partner, and they need to hear the Lord say, 'I am the true Bridegroom. There is only one set of arms that will give you all your heart's desire, and await you at the end of time, if only you turn to me. And know that I love you now.'

However, it is not just those without spouses who need to see that God is our ultimate spouse, but those *with* spouses as well. They need this in order to save their marriage from the crushing weight of their divine expectations. If you marry someone expecting them to be like a god, it is only inevitable that they will disappoint you. It's not that you should try to love your spouse less, but rather that you should know and love God more. How can we know God's love so deeply that we release our lovers and spouses from our stifling expectations? By looking at the one to whom Leah's life points.

Counterfeit Gods

A great mystery

This is a profound mystery—but I am talking about Christ and the church.

Ephesians 5:32

Paul declared that marriage is a 'great mystery.' [...] We cannot discard it, as it is too important, but it overwhelms us. However, the Greek word Paul used, *mysterion*, has a lexical range that also includes the idea of a 'secret.' In the Bible, this word is used to mean not some esoteric knowledge known only to insiders but rather some wondrous, unlooked-for truth that God is revealing through his Spirit.[12] Elsewhere, Paul uses the term to refer to other revelations of God's saving purposes in the gospel. But in Ephesians 5 he applies this rich term, surprisingly, to marriage. In verse 31 he quotes the final verse of the Genesis account of the first marriage: 'A man shall leave his father and mother and be united to his wife, and the two will become one flesh.' Then he says, literally, that this is a *mega-mysterion* (verse 32)—an extraordinarily great, wonderful and profound truth that can be understood only with the help of God's Spirit.

But what *is* the secret of marriage? Paul immediately adds, 'I am talking about Christ and the church,' referring to what he said earlier in verse 25: 'Husbands, love your wives, just as Christ loved the church and gave himself up for her.' In short, the 'secret' is not simply the fact of marriage per se. It is the message that what husbands should do for their wives is what Jesus did to bring us into union with himself.

The Meaning of Marriage

He gave himself up for us

Husbands, love your wives, just as Christ loved the church and gave himself up for her to make her holy, cleansing her by the washing with water through the word . . .

Ephesians 5:25–6

Jesus *gave himself up* for us. Jesus the Son, though equal with the Father, gave up his glory and took on our human nature (Phil. 2:5ff). But further, he willingly went to the cross and paid the penalty for our sins, removing our guilt and condemnation, so that we could be united with him (Rom. 6:5) and take on his nature (2 Pet. 1:4). He gave up his glory and power and became a servant. He died to his own interests and looked to our needs and interests instead (Rom. 15:1–3). Jesus' sacrificial service to us has brought us into a deep union with him and he with us. And *that*, Paul says, is the key not only to understanding marriage but to living it. That is why he is able to tie the original statement about marriage in Genesis 2 to Jesus and the church. [. . .]

Here we have a powerful answer to the objection that marriage is inherently oppressive and therefore obsolete. In Philippians 2, Paul tells us that the Son of God did not exploit his equality with the Father, but his greatness was revealed in his willingness to become the Father's servant. He went to the cross, but the Father raised him from the dead.

The Meaning of Marriage

More than we dare to fear or hope

. . . to present her to himself as a radiant church, without stain or wrinkle or any other blemish, but holy and blameless.

Ephesians 5:27

The reason that marriage is so painful and yet wonderful is because it is a reflection of the gospel, which is painful and wonderful at once.

The gospel is this: We are more sinful and flawed in ourselves than we ever dared believe, yet at the very same time we are more loved and accepted in Jesus Christ than we ever dared hope.

This is the only kind of relationship that will really transform us. Love without truth is sentimentality; it supports and affirms us but keeps us in denial about our flaws. Truth without love is harshness; it gives us information but in such a way that we cannot really hear it. God's saving love in Christ, however, is marked by both radical truthfulness about who we are and yet also radical, unconditional commitment to us. The merciful commitment strengthens us to see the truth about ourselves and repent. The conviction and repentance move us to cling to and rest in God's mercy and grace.

The Meaning of Marriage

The heart is an idol factory

Those who trust in their riches will fall, but the righteous will thrive like a green leaf.

Proverbs 11:28

Money can become a spiritual addiction, and like all addictions it hides its true proportions from its victims. We take more and greater risks to get an ever-diminishing satisfaction from the thing we crave, until a breakdown occurs. When we begin to recover, we ask, 'What were we thinking? How could we have been so blind?' We wake up like people with a hangover who can hardly remember the night before. But why? Why did we act so irrationally? Why did we completely lose sight of what is right?

The Bible's answer is that the human heart is an 'idol factory.'

When most people think of 'idols' they have in mind literal statues—or the next pop star anointed by Simon Cowell. Yet while traditional idol worship still occurs in many places of the world, internal idol worship, within the heart, is universal. In Ezekiel 14:3, God says about the elders of Israel, 'These men have set up idols in their *hearts*.' Like us, the elders must have responded to this charge, 'Idols? What idols? I don't see any idols.' God was saying that the human heart takes good things like a successful career, love, material possessions, even family, and turns them into ultimate things. Our hearts deify them as the center of our lives, because, we think, they can give us significance and security, safety and fulfillment, if we attain them.

Counterfeit Gods

Anything can be an idol

Dear children, keep yourselves from idols.

1 John 5:21

Anything can be an idol, and everything has been an idol. The most famous moral code in the world is the Decalogue, the Ten Commandments. The very first commandment is 'I am the LORD your God . . . you shall have no other gods before me' (Exod. 20:3). That leads to the natural question— 'What do you mean, "other gods"?' An answer comes immediately. 'You shall not make for yourself an idol in the form of anything in heaven above or on the earth beneath or in the waters below. You shall not bow down to them or worship them . . .' (Exod. 20:4–5) That includes everything in the world! Most people know you can make a god out of money. Most know you can make a god out of sex. However, *any*thing in life can serve as an idol, a God-alternative, a counterfeit god.

[. . .] We think that idols are bad things, but that is almost never the case. The greater the good, the more likely we are to expect that it can satisfy our deepest needs and hopes. Anything can serve as a counterfeit god, especially the very best things in life.

Counterfeit Gods

The worst thing that can happen

Although they claimed to be wise, they became fools and exchanged the glory of the immortal God for images made to look like a mortal human being and birds and animals and reptiles.

Romans 1:22–3

Why is getting your heart's deepest desire so often a disaster? In the book of Romans, Saint Paul wrote that one of the worst things God can do to someone is to give 'them over in the sinful desires of their hearts' (Rom. 1:24). Why would the greatest punishment imaginable be to allow someone to achieve their fondest dream? It is because our hearts fashion these desires into idols. In that same chapter, Paul summarized the history of the human race in one sentence: 'They worshipped and served created things rather than the Creator' (Rom. 1:25). Every human being must live for something. Something must capture our imaginations, our heart's most fundamental allegiance and hope. But, the Bible tells us, without the intervention of the Holy Spirit, that object will never be God himself.

If we look to some created thing to give us the meaning, hope, and happiness that only God himself can give, it will eventually fail to deliver and break our hearts.

Two Jewish philosophers who knew the Scriptures intimately concluded: 'The central ... principle of the Bible [is] the rejection of idolatry.'[13] The Bible is therefore filled with story after story depicting the innumerable forms and devastating effects of idol worship. Every counterfeit god a heart can choose—whether love, money, success, or power—has a powerful biblical narrative that explains how that particular kind of idolatry works itself out in our lives.

Counterfeit Gods

The call of Abraham

The Lᴏʀᴅ had said to Abram, 'Go from your country, your people and your father's household to the land I will show you'

Genesis 12:1–3

According to the Bible, God came to Abraham and made him a staggering promise. If he would obey him faithfully, God would bless all the nations of the earth through him and his descendants. For this to happen, however, Abraham had to *go*. [...] He was asked to give up, for God's sake, nearly all the worldly hopes and things that a human heart desires.

[...] As the years turned into decades, however, the divine promise became more and more difficult to believe. Finally, after Abraham was over a hundred years old, and Sarah over the age of ninety (Gen. 17:17, 21:5), she gave birth to a son, Isaac. This was clearly divine intervention, and so Isaac's name meant 'laughter,' a reference to both his parents' joy and to their difficulty in believing that God would ever give them what he had promised. [...]

But the question now was—had he been waiting and sacrificing for God, or for the boy? Was God just a means to an end? To whom was Abraham ultimately giving his heart? Did Abraham have the peace, humility, boldness, and unmovable poise that come to those who trust in God rather than in circumstances, public opinion, or their own competence? Had he learned to trust God *alone*, to love God for himself, not just for what he could get out of God?

Counterfeit Gods

The ultimate test

*Then God said, 'Take your son, your only son, whom you love—Isaac—
and go to the region of Moriah. Sacrifice him there as a burnt offering
on a mountain I will show you.'*

Genesis 22:2

This was the ultimate test. Isaac was now *everything* to Abraham, as God's call makes clear. He does not refer to the boy as 'Isaac,' but as 'your son, your only son, whom you love.' Abraham's affection had become adoration. Previously, Abraham's meaning in life had been dependent on God's word. Now it was becoming dependent on Isaac's love and well-being. The center of Abraham's life was shifting. God was not saying you cannot love your son, but that you must not turn a loved one into a counterfeit god. If anyone puts a child in the place of the true God, it creates an idolatrous love that will smother the child and strangle the relationship.

[. . .] Abraham was not just exercising 'blind faith.' He was not saying, 'This is crazy, this is murder, but I'm going to do it anyway.' Instead he was saying, 'I know God is *both* holy *and* gracious. I don't know how he is going to be both—but I know he will.' If he had not believed that he was in debt to a holy God, he would have been too angry to go. But if he had not also believed that God was a God of grace, he would have been too crushed and hopeless to go. He would have just lain down and died. It was only because he knew God was both holy and loving that he was able to put one foot after another up that mountain.

Counterfeit Gods

The danger of the best things in the world

*When they reached the place God had told him about, Abraham built
an altar there and arranged the wood on it. He bound his son Isaac
and laid him on the altar on top of the wood. Then he reached out his
hand and took the knife to slay his son.*

Genesis 22:9–10

B ut at that very moment, the voice of God came to him from
heaven, 'Abraham! Abraham!'

'Here I am,' he replied from the precipice.

'Do not lay a hand on the boy … now I know that you fear
God, because you have not withheld from me your son, your only
son' (Verse 12). And at that moment Abraham saw a ram caught by
its horns in a thicket. Abraham untied Isaac and sacrificed it in
place of his son.

[…] In the end the Lord said to him, 'Now I know that you
fear God.' […] This doesn't mean that God was trying to find out
if Abraham loved him. The all-seeing God knows the state of
every heart. Rather, God was putting Abraham through the
furnace, so his love for God could finally 'come forth as pure gold.'
It is not hard to see why God was using Isaac as the means for this.
If God had not intervened, Abraham would have certainly come
to love his son more than anything in the world, if he did not
already do so. That would have been idolatry, and all idolatry is
destructive.

From this perspective we see that God's extremely rough treatment of Abraham was actually merciful. Isaac was a wonderful gift
to Abraham, but he was not safe to have and hold until Abraham
was willing to put God first.

Counterfeit Gods

The substitute

He who did not spare his own Son, but gave him up for us all—how will he not also, along with him, graciously give us all things?

Romans 8:32

Many years later, in those same mountains, another firstborn son was stretched out on the wood to die. But there on Mount Calvary, when the beloved son of God cried, 'My God, my God—why hast thou forsaken me?' there was no voice from heaven announcing deliverance. Instead, God the Father paid the price in silence. Why? The true substitute for Abraham's son was God's only Son, Jesus, who died to bear our punishment. [...]

God saw Abraham's sacrifice and said, 'Now I know that you love me, because you did not withhold your only son from me.' But how much more can we look at *his* sacrifice on the cross, and say to God, 'Now, *we* know that you love *us*. For you did not withhold your son, your only son, whom you love, from us.' When the magnitude of what he did dawns on us, it makes it possible finally to rest our hearts in him rather than in anything else.

Jesus alone makes sense of this story. The only way that God can be both 'just' (demanding payment of our debt of sin) *and* 'justifier' (providing salvation and grace) is because years later another Father went up another 'mount' called Calvary with his firstborn and offered him there for us all. You will never be as great, as secure in God, as courageous, as Abraham became simply by trying hard, but only by believing in the Savior to whom this event points. Only if Jesus lived and died for us can you have a God of infinite love and holiness at once.

Counterfeit Gods

The King arrives

The beginning of the good news about Jesus the Messiah, the Son of God, as it is written in Isaiah the prophet:

'I will send my messenger ahead of you, who will prepare your way'— 'a voice of one calling in the wilderness "Prepare the way for the Lord, make straight paths for him."'

And so John the Baptist appeared in the wilderness, preaching a baptism of repentance for the forgiveness of sins.

Mark 1:1–4

Mark wastes no time in establishing the identity of his subject. He abruptly and bluntly asserts that Jesus is the 'Christ' and the 'Son of God.' *Christos* was a Greek word meaning 'an anointed royal figure.' It was another way of referring to the 'Messiah,' the one who would come and administer God's rule on earth, and rescue Israel from all its oppressors and troubles. Not just *a* king, but The King.

But Mark does not just call Jesus the 'Christ'; he goes further. 'Son of God' is an astonishingly bold term that goes beyond the popular understanding of the Messiah at the time. It is a claim of outright divinity. Mark then raises the stakes all the way and makes the ultimate claim. By quoting Isaiah's prophetic passage, Mark asserts that John the Baptist is the fulfillment of the 'voice' calling out in the desert. Since Mark equates John with the one who would 'prepare the way for the Lord,' by clear inference it means he is equating Jesus with the Lord himself, with God Almighty. The Lord God; the long-awaited divine King who would rescue his people; and Jesus—they are somehow one and the same person.

In making this audacious claim, Mark roots Jesus as deeply as possible in the historic, ancient religion of Israel. Christianity, he implies, is not a completely new thing. Jesus is the fulfillment of all the biblical prophets' longings and visions, and he is the one who will come to rule and renew the entire universe.

King's Cross

Jesus' baptism

At that time Jesus came from Nazareth in Galilee and was baptised by John in the Jordan. Just as Jesus was coming up out of the water, he saw heaven being torn open and the Spirit descending on him like a dove.

Mark 1:9–10

For the Spirit of God to be pictured as a dove is not particularly striking to us, but when Mark was writing, it was very rare. In the sacred writings of Judaism there is only one place where the Spirit of God is likened to a dove, and that is in the Targums, the Aramaic translation of the Hebrew Scriptures that the Jews of Mark's time read. In the creation account, the book of Genesis 1:2 says that the Spirit *hovered* over the face of the waters. The Hebrew verb here means 'flutter': the Spirit fluttered over the face of the waters. To capture this vivid image, the rabbis translated the passage for the Targums like this: 'And the earth was without form and empty, and darkness was on the face of the deep, and the Spirit of God fluttered above the face of the waters *like a dove*, and God spoke: "Let there be light."'

There are three parties active in the creation of the world: God, God's Spirit, and God's Word, through which he creates. The same three parties are present at Jesus' baptism: the Father, who is the voice; the Son, who is the Word; and the Spirit fluttering like a dove. Mark is deliberately pointing us back to the creation, to the very beginning of history. Just as the original creation of the world was a project of the triune God, Mark says, so the redemption of the world, the rescue and renewal of all things that is beginning now with the arrival of the King, is also a project of the triune God.

King's Cross

The dance of reality

And a voice came from heaven: 'You are my Son, whom I love; with you I am well pleased.'

Mark 1:11

[. . . W]hy is it important that creation and redemption are both products of a Trinity, one God in three persons?

The Christian teaching of the Trinity is mysterious and cognitively challenging. The doctrine of the Trinity is that God is one God, eternally existent in three persons. That's not tritheism, with three gods who work in harmony; neither is it unipersonalism, the notion that sometimes God takes one form and sometimes he takes another, but that these are simply different manifestations of one God. Instead, trinitarianism holds that there is one God in three persons who know and love one another. God is not more fundamentally one than he is three, and he is not more fundamentally three than he is one.

When Jesus comes out of the water, the Father envelops him and covers him with words of love: 'You are my Son, whom I love; with you I am well pleased.' Meanwhile the Spirit covers him with power. This is what has been happening in the interior life of the Trinity from all eternity. Mark is giving us a glimpse into the very heart of reality, the meaning of life, the essence of the universe. According to the Bible, the Father, the Son, and the Spirit glorify one another. Jesus says in his prayer recorded in John's Gospel: 'I have brought you glory on earth by completing the work you gave me to do. And now, Father, glorify me in your presence with the glory that I had with you before the world began' (John 17:4–5). Each person of the Trinity glorifies the other. It's a dance.

King's Cross

Dancing into battle

At once the Spirit sent him out into the wilderness, and he was in the wilderness forty days, being tempted by Satan. He was with the wild animals . . .

Mark 1:12–13

Mark is showing us in these two lines that even though ultimate reality is a dance, we're going to experience reality as a battle.

Mark weaves his account into the shared history of his readers by drawing parallels between the Hebrew Scriptures and the life of Jesus. In Genesis the Spirit moves over the face of the waters, God speaks the world into being, humanity is created, and history is launched. What's the very next thing that happens? Satan tempts the first human beings, Adam and Eve, in the Garden of Eden. [. . .]

We look at Adam and Eve and say, 'What fools—why did they listen to Satan?' Yet we know we still have Satan's lie in our own hearts, because we're afraid of trusting God—of trusting anybody, in fact. We're stationary, because Satan tells us we should be—that's the way he fights the battle.

But God didn't leave us defenseless. God said to Jesus, 'Obey me about the tree'—only this time the tree was a cross—'and you will die.' And Jesus did. He has gone before you into the heart of a very real battle, to draw you into the ultimate reality of the dance. What he has enjoyed from all eternity, he has come to offer to you. And sometimes, when you're in the deepest part of the battle, when you're tempted and hurt and weak, you'll hear in the depths of your being the same words Jesus heard: 'This is my beloved child—*you* are my beloved child, whom I love; with you I'm well pleased.'

King's Cross

The call

Jesus went into Galilee, proclaiming the good news of God. 'The time has come,' he said. 'The kingdom of God has come near. Repent and believe the good news!'

Mark 1:14–15

The first time we hear Jesus' voice in Mark's Gospel, he says, 'Repent and believe the good news!' The word *repent* here means 'to reverse course,' or 'to turn away from something.' In the Bible it refers specifically to turning away from the things that Jesus hates to the things he loves. *Euangelion* in Greek, which is translated as 'good news' or 'gospel,' combines *angelos*, the word for one announcing news, and the prefix *eu-*, which means 'joyful.' *Gospel* means 'news that brings joy.' This word had currency when Mark used it, but it wasn't religious currency. It meant history-making, life-shaping news, as opposed to just daily news. [...]

Right there you can see the difference between Christianity and all other religions, including no religion. The essence of other religions is advice; Christianity is essentially news. Other religions say, 'This is what you have to do in order to connect to God forever; this is how you have to live in order to earn your way to God.' But the gospel says, 'This is what has been done in history. This is how Jesus lived and died to earn the way to God for you.' Christianity is completely different. It's joyful news.

King's Cross

Following the King

As Jesus walked beside the Sea of Galilee, he saw Simon and his brother Andrew casting a net into the lake, for they were fishermen. 'Come, follow me,' Jesus said, 'and I will send you out to fish for people.' At once they left their nets and followed him. When he had gone a little farther, he saw James son of Zebedee and his brother John in a boat, preparing their nets. Without delay he called them, and they left their father Zebedee in the boat with the hired men and followed him.

Mark 1:16–20

Jesus immediately calls people to follow him. This is unique in Jewish tradition. Pupils chose rabbis; rabbis did not choose pupils. Those who wished to learn sought out a rabbi to say, 'I want to study with you.' But Mark is showing us that Jesus has a different type of authority than a regular rabbi's. You can't have a relationship with Jesus unless he calls you.

When Jesus says to Simon and Andrew, 'Come, follow me,' at once they leave their vocation as fishermen and follow him. When he calls James and John, they leave behind their father and friends, right there in the boat. We know from reading the rest of the Gospels that these men did fish again, and they did continue to relate to their parents. But what Jesus is saying is still disruptive. In traditional cultures you get your identity from your family. And so when Jesus says, 'I want priority over your family,' that's drastic. In our individualistic culture, on the other hand, saying goodbye to our parents isn't a big deal, but for Jesus to say, 'I want priority over your career'—*that's* drastic. Jesus is saying, 'Knowing me, loving me, resembling me, serving me must become the supreme passion of your life. Everything else comes second.'

King's Cross

The hands of the King are healing hands

As soon as they left the synagogue, they went with James and John to the home of Simon and Andrew. Simon's mother-in-law was in bed with a fever, and they immediately told Jesus about her. So he went to her, took her hand and helped her up. The fever left her and she began to wait on them.

Mark 1:29–31

The healing shows that Jesus is concerned with and king over the physical world—not just the spiritual. It is not simply a *claim* of authority (which we have in the calling of the disciples and the authoritative teaching) but is also a clear proof and exercise of Jesus' authority. He shows he has real power over sickness—just a touch of his hand and the fever is cured. And this happens over and over. Three lines later Mark records that Jesus cured whole crowds of people. A few days after that his touch cured a man with leprosy. By the middle of chapter 2 everyone is amazed, saying, 'We have never seen anything like this!' The deaf hear, the blind see, and the lame walk. There are, in fact, thirty healings recorded in the Gospels, all showing us that Jesus has authority over sickness. And over the first few chapters of his Gospel, Mark goes on to stack up layer upon layer of evidence to show that Jesus' authority extends to every realm of life.

Come, follow me. Jesus is saying, 'Follow me because I'm the King you've been looking for. Follow me because I have authority over everything, yet I have humbled myself for you. Because I died on the cross for you when you didn't have the right beliefs or the right behavior. Because I have brought you news, not advice. Because I'm your true love, your true life—follow me.'

King's Cross

Suffering can draw us closer to God

Not only so, but we also glory in our sufferings, because we know that suffering produces perseverance; perseverance, character; and character, hope. And hope does not put us to shame, because God's love has been poured out into our hearts through the Holy Spirit, who has been given to us.

Romans 5:3–5

It is an exaggeration to say that no one finds God unless suffering comes into their lives—but it is not a big one. When pain and suffering come upon us, we finally see not only that we are not in control of our lives but that we never were.

Over the years, I also came to realize that adversity did not merely lead people to believe in God's existence. It pulled those who already believed into a deeper experience of God's reality, love, and grace. One of the main ways we move from abstract knowledge about God to a personal encounter with him as a living reality is through the furnace of affliction. As C. S. Lewis famously put it, 'God whispers to us in our pleasures, speaks in our conscience, but shouts in our pain.'[14]

Believers understand many doctrinal truths in the mind, but those truths seldom make the journey down into the heart except through disappointment, failure, and loss. As a man who seemed about to lose both his career and his family once said to me, 'I always knew, in principle, that 'Jesus is all you need' to get through. But you don't really know Jesus is all you need until Jesus is all you have.'

Walking with God through Pain and Suffering

Suffering is a key Bible theme

Therefore, since we have a great high priest who has ascended into heaven, Jesus the Son of God, let us hold firmly to the faith we profess. For we do not have a high priest who is unable to empathize with our weaknesses, but we have one who has been tempted in every way, just as we are – yet he did not sin.

Hebrews 4:14–15

As I grew in my understanding of the Bible itself, I came to see that the reality of suffering was one of its main themes. The book of Genesis begins with an account of how evil and death came into the world. The book of Exodus recounts Israel's forty years in the wilderness, a time of intense testing and trial. The wisdom literature of the Old Testament is largely dedicated to the problem of suffering. The book of Psalms provides a prayer for every possible situation in life, and so it is striking how filled it is with cries of pain and with blunt questions to God about the seeming randomness and injustice of suffering. In Psalm 44, the writer looks at the devastation of his country and calls, 'Awake, Lord! Why do you sleep? ... Why do you hide your face and forget our misery and oppression?' (Ps. 44:23–4). The books of Job and Ecclesiastes are almost wholly dedicated to deep reflection on unjust suffering and on the frustrating pointlessness that characterizes so much of life. The prophets Jeremiah and Habakkuk give searing expression to the human complaint that evil seems to rule history. New Testament books such as Hebrews and 1 Peter are almost entirely devoted to helping people face relentless sorrows and troubles. And towering over all, the central figure of the whole of Scripture, Jesus Christ, is a man of sorrows. The Bible, therefore, is about suffering as much as it is about anything.

Walking with God through Pain and Suffering

Not just despite but through suffering

The righteous cry out, and the LORD hears them; he delivers them from all their troubles. The LORD is close to the broken-hearted and saves those who are crushed in spirit.

Psalm 34:17–18

Looking back on our lives, Kathy and I came to realize that at the heart of why people disbelieve and believe in God, of why people decline and grow in character, of how God becomes less real and more real to us—is suffering. And when we looked to the Bible to understand this deep pattern, we came to see that the great theme of the Bible itself is how God brings fullness of joy not just despite but through suffering, just as Jesus saved us not in spite of but because of what he endured on the cross. And so there is a peculiar, rich, and poignant joy that seems to come to us only through and in suffering.

What we have learned from these years of ministry to 'the afflicted' is in this volume. Simone Weil writes that suffering makes God 'appear to be absent.' She is right. But in Psalm 34, David counters that though God feels absent, it does not mean he actually is. Looking back at a time when his life had been in grave danger and all seemed lost, David concludes, 'The LORD is close to the broken-hearted and saves those who are crushed in spirit' (v. 18).

Walking with God through Pain and Suffering

God is with us in the furnace

'If we are thrown into the blazing furnace, the God we serve is able to deliver us from it, and he will deliver us from Your Majesty's hand.'

Daniel 3:17

In perhaps the most vivid depiction of suffering in the Bible, in the third chapter of the book of Daniel, three faithful men are thrown into a furnace that is supposed to kill them. But a mysterious figure appears beside them. The astonished observers discern not three but four persons in the furnace, and one who appears to be 'the son of the gods.' And so they walk through the furnace of suffering and are not consumed. From the vantage of the New Testament, Christians know that this was the Son of God himself, one who faced his own, infinitely greater furnace of affliction centuries later when he went to the cross. This raises the concept of God 'walking with us' to a whole new level. In Jesus Christ we see that God actually experiences the pain of the fire as we do. He truly is God with us, in love and understanding, in our anguish.

He plunged himself into our furnace so that, when we find ourselves in the fire, we can turn to him and know we will not be consumed but will be made into people great and beautiful. 'I will be with you, your troubles to bless, and sanctify to you your deepest distress.'[15]

Walking with God through Pain and Suffering

Purification, not punishment

Son though he was, he learned obedience from what he suffered and, once made perfect, he became the source of eternal salvation for all who obey him.

Hebrews 5:8–9

Unlike believers in karma, Christians believe that suffering is often unjust and disproportionate. Life is simply not fair. People who live well often do not do well. Scheler writes that Christianity succeeded in doing justice to the full gravity and misery of suffering by acknowledging this, as the doctrine of karma does not, which insists that all an individual's suffering is fully deserved. The book of Job is of course the first place this is clearly stated, when God condemns Job's friends for their insistence that Job's pain and suffering had to be caused by a life of moral inferiority.

We see this most of all in Jesus. If anyone ever deserved a good life on the basis of character and behavior, Jesus did, but he did not get it. As Scheler writes, the entire Christian faith is centered on 'the paragon of the innocent man who freely receives suffering for others' debts ... Suffering ... acquires, through the divine quality of the suffering person, a wonderful, new nobility.' In the light of the cross, suffering becomes 'purification, not punishment.'[16]

Walking with God through Pain and Suffering

Suffering and grace

For all have sinned and fall short of the glory of God, and all are justified freely by his grace through the redemption that came by Christ Jesus.

Romans 3:23–4

Unlike the dualistic (and to some degree, the moralistic) view, Christianity does not see suffering as a means of working off your sinful debts by virtue of the quality of your endurance of pain. Christianity does not teach 'that an ascetic, voluntary self-affliction ... makes one more spiritual and brings one closer to God ... The interpretation that suffering *in itself* brings men nearer to God is far more Greek and Neoplatonic than Christian.'[17] Also, dualism divides the world into the good people and the evil people, with suffering as a badge of virtue and the mark of moral superiority that warrants the demonization of groups that have mistreated you. In stark contrast, Christians believe, as Aleksandr Solzhenitsyn wrote famously, 'The line dividing good and evil cuts through the heart of every human being.'[18]

No, the Christian understanding of suffering is dominated by the idea of grace. In Christ we have received forgiveness, love, and adoption into the family of God.

Walking with God through Pain and Suffering

The *Logos* is a person

In the beginning was the Word, and the Word was with God, and the Word was God.

John 1:1

There is no more striking statement of this difference between Christianity and ancient paganism than that found in the first chapter of the New Testament Gospel of John. There, John brilliantly co-opts one of Greek philosophy's main themes when he begins his account saying that 'in the beginning [of time] was *the Logos*' (John 1:1). But then he goes on to say, 'The *Logos* became flesh, and made his dwelling among us, and we have seen his glory' (John 1:14). This was an electrifying claim. John was saying, 'We agree that there is an ordering structure behind the universe, and that the meaning of life is to be found in aligning oneself with it.' But John was also saying that the *Logos* behind the universe was not an abstract, rational principle that could be known only through high contemplation by the educated elite. Rather, the *Logos* of the universe is a person—Jesus Christ—who can be loved and known in a personal relationship by anyone at all. Ferry summarizes John's message to the culture like this: 'The divine ... was no longer an impersonal structure, but an extraordinary individual.' This, Ferry said, was an 'unfathomable shift' which had an 'incalculable effect on the history of ideas.'[19]

Walking with God through Pain and Suffering

Room for grief and tears

When Jesus saw her weeping, and the Jews who had come along with her also weeping, he was deeply moved in spirit and troubled. 'Where have you laid him?' he asked. 'Come and see, Lord,' they replied. Jesus wept.

John 11:33–5

The other major difference between the Greek philosophers and Christianity was seen in how Christian consolation gave far more scope to expressions of sorrow and grief. Tears and cries are not to be stifled or even kept under strict limits—they are natural and good. Cyprian cites St. Paul, saying that Christians are to really grieve—but to do so bathed in hope (1 Thess. 4:13).[20] Christians did not see grief as a useless thing to be suppressed at all costs. Ambrose did not apologize for his tears and grief over the death of his brother. Pointing to Jesus' tears at the tomb of Lazarus, he wrote: 'We have not incurred any grievous sin by our tears. Not all weeping proceeds from unbelief or weakness ... The Lord also wept. He wept for one not related to Him, I for my brother. He wept for all in weeping for one, I will weep for the all, in my brother.'[21]

For Christians, suffering was not to be dealt with primarily through the control and suppression of negative emotions with the use of reason or willpower. Ultimate reality was known not primarily through reason and contemplation but through relationship. Salvation was through humility, faith, and love rather than reason and control of emotions. And therefore, Christians don't face adversity by stoically decreasing our love for the people and things of this world so much as by increasing our love and joy in God.

Walking with God through Pain and Suffering

God is for us, even when we suffer

What, then, shall we say in response to these things? If God is for us, who can be against us?

Romans 8:31

In ancient times, Christianity was widely recognized as having superior resources for facing evil, suffering, and death. In modern times— though it is not as publicly discussed—it continues to have assets for sufferers arguably far more powerful than anything secular culture can offer. Those assets, however, reside in robust, distinctive Christian beliefs.

The first relevant Christian belief is in a personal, wise, infinite, and therefore inscrutable God who controls the affairs of the world—and that is far more comforting than the belief that our lives are in the hands of fickle fate or random chance. The second crucial tenet is that, in Jesus Christ, God came to earth and suffered with and for us sacrificially—and that is far more comforting than the idea that God is remote and uninvolved. The cross also proves that, despite all the inscrutability, God is for us. The third doctrine is that through faith in Christ's work on the cross, we can have assurance of our salvation—that is far more comforting than the karmic systems of thought. We are assured that the difficulties of life are not payment for our past sins, since Jesus has paid for them. As Luther taught, suffering is unbearable if you aren't certain that God is for you and with you. Secularity cannot give you that, and religions that provide salvation through virtue and good works cannot give it, either.

Walking with God through Pain and Suffering

The stain

*So the Pharisees and teachers of the law asked Jesus, 'Why don't your
disciples live according to the tradition of the elders instead of eating
their food with defiled hands?'*

Mark 7:5

According to the cleanliness laws, if you touched a dead animal
or human being, if you had an infectious skin disease like boils
or rashes or sores, if you came into contact with mildew (on your
clothes, articles in your home, or your house itself), if you had any
kind of bodily discharge, or if you ate meat from an animal desig-
nated as unclean, you were considered ritually impure, defiled,
stained, unclean. That meant you couldn't enter the temple—and
therefore you couldn't worship God with the community. [. . .] So
the washings and efforts to stay clean and free from dirt and disease
that were used by religious people in Jesus' day were a kind of
visual aid that enabled them to recognize that they were spiritually
and morally unclean and couldn't enter the presence of God unless
there was some kind of spiritual purification.

If you're going to meet up with somebody who is particularly
important to you—for that big date or important job interview—
you wash, you brush your teeth, you comb your hair. What are you
doing? Getting rid of the uncleanness, of course. You don't want a
speck or stain on you. You don't want to smell bad. The cleanliness
laws were the same idea. Spiritually, morally, unless you're clean,
you can't be in the presence of a perfect and holy God.

Jesus couldn't have agreed more with the religious leaders of
his day about the fact that we are unclean before God, unfit for
the presence of God. But he disagreed with them about the source
of the uncleanness, and about how to address it.

King's Cross

Outside-in cleansing

*After [Jesus] had left the crowd and entered the house, his disciples
asked him about this parable. 'Are you so dull?' he asked. 'Don't you
see that nothing that enters a person from the outside can defile them?
For it doesn't go into their heart but into their stomach, and then out of
the body.'*

Mark 7:17–9

Jesus' language is quite graphic here: Whether you eat clean or
unclean food it goes into the mouth, down to the stomach, and
then (literally) out into the latrine. It never gets to the heart.
Nothing that comes in from the outside makes us unclean.

What's really wrong with the world? Why can the world be
such a miserable place? Why is there so much strife between
nations, races, tribes, classes? Why do relationships tend to fray and
fall apart? Jesus is saying: *We are what's wrong.* It's what comes out
from the inside. It's the self-centeredness of the human heart. It's
sin. [. . .]

If the problem were the foot or the eye, although the solution
would be drastic, it would be possible to deal with it. But we can't
cut out our heart. No matter what we do, or how hard we try,
external solutions don't deal with the soul. Outside-in will never
work, because most of what causes our problems works from the
inside out. We will never shake that sense that we are unclean.

As Aleksandr Solzhenitsyn said, 'The line between good and
evil passes not through states, nor between classes, nor between
political parties either—but right through every human heart—
and through all human hearts.'[22]

King's Cross

Inside-out cleansing

God made him who had no sin to be sin for us, so that in him we might become the righteousness of God.

2 Corinthians 5:21

God clothed Jesus in our sin. He took our penalty, our punishment so that we, like Joshua, the high priest, can get what Revelation 19:7–8 pictures: 'Let us rejoice and be glad ... Fine linen, bright and clean, [is] given [to us] to wear.' Pure linen—perfectly clean—without stain or blemish. Hebrews 13 says Jesus was crucified outside the gate where bodies are burned—the garbage heap, a place of absolute uncleanliness—so that we can be made clean. Through Jesus Christ, at infinite cost to himself, God has clothed us in costly clean garments. It cost him his blood. And it is the only thing that can deal with the problem of your heart.

Are you living with a specific failure in your past that you feel guilty about and that you have spent your life trying to make up for? [...] You might be doing it through religion or politics or beauty. You might even be doing it through Christian ministry. Doing, doing, doing from the outside in. *It won't work.*

Cast your deadly 'doing' down—
Down at Jesus' feet;
Stand in Him, in Him alone,
Gloriously complete.[23]

King's Cross

The turn

Jesus and his disciples went on to the villages around Caesarea Philippi. On the way he asked them, 'Who do people say I am?' They replied, 'Some say John the Baptist; others say Elijah; and still others, one of the prophets.' 'But what about you?' he asked. 'Who do you say I am?' Peter answered, 'You are the Messiah.' Jesus warned them not to tell anyone about him.

Mark 8:27–30

Chapter 8 of Mark's Gospel is a pivotal chapter. It's the climax of the first act, in which the disciples finally begin to see the true identity of the one they have been following. In it Jesus says two things: *I'm a King, but a King going to a cross*; and *If you want to follow me, you've got to come to the cross too.* [...]

Here at last Peter begins to get the answer to the big question, 'Who is Jesus?' He proposes to Jesus, 'You are the Christ.' Peter is using a word that literally means 'anointed one.' Kings were traditionally anointed with oil as a kind of coronation, but the word *Christos* had come to mean *the* Anointed One, the Messiah, the King to end all kings, the King who's going to put everything right. *You are the Messiah,* Peter says. Jesus accepts the title—but then immediately turns around and begins to say things they find appalling and shocking. 'Yes, I'm the King,' he says, 'but I'm not anything like the king you were expecting':

He then began to teach them that the Son of Man must suffer many things and be rejected by the elders, the chief priests and the teachers of the law, and that he must be killed and after three days rise again.   Mark 8:31

[...] The notion that the Messiah would suffer made no sense at all, because the Messiah was supposed to defeat evil and injustice and make everything right in the world. How could he defeat evil by suffering and dying? That seemed ridiculous, impossible. By using the word *must,* Jesus is also indicating that he is planning to die—that he is doing it voluntarily.

King's Cross

The Son of Man must suffer

He spoke plainly about this, and Peter took him aside and began to rebuke him.

Mark 8:32

[... T]he minute Jesus says [he must suffer and die], Peter begins to 'rebuke' him. This is the verb used elsewhere for what Jesus does to demons. This means Peter is condemning Jesus in the strongest possible language. Why is Peter so undone, that he would turn on Jesus like this right after identifying him as the Messiah? From his mother's knee Peter had always been told that when the Messiah came he would defeat evil and injustice by ascending the throne. But here is Jesus saying, 'Yes, I'm the Messiah, the King, but I came not to live but to die. I'm not here to take power but to lose it; I'm here not to rule but to serve. And that's how I'm going to defeat evil and put everything right.'

[...] If we know that forgiveness always entails suffering for the forgiver and that the only hope of rectifying and righting wrongs comes by paying the cost of suffering, then it should not surprise us when God says, 'The only way I can forgive the sins of the human race is to suffer—either you will have to pay the penalty for sin or I will.' Sin always entails a penalty. Guilt can't be dealt with unless someone pays.

The only way God can pardon us and not judge us is to go to the cross and absorb it into himself. 'I *must* suffer,' Jesus said.

King's Cross

Take up your cross

Then he called the crowd to him along with his disciples and said:
'Whoever wants to be my disciple must deny themselves and take up
their cross and follow me. For whoever wants to save their life will lose
it, but whoever loses their life for me and for the gospel will save it.
What good is it for someone to gain the whole world, yet forfeit their
soul?'

Mark 8:34–6

Jesus is saying, 'Since I am a King on a cross, if you want to follow me *you* must go to a cross.' What does it mean to take up our cross? What does it mean to lose our life for the gospel in order to save it?

The deliberately chosen Greek word for 'life' here is *psyche*, from which we get our word *psychology*. It denotes your identity, your personality, your selfhood—what makes you distinct. Jesus is not saying, 'I want you to lose your sense of being an individual self.' That's a teaching of Eastern philosophy, and if he meant that he would have said, 'You must lose yourself to lose yourself.' Jesus is saying, 'Don't build your identity on gaining things in the world.' His exact words are, 'What good is it for a man to gain the whole world, yet forfeit his soul?'

[. . .] Once you see the Son of God loving you [by going to the cross for you], once you are moved by that viscerally and existentially, you begin to get a strength, an assurance, a sense of your own value and distinctiveness that is not based on what you're doing or whether somebody loves you, whether you've lost weight or how much money you've got. You're free—the old approach to identity is gone.

King's Cross

Seeing the kingdom

And he said to them, 'Truly I tell you, some who are standing here will not taste death before they see that the kingdom of God has come with power.'

Mark 9:1

Some people have interpreted this to mean that the current generation wouldn't pass away before he returned to earth. But that's not what he's saying. The early church cherished this passage well beyond the death of Jesus' generation. They knew that Jesus meant something else. They understood him to mean that although the kingdom of God began in weakness—on the cross— it would not end that way. They would see the power of his resurrection, and see the church multiply and grow in love, and service, and influence in the world.

For us, the kingdom of God begins with weakness, relinquishment, giving up our rights to our own life; it begins with admitting that we need a Savior. We need someone to actually fulfill all the requirements and pay for our sin. That's weakness. Jesus started in weakness—first, by becoming human, and second, by going to a cross. And if we want him in our life, we have to start in weakness too. The kingdom begins there, but it won't end there. Someday, when Jesus returns and ushers in a renewed creation, love will totally triumph over hate and life will totally triumph over death.

King's Cross

The mountain

After six days Jesus took Peter, James and John with him and led them up a high mountain, where they were all alone. There he was transfigured before them. His clothes became dazzling white, whiter than anyone in the world could bleach them. And there appeared before them Elijah and Moses, who were talking with Jesus.

Mark 9:2–4

Centuries prior to this event, according to the book of Exodus in the Old Testament, God came down on Mount Sinai in a cloud. The voice of God spoke out of the cloud, and everyone was afraid. Moses went to the top of the mountain and begged to see God's glory: 'Show me your glory—your infinite greatness and unimaginable beauty.' And God responded, 'When my glory passes by, I will put you in a cleft in the rock and cover you with my hand until I have passed by, but my face cannot be seen. No one may see me and live' (Exod. 33:18–23, paraphrased). Moses was not able to see God's glory directly. But even getting near was enough to make Moses' face shine with the reflected glory of God.

Now, centuries later, we're on top of another mountain and there's glory again. This dazzling brightness makes Jesus' clothes 'whiter than anyone in the world could bleach them.' There's a mountain, a voice out of a cloud—and even Moses makes an appearance. Is this Mount Sinai all over again? No, because there's a head-snapping twist. Moses had reflected the glory of God as the moon reflects the light of the sun. But Jesus *produces* the unsurpassable glory of God; it emanates from him. Jesus does not *point to* the glory of God as Elijah, Moses, and every other prophet has done; Jesus *is* the glory of God in human form.

King's Cross

The face of God

Peter said to Jesus, 'Rabbi, it is good for us to be here. Let us put up three shelters—one for you, one for Moses and one for Elijah.' (He did not know what to say, they were so frightened.) Then a cloud appeared and covered them, and a voice came from the cloud: 'This is my Son, whom I love. Listen to him!'

Mark 9:5–7

Something else happens here that never happened on Mount Sinai—Peter, James, and John are in the presence of God and yet they do not die. [. . .] This is why, here on the mountain where Jesus is 'transfigured' (this scene is generally known as the trans-figuration), Peter is scared. So scared he doesn't know what he's saying, according to Mark. He stammers out, 'Rabbi . . . let us put up three shelters—one for you, one for Moses, and one for Elijah.' To us that's a baffling proposal—so let's explore it. [. . .]

What Peter is actually saying here is, 'We need a tabernacle, we need to set up rituals, to protect us from the presence of God.' Immediately after Peter says this, a cloud appears and envelops Jesus, Moses, and Elijah. And from within the *shekinah* glory cloud, God says, 'This is my Son, whom I love. Listen to him!' They are in the very presence of God. [. . .]

Worship is not just believing. Before they went up the mountain, Peter, James, and John already believed in God. And Peter had already said, 'You are the Christ.' But now they have sensed it. The presence of God has enveloped them. They have had a foretaste of what [. . .] all of us are longing for: the very face and embrace of God.

King's Cross

Caught in the trap

As Jesus started on his way, a man ran up to him and fell on his knees before him. 'Good teacher,' he asked, 'what must I do to inherit eternal life?'

Mark 10:17

Consider how Jesus counseled this young man. Yes, this man needed counseling, though on the outside he looked completely pulled together. He was rich, he was young, and he was probably good-looking—it's hard to be rich and young and *not* be good-looking. But he didn't have it all together. If he had, he would never have come to Jesus and asked, 'What must I do to inherit eternal life?'

Any devout Jew would have known the answer to this question. [. . .] The answer was 'Obey the statutes of God and avoid all sin.' The young man would have known this answer. Why then was he asking Jesus?

Jesus' perceptive statement 'One thing you lack' allows us to capture the gist of the young man's struggle. The man was saying, 'You know what, I've done everything right: I've been successful economically, successful socially, successful morally, successful religiously. I've heard you're a good rabbi, and I'm wondering if there's something I've missed, something I'm overlooking. I sense that something is lacking.'

Of course he was missing something. Because anyone who counts on what they are *doing* to get eternal life will find that, in spite of everything they've accomplished, there's an emptiness, an insecurity, a doubt. Something is bound to be missing. How can anyone ever know whether they are good enough?

King's Cross

Repenting of our good things

'One thing you lack,' he said. 'Go, sell everything you have and give to the poor, and you will have treasure in heaven. Then come, follow me.'

Mark 10:21

But then the blow comes. Jesus has already accepted what the man said about having obeyed the commandments, having lived an ethical life. What Jesus says to the man goes further. [. . .]

In other words, Jesus says: [. . .] 'You shouldn't do bad things. But if you just repent of doing bad things, all it will do is make you a religious person. If you want eternal life, if you want intimacy with God, if you want to get over that nagging sense that there's still something missing, if you can't find a way to get the stain out, then you have to change how you relate to your gifts and your successes. You have to repent of how you've been using your *good things*.'

And there are many ways that we use these 'good things.' [. . .] Most of all, we may point to our good things—our achievements and our attainments—and say to God, 'Look at what I've accomplished! You owe it to me to answer my prayers.' We may use our good things to get control of God and other people.

So Jesus is saying to the man in this passage, 'You have put your faith and trust in your wealth and accomplishments. But the effort is alienating you from God. Right now God is your boss; but God is not your Savior, and here's how you can see it: *I want you to imagine life without money.* I want you to imagine all of it gone. No inheritance, no inventory, no servants, no mansions—all of that is gone. All you have is me. Can you live like that?'

King's Cross

79

The center of our identity

At this the man's face fell. He went away sad, because he had great wealth.

Mark 10:22

The word *sad* translated here is better translated 'grieved'—he *grieved*. Let me tell you why that translation is better. There's a place where the same Greek word is applied to Jesus. Matthew records in his Gospel that in the Garden of Gethsemane Jesus started to sweat blood as he *grieved in deep distress*. Why? He knew he was about to experience the ultimate dislocation, the ultimate disorientation. He was about to lose the joy of his life, the core of his identity. He was going to lose his Father. Jesus was losing his spiritual center, his very self.

When Jesus called this young man to give up his money, the man started to grieve, because money was for him what the Father was for Jesus. It was the center of his identity. To lose his money would have been to lose himself—to lose what little sense he had of having covered the stain.

It's one thing to have God as a boss, an example, a mentor; but if you want God to be your Savior, you have to replace what you're already looking to as a savior. Everybody's got something. What is it for you?

If you want to be a Christian, of course you'll repent of your sins. But after you've repented of your sins you'll have to repent of how you have used the good things in your life to fill the place where God should be. If you want intimacy with God, if you want to get over this sense that something is missing, it will have to become God that you love with all your heart and strength.

King's Cross

A ransom for many

'For even the Son of Man did not come to be served, but to serve, and to give his life as a ransom for many.'

Mark 10:45

Jesus Christ came not to be served but to die, to give his life. That sets him apart from the founder of every other major religion. Their purpose was to live and be an example; Jesus' purpose was to die and be a sacrifice.

Jesus' choice of the word *come* is a strong giveaway that he existed before he was born: He came into the world. By saying 'did not come to be served,' he assumes that he had every right to expect to be honored and served when he came, though he did not exercise that privilege.

The final phrase, 'to give his life as a ransom for many,' sums up the reason why he has to die. Jesus came to be a substitutionary sacrifice. Consider the little preposition *for* in the phrase 'a ransom *for* many.' In Greek it's the word *anti*, which means 'instead of,' 'in place of,' 'substitute.' What about *ransom*? In English we don't even use that word nowadays except in relation to kidnapping. But here it translates a Greek word, *lutron*, that meant 'to buy the freedom of a slave or a prisoner.' The ransomer would make a huge sacrificial payment that matched the value, or paid the debt of the slave or the prisoner in order to procure his or her freedom.

Jesus came to pay that kind of ransom. But since the slavery he is dealing with is of a cosmic kind—that is, cosmic evil—it required a cosmic payment. Jesus is saying, 'I will pay the ransom that you couldn't possibly pay, and it will procure your freedom.' The payment is Jesus' death on the cross.

King's Cross

Love and sacrifice

Greater love has no one than this: to lay down one's life for one's friends.

John 15:13

All real, life-changing love is substitutionary sacrifice. Remember Lily Potter, the mother of Harry Potter? In the first book of the series, the evil Lord Voldemort tries to kill Harry, but he can't touch him. When the Voldemort-possessed villain tries to lay hands on Harry, he experiences agonizing pain, and so he is thwarted. Harry later goes to Dumbledore, his mentor, and asks, 'Why couldn't he touch me?' Dumbledore replies that 'Your mother died to save you . . . love as powerful as your mother's for you leaves its own mark. Not a scar, no visible sign . . . [but] to have been loved so deeply . . . will give us some protection forever.'[24] Why is Dumbledore's statement so moving? Because we know from experience, from the mundane to the dramatic, that sacrifice is at the heart of real love. [. . .]

Therefore, it makes sense that a God who is more loving than you and me, a God who comes into the world to deal with the ultimate evil, the ultimate sin, would have to make a substitutionary sacrifice. Even we flawed human beings know that you can't just overlook evil. It can't be dealt with, removed, or healed just by saying, 'Forget it.' It must be paid for, and dealing with it is costly. How much more should we expect that God could not just shrug off evil? The debt had to be paid. But he was so incredibly loving that he was willing to die in order to do it himself.

King's Cross

Meekness and majesty

When they brought the colt to Jesus and threw their cloaks over it, he sat on it. Many people spread their cloaks on the road, while others spread branches they had cut in the fields. Those who went ahead and those who followed shouted, 'Hosanna!' 'Blessed is he who comes in the name of the Lord!' 'Blessed is the coming kingdom of our father David!' 'Hosanna in the highest!'

Mark 11:7–9

When Jesus rode into Jerusalem, people laid down their cloaks on the road in front of him and hailed him as a king coming in the name of the house of David. This type of parade was culturally appropriate in that era: A king would ride into town publicly and be hailed by cheering crowds. But Jesus deliberately departed from the script and did something very different. He didn't ride in on a powerful war horse the way a king would; he was mounted on a *polos*, that is, a colt or a small donkey. Here was Jesus Christ, the King of authoritative, miraculous power, riding into town on a steed fit for a child or a hobbit. In this way, Jesus let it be known that he was the One prophesied in Zechariah, the great Messiah to come:

Rejoice greatly, Daughter Zion! Shout, Daughter Jerusalem! See, your king comes to you, righteous and victorious, lowly and riding on a donkey, on a colt, the foal of a donkey.

Zechariah 9:9

This odd juxtaposition demonstrates that Jesus was King, but that he didn't fit into the world's categories of kingship. He brought together majesty and meekness.

King's Cross

83

Destroying the ring

'I am the LORD; that is my name! I will not yield my glory to another or my praise to idols.'

Isaiah 42:8

When J. R. R. Tolkien's *The Lord of the Rings* was published in the 1950s, a woman named Rhona Beare wrote Tolkien and asked him about the chapter in which the Ring of Power is destroyed in the fires of Mount Doom. When the ring is melted, the Dark Lord's entire power collapses and melts away with it. She found it inexplicable that this unassailable, overwhelming power would be wiped out by the erasure of such a little object. Tolkien replied that at the heart of the plot was the Dark Lord's effort to magnify and maximize his power by placing so much of it in the ring. He wrote: 'The Ring of Sauron is only one of the various mythical treatments of the placing of one's life, or power, in some external object, which is thus exposed to capture or destruction with disastrous results to oneself.'[25]

Tolkien means something like this: It is one thing to love somebody and get a lot of joy out of the relationship. But if that person breaks up with you and you want to kill yourself, it means you have given that person too much glory, too much weight in your life. You may have said in your heart, 'If that person loves me, then I know I am somebody.' But if that person then takes the relationship away, you collapse and melt down because you have ascribed more glory and honor to him or her than to God. If anything matters more to you than God, you are placing yourself and your heart into something external. Only if you make God matter the most—which means only if you glorify him and give him the glory—will you have a safe life.

Walking with God through Pain and Suffering

Opening the temple

On reaching Jerusalem, Jesus entered the temple courts and began driving out those who were buying and selling there. He overturned the tables of the money-changers and the benches of those selling doves, and would not allow anyone to carry merchandise through the temple courts. And as he taught them, he said, 'Is it not written: "My house will be called a house of prayer for all nations"? But you have made it a den of robbers.'

Mark 11:15–17

When you stepped inside the temple door, the first area you got to was the court of the Gentiles—the *ethne* or 'nations.' This was the only part where non-Jews were allowed. It was the biggest section of the temple, and you had to go through it to get to the rest. All the business operations of the temple were set up there. And what an operation it was! [...] Think of how tumultuous, loud, and confusing our financial trading floors are—and then add livestock. And this was the place where the Gentiles were supposed to find God through quiet reflection and prayer.

Jesus' reaction to all this was to start throwing the furniture over. Imagine the leaders hurrying to him in panic: 'What's going on? Why are you doing this?' He quoted from the prophet Isaiah in reply: 'My house will be called a house of prayer for all nations'—that is, for the Gentiles. We are told this amazed those who heard him. Why? For one thing, it was popularly believed that when the Messiah showed up he would purge the temple of foreigners. Instead, here is Jesus clearing the temple *for* the Gentiles—acting as their advocate. In our multicultural society it's easy to like that about Jesus. But what he was doing was even more subversive. Jesus was challenging the sacrificial system altogether and saying that the Gentiles—the pagan, unwashed Gentiles—could now go directly to God in prayer.

King's Cross

The feast

While they were eating, Jesus took bread, and when he had thanks, he broke it and gave it to his disciples, saying, 'Take it; this is my body.' Then he took the cup, and when he had given thanks, he gave it to them, and they all drank from it. 'This is my blood of the covenant, which is poured out for many,' he said to them. 'Truly I tell you, I will not drink again from the fruit of the vine until that day when I drink it anew in the kingdom of God.'

Mark 14:22–5

Imagine the astonishment of the disciples when, blessing the elements and explaining their symbolism, Jesus departs from the script that has been re-enacted by generation after generation. He shows them the bread and says, 'This is my body.' What does that mean? Jesus is saying, 'This is the bread of *my* affliction, the bread of *my* suffering, because I'm going to lead the ultimate exodus and bring you the ultimate deliverance from bondage.' [...]

Jesus' words mean that as a result of his substitutionary sacrifice there is now a new covenant between God and us. And the basis of this relationship is Jesus' own blood: 'my blood of the covenant.' When he announces that he will not eat or drink until he meets us in the kingdom of God, Jesus is promising that he is unconditionally committed to us: 'I am going to bring you into the Father's arms. I'm going to bring you to the feast of the King.' Jesus often compares God's kingdom to sitting at a big feast. In Matthew 8 verse 11, Jesus says, 'I say to you that many will come from the east and the west, and will take their places at the feast ... in the kingdom of heaven.' Jesus promises that we will be at this kingdom feast with him.

King's Cross

The Lamb of God

The LORD has laid on him the iniquity of us all. He was oppressed and afflicted, yet he did not open his mouth; he was led like a lamb to the slaughter . . . He poured out his life unto death, and was numbered with the transgressors.

Isaiah 53:6–7, 12

Jesus' last meal with his disciples departed from the script in another way too. When Jesus stood up to bless the food, he held up bread. All Passover meals had bread. He blessed the wine—all Passover meals had wine. But not one of the Gospels mentions a main course. There is no mention of lamb at this Passover meal. Passover was not a vegetarian meal, of course. What kind of Passover would be celebrated without lamb? There was no lamb *on* the table because the Lamb of God was *at* the table. Jesus was the main course. That's the reason that when John the Baptist saw Jesus for the first time, he said, 'Look, the Lamb of God, who takes away the sin of the world!' (John 1:29). [. . .]

In Mark, when Jesus says, 'This is my body . . . This is my blood . . . poured out,' he means: *I'm the One that Isaiah and John spoke about. I am the Lamb of God to which all the other lambs pointed, the Lamb that takes away the sin of the world.*

On the cross Jesus got what *we* deserved: The sin, guilt, and brokenness of the world fell upon him. He loved us so much he took divine justice on himself so that we could be passed over, forever.

It bears repeating: All love, all real, life-changing love, is substitutionary sacrifice.

King's Cross

The curtain torn in two

With a loud cry, Jesus breathed his last. The curtain of the temple was torn in two from top to bottom. And when the centurion, who stood there in front of Jesus, heard his cry and saw how he died, he said, 'Surely this man was the Son of God!'

Mark 15:37–9

Remember that the curtain in the temple was not a flimsy little veil; it was heavy and thick, almost as substantial as a wall. The curtain separated the holy of holies, where God's *shekinah* glory dwelled, from the rest of the temple—it separated the people from the presence of God. And remember that only the holiest man, the high priest, from the holiest nation, the Jews, could enter the holy of holies—and only on the holiest day of the year, Yom Kippur, and he had to bring a blood sacrifice, an atonement for sins. The curtain said loudly and clearly that it is impossible for anyone sinful—anyone in spiritual darkness—to come into God's presence.

At the moment Jesus Christ died, this massive curtain was ripped open. The tear was from top to bottom, just to make clear who did it. This was God's way of saying, 'This is the sacrifice that ends all sacrifices, the way is now open to approach me.' Now that Jesus has died, anybody who believes in him can see God, connect to God. The barrier is gone for good. Our trajectory has been permanently redirected toward God. And that's only possible because Jesus has just paid the price for our sin. Anybody who believes can go in now.

King's Cross

The shadow is only a small and passing thing

For Christ also suffered once for sins, the righteous for the unrighteous, to bring you to God. He was put to death in the body but made alive in the Spirit.

1 Peter 3:18

The only time I ever faced death personally was when I had thyroid cancer. From the beginning the doctors told me it was treatable. Still, when I was going under anesthesia for the surgery, I wondered what would happen. You may be curious about what passage from the Bible came to my mind. True confession: What I thought of was a passage from *The Lord of the Rings*. It comes near the end of the third book, when evil and darkness seem overwhelming. Here is what Tolkien tells us about the thoughts of Sam, one of the heroes:

Sam saw a white star twinkle for a while. The beauty of it smote his heart, as he looked up out of the forsaken land, and hope returned to him. For like a shaft, clear and cold, the thought pierced him that in the end the Shadow was only a small and passing thing: there was light and high beauty forever beyond its reach. His song in the Tower had been defiance rather than hope; for then he was thinking of himself. Now, for a moment, his own fate . . . ceased to trouble him . . . [P]utting away all fear, he cast himself into a deep, untroubled sleep.[26]

I remember thinking at that moment: It's really true. Because of Jesus' death evil is a passing thing—a shadow. There is light and high beauty forever beyond its reach because evil fell into the heart of Jesus. The only darkness that could have destroyed us forever fell into his heart. It didn't matter what happened in my surgery—it was going to be all right. And it *is* going to be all right.

King's Cross

A remembrance of the future

*'Don't be alarmed,' he said. 'You are looking for Jesus the Nazarene,
who was crucified. He has risen! He is not here. See the place where
they laid him.'*

Mark 16:6

What if you believe the resurrection is true? You believe that Jesus has died to save you—to redirect your eternal trajectory irrevocably toward God. You believe that God has accepted you, for Jesus' sake, through an act of supreme grace. You are part of the kingdom of God. What then? Does the resurrection mean anything for your life *now*? Oh my, yes. [...]

Only in the gospel of Jesus Christ do people find such enormous hope to live. Only the resurrection promises us not just new minds and hearts, but also new bodies. They are going to be more indissoluble, more perfect, more beautiful. They will be able to be and do and bear the burden of what bodies are supposed to do in a way in which our present bodies cannot.

If you can't dance and you long to dance, in the resurrection you'll dance perfectly. If you're lonely, in the resurrection you will have perfect love. If you're empty, in the resurrection you will be fully satisfied. Ordinary life is what's going to be redeemed. There is nothing better than ordinary life, except that it's always going away and always falling apart. Ordinary life is food and work and chairs by the fire and hugs and dancing and mountains—this world. God loves it so much that he gave his only Son so we—and the rest of this ordinary world—could be redeemed and made perfect. And that's what is in store for us.

King's Cross

Easter hope for the world

This is how we know what love is: Jesus Christ laid down his life for us.
And we ought to lay down our lives for our brothers and sisters.

1 John 3:16

Each year at Easter I get to preach on the resurrection. In my sermon I always say to my skeptical, secular friends that, even if they can't believe in the resurrection, they should want it to be true. Most of them care deeply about justice for the poor, alleviating hunger and disease, and caring for the environment. Yet many of them believe that the material world was caused by accident and that the world and everything in it will eventually simply burn up in the death of the sun. They find it discouraging that so few people care about justice without realizing that their own worldview undermines any motivation to make the world a better place. Why sacrifice for the needs of others if in the end nothing we do will make any difference?

If the resurrection of Jesus happened, however, that means there's infinite hope and reason to pour ourselves out for the needs of the world.

The Reason for God

The empty tomb and the witnesses

For what I received I passed on to you as of first importance: that Christ died for our sins according to the Scriptures, that he was buried, that he was raised on the third day according to the Scriptures, and that he appeared to Cephas, and then to the Twelve. After that, he appeared to more than five hundred of the brothers and sisters at the same time, most of whom are still living, though some have fallen asleep.

1 Corinthians 15:3–6

The first accounts of the empty tomb and the eyewitnesses are not found in the Gospels, but in the letters of Paul, which every historian agrees were written just fifteen to twenty years after the death of Jesus.

Here Paul not only speaks of the empty tomb and resurrection on the 'third day' (showing he is talking of a historical event, not a symbol or metaphor) but he also lists the eyewitnesses. Paul indicates that the risen Jesus not only appeared to individuals and small groups, but he also appeared to five hundred people at once, most of whom were still alive at the time of his writing and could be consulted for corroboration. Paul's letter was to a church, and therefore it was a public document, written to be read aloud. Paul was inviting anyone who doubted that Jesus had appeared to people after his death to go and talk to the eyewitnesses if they wished.

[. . .] Paul's letters show that Christians proclaimed Jesus' bodily resurrection from the very beginning. That meant the tomb *must* have been empty.

The Reason for God

Was the resurrection a hoax?

For we did not follow cleverly devised stories when we told you about the coming of our Lord Jesus Christ in power, but we were eyewitnesses of his majesty.

2 Peter 1:16

Over the years, skeptics about the resurrection have proposed that the followers of Jesus may have had hallucinations, that they may have imagined him appearing to them and speaking to them. This assumes that their master's resurrection was imaginable for his Jewish followers, that it was an option in their worldview. It was not. Others have put forth the conspiracy theory, that the disciples stole the body and claimed he was alive to others. This assumes that the disciples would expect other Jews to be open to the belief that an individual could be raised from the dead. But none of this is possible. The people of that time would have considered a bodily resurrection to be as impossible as the people of our own time, though for different reasons.

[...] There were dozens of other messianic pretenders whose lives and careers ended the same way Jesus' did. Why would the disciples of Jesus have come to the conclusion that his crucifixion had not been a defeat but a triumph—unless they had seen him risen from the dead?

The Reason for God

God's grace shown through his suffering

But God demonstrates his own love for us in this: while we were still sinners, Christ died for us.

Romans 5:8

The religious leaders of Jesus' day expected a nice, easy-to-understand Messiah who would defeat the Roman power and lead Israel to political independence. A weak, suffering, and crucified Messiah made no sense to them. Those looking at Jesus as he was dying on the cross had no idea that they were looking at the greatest act of salvation in history. Could the observers of the crucifixion 'clearly perceive' the ways of God? No—even though they were looking right at a wonder of grace. They saw only darkness and pain, and the categories of human reason are sure God cannot be working in and through *that*. So they called Jesus to 'come down now from the cross,' sneering, 'He saved others . . . but he can't save himself.' (Matt 27:42). But they did not realize he could save others only because he did *not* save himself.

Only through weakness and pain did God save us and show us, in the deepest way possible, the infinite depths of his grace and love for us. For indeed, here was infinite wisdom—in one stroke, the just requirement of the law was fulfilled *and* the forgiveness of lawbreakers secured. In one moment, God's love and justice were fully satisfied. This Messiah came to die in order to put an end to death itself. Only through weakness and suffering could sin be atoned—it was the only way to end evil without ending us.

Walking with God through Pain and Suffering

Restoration, not just consolation

Listen, I tell you a mystery: we will not all sleep, but we will all be changed – in a flash, in the twinkling of an eye, at the last trumpet. For the trumpet will sound, the dead will be raised imperishable, and we will be changed.

1 Corinthians 15:51–2

... [Another] great doctrine is that of the bodily resurrection from the dead for all who believe. This completes the spectrum of our joys and consolations. One of the deepest desires of the human heart is for love without parting. Needless to say, the prospect of the resurrection is far more comforting than the beliefs that death takes you into nothingness or into an impersonal spiritual substance. The resurrection goes beyond the promise of an ethereal, disembodied afterlife. We get our bodies back, in a state of beauty and power that we cannot today imagine. Jesus' resurrection body was corporeal—it could be touched and embraced, and he ate food. And yet he passed through closed doors and could disappear. This is a material existence, but one beyond the bounds of our imagination. The idea of heaven can be a consolation for suffering, a compensation for the life we have lost. But resurrection is not just consolation—it is restoration. We get it all back— the love, the loved ones, the goods, the beauties of this life—but in new, unimaginable degrees of glory and joy and strength.

Walking with God through Pain and Suffering

Living with hope and grace

You, then, why do you judge your brother or sister? Or why do you treat them with contempt? For we will all stand before God's judgment seat.

Romans 14:10

[...] the biblical doctrine of Judgment Day, far from being a gloomy idea, enables us to live with both hope and grace. If we accept it, we get hope and incentive to work for justice. For no matter how little success we may have now, we know that justice will be established—fully and perfectly. All wrongs—what we have called moral evil—will be redressed. But it also enables us to be gracious, to forgive, and to refrain from vengefulness and violence. Why? If we are not sure that there will be a final judgment, then when we are wronged, we will feel an almost irresistible compulsion to take up the sword and smite the wrongdoers. But if we know that no one will get away with anything, and that all wrongs will be ultimately redressed, then we can live in peace. The doctrine of Judgment Day warns us that we have neither the knowledge to know exactly what people deserve, nor the right to mete out punishment when we are sinners ourselves (Rom 2:1–16, 12:17–21). So belief in Judgment Day keeps us from being too passive or too violently aggressive in our pursuit of truth and justice.

Walking with God through Pain and Suffering

God brings about good from evil

And we know that in all things God works for the good of those who love him, who have been called according to his purpose.

Romans 8:28

Often we can see how bad things 'work together for good' (Rom 8:28). The problem is that we can only glimpse this sometimes, in a limited number of cases. But why could it not be that God allowed evil because it will bring us all to a far greater glory and joy than we would have had otherwise? Isn't it possible that the eventual glory and joy we will know will be infinitely greater than it would have been had there been no evil? What if that future world will somehow be greater for having once been broken and lost? If such is the case, that would truly mean the utter defeat of evil. Evil would not just be an obstacle to our beauty and bliss, but it will have only made it better. Evil would have accomplished the very opposite of what it intended.

How might that come about? At the simplest level, we know that only if there is danger can there be courage. And apart from sin and evil, we would never have seen the courage of God, or the astonishing extent of his love, or the glory of a deity who lays aside his glory and goes to the cross.

Walking with God through Pain and Suffering

Nothing compared to seeing God

It was revealed to them that they were not serving themselves but you, when they spoke of the things that have now been told you by those who have preached the gospel to you by the Holy Spirit sent from heaven. Even angels long to look into these things.

1 Peter 1:12

For us here in this life, the thought of God's glory is rather remote and abstract. But we must realize that the most rapturous delights you have ever had—in the beauty of a landscape, or in the pleasure of food, or in the fulfillment of a loving embrace— are like dewdrops compared to the bottomless ocean of joy that it will be to see God face-to-face (1 John 3:1–3). That is what we are in for, nothing less. And according to the Bible, that glorious beauty, and our enjoyment of it, has been immeasurably enhanced by Christ's redemption of us from evil and death. We are told that the angels long to endlessly gaze into the gospel, into the wonder of what Jesus did in his Incarnation and atonement (1 Pet. 1:12).

Paul speaks mysteriously that we who know Christ and the power of his resurrection also know 'the fellowship of sharing in his sufferings' (Phil .3:10–11, NIV–1984). Alvin Plantinga points to the teachings of older Reformed theologians, such as Jonathan Edwards and Abraham Kuyper, who believed that because of our fall and redemption, we will achieve a level of intimacy with God that cannot be received any other way. And therefore the angels are envious of it.[27] What if, in the future, we came to see that just as Jesus could not have displayed such glory and love any other way except through his suffering, we would not have been able to experience such transcendent glory, joy, and love any other way except by going through a world of suffering?

Walking with God through Pain and Suffering

Jesus' glory in his suffering

The Word became flesh and made his dwelling among us. We have seen his glory, the glory of the one and only Son, who came from the Father, full of grace and truth.

John 1:14

The New Testament teaches that Jesus was God come in the flesh— 'in Christ all the fullness of the Deity lives in bodily form' (Col. 2:9). He was God yet he suffered. He experienced weakness, a life filled 'with fervent cries and tears' (Heb. 5:7). He knew first-hand rejection and betrayal, poverty and abuse, disappointment and despair, bereavement, torture, and death. And so he is able to empathize with our weaknesses for he 'has been tempted in every way, just as we are—yet he did not sin' (Heb. 4:15). On the cross, he went beyond even the worst human suffering and experienced cosmic rejection and a pain that exceeds ours as infinitely as his knowledge and power exceeds ours. There is no greater inner agony than the loss of a love relationship. We cannot imagine, however, what it would be like to lose not just a human relationship that has lasted for some years but the infinite love of the Father that Jesus had from all eternity. The separation would have been infinitely unbearable. And so Jesus experienced Godforsakenness itself on the cross when he cried out, 'My God, my God! Why have you forsaken me?'

Here we see the ultimate strength—a God who is strong enough to voluntarily become weak and plunge himself into vulnerability and darkness out of love for us. And here we see the greatest possible glory—the willingness to lay aside all his glory out of love for us.

Walking with God through Pain and Suffering

Suffering is within God's control

In him we were also chosen, having been predestined according to the plan of him who works out everything in conformity with the purpose of his will . . .

Ephesians 1:11

God is called the one 'who works out everything in conformity with the purpose of his will' (Eph. 1:11). '*Everything*' that happens fits in accord with, in harmony with, God's plan. This means that God's plan includes 'little things.' Proverbs 16:33 (KJV) says, 'The lot is cast into the lap, but the whole disposing thereof is of the LORD.' Even the flip of the coin is part of his plan. Ultimately, there are no accidents. His plan also includes bad things. Psalm 60:3 (ESV) reads, 'You have made your people see hard things; you have given us wine to drink that made us stagger.'

Suffering then is not outside God's plan but a part of it. In Acts 4:27–8 (ESV), the Christian disciples pray to God, 'In this city, there were gathered together against your holy servant Jesus . . . Herod and Pontius Pilate, along with the Gentiles and the peoples of Israel, to do whatever your hand and your plan had predestined to take place.' Jesus' suffering and death was a great act of injustice, but it was also part of the set plan of God.

Walking with God through Pain and Suffering

God plans our plans

In their hearts humans plan their course, but the LORD establishes their steps.

Proverbs 16:9

According to the Bible, God plans our plans. The author of Proverbs assumes that while we make our plans, they only fit into the larger plans of God.

There are many texts that weave freewill and divine sovereignty together in ways that startle us. In Genesis 50:20, Joseph explains how his brothers' evil action of selling him into slavery was used by God to do great good. 'You intended to harm me, but God intended it for good to accomplish what is now being done, the saving of many lives.' Notice Joseph assuming that what they did was evil—they 'intended' harm, it was deliberate. Yet he says God's plan overruled and he used Joseph's troubles and sorrows for his own good purposes. The New Testament version of Joseph's saying is Romans 8:28 (NKJV)—'All things work together for good to those who love God.'

In Acts 2:23, Peter again tells us Jesus was crucified 'according to the definite plan' of God, and yet the hands that put him to death were guilty of injustice and 'lawlessness.' In other words, the death of Jesus was destined to happen by God's will—it was not possible that it would not happen. Yet no one who betrayed and put Jesus to death was forced to do it. They all freely chose what they did and were fully liable and responsible for their decisions. Jesus himself puts these truths together in one sentence: 'The Son of Man will go [to his death] as it has been decreed, but woe to that man who betrays him!' (Luke 22:22).

Walking with God through Pain and Suffering

Our deepest need

Some men came, bringing to him a paralyzed man, carried by four of them. Since they could not get him to Jesus because of the crowd, they made an opening in the roof above Jesus by digging through it and then lowered the mat the man was lying on. When Jesus saw their faith, he said to the paralyzed man, 'Son, your sins are forgiven.'

Mark 2:3–5

What a dramatic scene! If somebody suddenly came down through the roof as I was preaching, everything would stop—I would be speechless. What were these men so determined to get from Jesus? Well, it doesn't seem at first that Jesus understands. Jesus turns to the paralyzed man, and instead of saying 'Rise up, be healed,' he says, 'Your sins are forgiven.' If this man were from our time and place, I believe he would have said something like this: 'Um, thanks, but that's not what I asked for. I'm paralyzed. I've got a more immediate problem here.'

But in fact Jesus knows something the man doesn't know—that he has a much bigger problem than his physical condition. Jesus is saying to him, 'I understand your problems. I have seen your suffering. I'm going to get to that. But please realize that the main problem in a person's life is never his suffering; it's his sin.' [...] When the Bible talks about sin it is not just referring to the bad things we do. It's not just lying or lust or whatever the case may be—it is ignoring God in the world he has made; it's rebelling against him by living without reference to him. It's saying, 'I will decide exactly how I live my life.' And Jesus says that is our main problem.

King's Cross

Jesus' patience

But for that very reason I was shown mercy so that in me, the worst of sinners, Christ Jesus might display his immense patience as an example for those who would believe in him and receive eternal life.

1 Timothy 1:16

'Grant that we may follow the example of Jesus' patience.' That is what Thomas Cranmer, the author of the original *Book of Common Prayer*, wrote as a prayer to be used on Palm Sunday—the Sunday before Easter. What does he mean by patience? Patience is love for the long haul; it is bearing up under difficult circumstances, without giving up or giving in to bitterness. Patience means working when gratification is delayed. It means taking what life offers—even if it means suffering—without lashing out. And when you're in a situation that you're troubled over or when there's a delay or pressure on you or something's not happening that you want to happen, there's always a temptation to come to the end of your patience. You may well have lost your patience before you're even aware of it.

Cranmer's prayer is particularly poignant because it is prayed the week before Easter, the time when we remember Jesus' sacrificial death on the cross. Jesus displayed patience not just in the way he faced his execution and his enemies. [. . .] The complete prayer actually says, 'Grant that we may both follow the example of his patience, and also be made partakers of his resurrection.' Jesus Christ knew the only way to the crown was through the cross. The only way to resurrection was through death.

King's Cross

Who can forgive sins but God alone?

Now some teachers of the law were sitting there, thinking to themselves, 'Why does this fellow talk like that? He's blaspheming! Who can forgive sins but God alone?'

Mark 2:6–7

Jesus can read the motives of the hearts of those around him—in this case the religious leaders. When Jesus says to the paralyzed man, 'Son, your sins are forgiven,' they are shocked and angry. They believe Jesus is blaspheming—showing contempt or irreverence toward God—because he claims to do something only God can do. They think to themselves: 'Who can forgive sins but God alone?' They're totally right.

Let's say Tom, Dick, and Harry are talking. Tom punches Dick smack in the mouth. There's blood everywhere. Then Harry goes up to Tom and says, 'Tom, I forgive you for punching Dick in the mouth. It's all right. It's over.' What is Dick going to say, once he's calmed down? 'Harry, you can't forgive him. Only I can forgive him. He didn't wrong you; he wronged me.' You can only forgive a sin if it's against *you*. That's why, when Jesus looks at the paralyzed man and says, 'Your sins are forgiven,' he's actually saying, 'Your sins have really been against me.' The only person who can possibly say that to a human being would be their Creator. Jesus Christ, by forgiving the man, is claiming to be God Almighty. The religious leaders know it: This man is not just claiming to be a miracle worker, he is claiming to be the Lord of the universe—and they are understandably furious about it.

King's Cross

The price of forgiveness

*'Which is easier: to say to this paralyzed man, "Your sins are forgiven,"
or to say, "Get up, take your mat and walk"? But I want you to know
that the Son of Man has authority on earth to forgive sins.' So he said to
the man, 'I tell you, get up, take your mat and go home.'*

Mark 2:9–11

Many biblical scholars say that here, as early as chapter 2 of
Mark, the shadow of the cross falls across Jesus' path. Jesus
knows what the religious leaders are thinking, so he knows that if
he begins to let on that he's not just a miracle worker but also the
Savior of the world, they're eventually going to kill him. If he not
only heals this man but forgives his sins as well, he's taking a deci-
sive, irreversible step down the path to his death. By taking that
step, he is putting a down payment on our forgiveness.

You see, at that moment Jesus had the power to heal the man's
body, just as he has the power to give you that career success, that
relationship, that recognition you've been longing for. He actually
has the power and authority to give each of us what we've been
asking for, on the spot, no questions asked.

But Jesus knows that's not nearly deep enough. [...] We need
someone who can go deeper than that. Someone who will [...]
pierce our self-centeredness and remove the sin that enslaves us
and distorts even our beautiful longings. In short, we need to be
forgiven. That's the only way for our discontent to be healed. It
will take more than a miracle worker or a divine genie—it will
take a Savior. Jesus knows that to be our Savior he is going to have
to die.

King's Cross

Jesus vs religion

One Sabbath Jesus was going through the grainfields, and as his disciples walked along, they began to pick some heads of grain. The Pharisees said to him, 'Look, why are they doing what is unlawful on the Sabbath?'

Mark 2:23–4

Jesus claimed to be able to forgive sins, and the religious leaders called that blasphemy. But Jesus goes on to make a claim so outrageous that the leaders don't have a word for it. Jesus declares not that he has come to reform religion but that he's here to *end* religion and to replace it with himself.

The law of God directed that you had to rest from your work one day in seven. That was wonderful, of course, but the religious leaders of the day had fenced in this law with a stack of specific regulations. There were thirty-nine types of activity that you could not do on the Sabbath, including reaping grain, which is what the Pharisees accused the disciples of doing. Mark goes on to record a second incident that took place on the Sabbath day [in Mark 3:1–6, where they look on stubbornly as Jesus heals a man with a shrivelled hand].

Why does Jesus become angry with the religious leaders? Because the Sabbath is about restoring the diminished. It's about replenishing the drained. It's about repairing the broken. To heal the man's shriveled hand is to do exactly what the Sabbath is all about. Yet because the leaders are so concerned that Sabbath regulations be observed, they don't want Jesus to heal this man—an incredible example of missing the forest for the trees. Their hearts are as shriveled as the man's hand. They're insecure and anxious about the regulations. They're tribal, judgmental, and self-obsessed instead of caring about the man. Why? *Religion.*

King's Cross

Lord of rest

Then he said to them, 'The Sabbath was made for man, not man for the Sabbath. So the Son of Man is Lord even of the Sabbath.'

Mark 2:27–8

In the face of this self-righteous religious preoccupation Jesus says, 'The Sabbath was made for man, not man for the Sabbath. So the Son of Man is Lord even of the Sabbath.' He affirms, even celebrates, the original principle of the Sabbath—the need for rest. Yet he squashes the legalism around its observance. He dismantles the whole religious paradigm. And he does it by pointing to his identity.

Jesus could have claimed divine authority to change the Sabbath, by saying something along the lines of 'I'm Lord *over* the Sabbath.' But he is saying even more.

The word *Sabbath* means a deep rest, a deep peace. It's a near synonym for *shalom*—a state of wholeness and flourishing in every dimension of life. When Jesus says, 'I am the Lord *of* the Sabbath,' Jesus means that he *is* the Sabbath. [. . .]

Most of us work and work trying to prove ourselves, to convince God, others, and ourselves that we're good people. That work is never over unless we rest in the gospel. At the end of his great act of creation the Lord said, 'It is finished,' and he could rest. On the cross at the end of his great act of redemption Jesus said, 'It is finished'—and we can rest.

King's Cross

Be still

*He got up, rebuked the wind and said to the waves, 'Quiet! Be still!'
Then the wind died down and it was completely calm.*

Mark 4:39

Jesus woke up, and two amazing things happened. The first was his words themselves are a command of utter simplicity. He didn't brace himself, roll up his sleeves, and raise a wand. There were no incantations. He said: *Quiet! Be still!* That's it. To a hurricane, Jesus simply says, *Quiet! Be still!*—just as you would talk to an unruly child. [...]

Now by his actions here Jesus is demonstrating, 'I am not just someone who *has* power; I am power *itself*. Anyone and anything in the whole universe that has any power has it on loan from me.'

That is a mighty claim. And if it's true, who is this and what does this mean for us? There are two options. You could argue that this world is just the result of a monumental 'storm'—you're here by accident, through blind, violent forces of nature, through the big bang—and when you die, you'll turn to dust. And when the sun goes out, there won't be anyone around to remember anything that you've done, so in the end whether you're a cruel person or loving person makes no lasting difference at all.

However, if Jesus is who he says he is, there's another way to look at life. If he's Lord of the storm, then no matter what shape the world is in—or your life is in—you will find Jesus provides all the healing, all the rest, all the power you could possibly want.

King's Cross

Unmanageable power

He said to his disciples, 'Why are you so afraid? Do you still have no faith?' They were terrified and asked each other, 'Who is this? Even the wind and the waves obey him!'

Mark 4:40–1

Why were they more terrified in the calm than they were in the storm? Because Jesus was as unmanageable as the storm itself. The storm had immense power—they couldn't control it. Jesus had infinitely more power, so they had even less control over him.

But there's a huge difference. A storm doesn't love you. Nature is going to wear you down, destroy you. If you live a long time, eventually your body will give out and you'll die. And maybe it will happen sooner—through an earthquake, a fire, or some other disaster. Nature is violent and overwhelming—it's unmanageable power, and it's going to get you sooner or later.

You may say, that's true, but if I go to Jesus, he's not under my control either. He lets things happen that I don't understand. He doesn't do things according to my plan, or in a way that makes sense to me. But if Jesus is God, then he's got to be great enough to have some reasons to let you go through things you can't understand. His power is unbounded, but so are his wisdom and his love. Nature is indifferent to you, but Jesus is filled with untamable love for you. [...]

If you have a God great enough and powerful enough to be mad at because he doesn't stop your suffering, you also have a God who's great enough and powerful enough to have reasons that you can't understand.

King's Cross

Costly power

Then they took Jonah and threw him overboard, and the raging sea grew calm. At this the men greatly feared the LORD, and they offered a sacrifice to the LORD and made vows to him.

Jonah 1:15–16

Mark has deliberately laid out this account [of Jesus calming the storm] using language that is parallel, almost identical, to the language of the famous Old Testament account of Jonah. [...] Two almost identical stories—with just one difference. In the midst of the storm, Jonah said to the sailors, in effect: 'There's only one thing to do. If I perish, you survive. If I die, you will live' (Jonah 1:12). And they threw him into the sea. Which doesn't happen in Mark's story. Or does it?

I think Mark is showing that the stories aren't actually different when you stand back a bit and look at them with the rest of the story of Jesus in view. In Matthew's Gospel, Jesus says, 'One greater than Jonah is here,' and he's referring to himself: *I'm the true Jonah.*

He meant this: Someday I'm going to calm all storms, still all waves. I'm going to destroy destruction, break brokenness, kill death. How can he do that? He can do it only because when he was on the cross he was thrown—willingly, like Jonah—into the ultimate storm, under the ultimate waves, the waves of sin and death. Jesus was thrown into the only storm that can actually sink us—the storm of eternal justice, of what we owe for our wrongdoing. That storm wasn't calmed—not until it swept him away.

King's Cross

A trustworthy Bible or a Stepford God?

All Scripture is God-breathed and is useful for teaching, rebuking, correcting and training in righteousness . . .

2 Timothy 3:16

If we let our unexamined beliefs undermine our confidence in the Bible, the cost may be greater than we think.

If you don't trust the Bible enough to let it challenge and correct your thinking, how could you ever have a *personal* relationship with God? In any truly personal relationship, the other person has to be able to contradict you. For example, if a wife is not allowed to contradict her husband, they won't have an intimate relationship. Remember the (two!) movies *The Stepford Wives*? The husbands of Stepford, Connecticut, decide to have their wives turned into robots who never cross the wills of their husbands. A Stepford wife was wonderfully compliant and beautiful, but no one would describe such a marriage as intimate or personal.

Now, what happens if you eliminate anything from the Bible that offends your sensibility and crosses your will? If you pick and choose what you want to believe and reject the rest, how will you ever have a God who can contradict you? You won't! You'll have a Stepford God! A God, essentially, of your own making, and not a God with whom you can have a relationship and genuine interaction. Only if your God can say things that outrage you and make you struggle (as in a real friendship or marriage!) will you know that you have got hold of a real God and not a figment of your imagination. So an authoritative Bible is not the enemy of a personal relationship with God. It is the precondition for it.

The Reason for God

Acknowledging and wrestling with doubts

Immediately the boy's father exclaimed, 'I do believe; help me overcome my unbelief!'

Mark 9:24

I want to make a proposal that I have seen bear much fruit in the lives of young New Yorkers over the years. I recommend that each side look at *doubt* in a radically new way.

Let's begin with believers. A faith without some doubts is like a human body without any antibodies in it. People who blithely go through life too busy or indifferent to ask hard questions about why they believe as they do will find themselves defenseless against either the experience of tragedy or the probing questions of a smart skeptic. A person's faith can collapse almost overnight if she has failed over the years to listen patiently to her own doubts, which should only be discarded after long reflection.

Believers should acknowledge and wrestle with doubts – not only their own but their friends' and neighbors'. It is no longer sufficient to hold beliefs just because you inherited them. Only if you struggle long and hard with objections to your faith will you be able to provide grounds for your beliefs to skeptics, including yourself, that are plausible rather than ridiculous or offensive. And, just as important for our current situation, such a process will lead you, even after you come to a position of strong faith, to respect and understand those who doubt.

The Reason for God

Doubt your doubts

'Come now, let us reason together,' says the LORD: 'though your sins are like scarlet, they shall be as white as snow; though they are red as crimson, they shall be like wool.'

Isaiah 1:18 (NIV 1984)

But even as believers should learn to look for reasons behind their faith, skeptics must learn to look for a type of faith hidden within their reasoning.

Some will respond to all this, 'My doubts are not based on a leap of faith. I have no beliefs about God one way or another. I simply feel no need for God and I am not interested in thinking about it.' But hidden beneath this feeling is the very modern belief that the existence of God is a matter of indifference unless it intersects with my emotional needs. The speaker is betting his or her life that no God exists who would hold you accountable for your beliefs and behavior if you didn't feel the need for him. That may be true or it may not be true, but, again, it is quite a leap of faith.[28]

The only way to doubt Christianity rightly and fairly is to discern the alternative belief under each of your doubts and then to ask yourself what reasons you have for believing it. How do you know your belief is true? It would be inconsistent to require more justification for Christian belief than you do for your own, but that is frequently what happens. In fairness you must doubt your doubts.

The Reason for God

Help my unbelief

Now Thomas (also known as Didymus), one of the Twelve, was not with the disciples when Jesus came. So the other disciples told him, 'We have seen the Lord!'

But he said to them, 'Unless I see the nail marks in his hands and put my finger where the nails were, and put my hand into his side, I will not believe.'

A week later his disciples were in the house again, and Thomas was with them. Though the doors were locked, Jesus came and stood among them and said, 'Peace be with you!' Then he said to Thomas, 'Put your finger here; see my hands. Reach out your hand and put it into my side. Stop doubting and believe.'

Thomas said to him, 'My Lord and my God!'

Then Jesus told him, 'Because you have seen me, you have believed; blessed are those who have not seen and yet have believed.'

John 20:24–9

Jesus modeled a view of doubt more nuanced than those of either modern skeptics or modern believers. When Jesus confronted 'doubting Thomas' he challenged him not to acquiesce in doubt ('believe!') and yet responded to his request for more evidence. In another incident, Jesus meets a man who confesses that he is filled with doubts (Mark 9:24), who says to Jesus, 'Help my unbelief'—help me with my doubts! In response to this honest admission, Jesus blesses him and heals his son. Whether you consider yourself a believer or a skeptic, I invite you to seek the same kind of honesty and to grow in an understanding of the nature of your own doubts. The result will exceed anything you can imagine.

The Reason for God

Faith and violence?

Do not repay anyone evil for evil. Be careful to do what is right in the eyes of everyone. If it is possible, as far as it depends on you, live at peace with everyone.

Romans 12:17–18

Christianity provides a firm basis for respecting people of other faiths. Jesus assumes that nonbelievers in the culture around them will gladly recognize much Christian behavior as 'good' (Matt. 5:16; cf. 1 Pet. 2:12). That assumes some overlap between the Christian constellation of values and those of any particular culture[29] and of any other religion.[30] Why would this overlap exist? Christians believe that all human beings are made in the image of God, capable of goodness and wisdom. The biblical doctrine of the universal image of God, therefore, leads Christians to expect nonbelievers will be better than any of their mistaken beliefs could make them. The biblical doctrine of universal sinfulness also leads Christians to expect believers will be worse in practice than their orthodox beliefs should make them. So there will be plenty of ground for respectful co-operation.

[. . .] It is common to say that 'fundamentalism' leads to violence, yet as we have seen, all of us have fundamental, unprovable faith commitments that we think are superior to those of others. The real question, then, is *which fundamentals will lead their believers to be the most loving and receptive to those with whom they differ?* Which set of unavoidably exclusive beliefs will lead us to humble, peace-loving behaviour?

The Reason for God

Redemption and suffering

About three in the afternoon Jesus cried out in a loud voice, 'Eli, Eli, lema sabachthani?' (which means 'My God, my God, why have you forsaken me?')

Matthew 27:46

The death of Jesus was qualitatively different from any other death. The physical pain was nothing compared to the spiritual experience of cosmic abandonment.[31] Christianity alone among the world religions claims that God became uniquely and fully human in Jesus Christ and therefore knows first-hand despair, rejection, loneliness, poverty, bereavement, torture and imprisonment. On the cross he went beyond even the worst human suffering and experienced cosmic rejection and pain that exceeds ours as infinitely as his knowledge and power exceeds ours. In his death, God suffers in love, identifying with the abandoned and godforsaken. Why did he do it? The Bible says that Jesus came on a rescue mission for creation. He had to pay for our sins so that some day he can end evil and suffering without ending us.

Let's see where this has brought us. If we again ask the question: 'Why does God allow evil and suffering to continue?' and we look at the cross of Jesus, we still do not know what the answer is. However, we now know what the answer isn't. It can't be that he doesn't love us. It can't be that he is indifferent or detached from our condition. God takes our misery and suffering *so* seriously that he was willing to take it on himself.

The Reason for God

Resurrection and suffering

And I heard a loud voice from the throne saying, 'Look! God's dwelling-place is now among the people, and he will dwell with them. They will be his people, and God himself will be with them and be their God. He will wipe every tear from their eyes. There will be no more death or mourning or crying or pain, for the old order of things has passed away.'

Revelation 21:3–4

For the one who suffers, the Christian faith provides as a resource not just its teaching on the cross but also the fact of the resurrection. The Bible teaches that the future is not an immaterial 'paradise' but a new heaven and a new earth. In Revelation 21, we do not see human beings being taken out of this world into heaven, but rather heaven coming down and cleansing, renewing and perfecting this material world. The secular view of things, of course, sees no future restoration after death or history. And Eastern religions believe we lose our individuality and return to the great All-soul, so our material lives in this world are gone for ever. Even religions that believe in a heavenly paradise consider it a consolation for the losses and pain of this life and all the joys that might have been.

The biblical view of things is resurrection—not a future that is just a *consolation* for the life we never had but a *restoration* of the life you always wanted. This means that every horrible thing that ever happened will not only be undone and repaired but will in some way make the eventual glory and joy even greater.

The Reason for God

Everything sad will come untrue

He who was seated on the throne said, 'I am making everything new!' Then he said, 'Write this down, for these words are trustworthy and true.'

Revelation 21:5

In Greek (specifically Stoic) philosophy there was a belief that history was an endless cycle. Every so often the universe would wind down and burn up in a great conflagration called a *palengenesia*, after which history, having been purified, started over. But in Matthew 19:28 Jesus spoke of his return to earth as *the* palingenesis. 'I tell you the truth, at the renewal of all things (Greek *palingenesis*), the Son of Man will sit on his glorious throne.' This was a radically new concept. Jesus insisted that his return will be with such power that the very material world and universe will be purged of all decay and brokenness. All will be healed and all might-have-beens will *be*.

Just after the climax of the trilogy, *The Lord of the Rings*, Sam Gamgee discovers that his friend Gandalf was not dead (as he thought) but alive. He cries, 'I thought you were dead! But then I thought I was dead myself! *Is everything sad going to come untrue?*'[32] The answer of Christianity to that question is—yes. Everything sad is going to come untrue and it will somehow be *greater* for having once been broken and lost.

The Reason for God

Form and freedom

For Christ's love compels us, because we are convinced that one died for all, and therefore all died. And he died for all, that those who live should no longer live for themselves but for him who died for them and was raised again.

2 Corinthians 5:14–15

Freedom is not the absence of limitations and constraints but it is finding the right ones, those that fit our nature and liberate us.

For a love relationship to be healthy there must be a mutual loss of independence. It can't be just one way. [. . .] At first sight, then, a relationship with God seems inherently dehumanizing. Surely it will have to be 'one way', God's way. God, the divine being, has all the power. I must adjust to God—there is no way that God could adjust to and serve me.

While this may be true in other forms of religion and belief in God, it is not true in Christianity. In the most radical way, God has adjusted to us—in his incarnation and atonement. In Jesus Christ he became a limited human being, vulnerable to suffering and death. On the cross, he submitted to our condition—as sinners—and died in our place to forgive us. In the most profound way, God has said to us, in Christ, 'I will adjust to you. I will change for you. I'll serve you though it means a sacrifice for me.' If he has done this for us, we can and should say the same to God and others.

The Reason for God

No needy among them

... there were no needy persons among them. For from time to time those who owned lands or houses sold them, brought the money from the sales, and put it at the apostles' feet, and it was distributed to anyone who had need.

Acts 4:34–5

This statement [about the early church] is more significant than it looks. Remember the key Old Testament text, Deuteronomy 15, in which God declared that if his people obeyed him as they should, no permanent poverty could exist in their midst. 'There need be no poor among you' (Deut. 15:4). This was the pinnacle of the 'social righteousness' legislation of the Old Testament, which expressed God's love for the vulnerable and his zeal to see poverty and want eliminated. It is remarkable, then, that Acts 4:34 is a direct quote from Deuteronomy 15:4. It cannot be accidental that Luke, in his portrayal of the beginnings of the ... community of the Holy Spirit, chose to describe them in words taken almost directly from [Deuteronomy 15:4]. In Deuteronomy, believers were called to open their hands to the needy as far as there was need, until they were self-sufficient. The New Testament calls Christians to do the same (1 John 3:16–17; cf. Deut. 15:7–8).

Generous Justice

Do good to all people

Let us not become weary in doing good, for at the proper time we will reap a harvest if we do not give up. Therefore, as we have opportunity, let us do good to all people, especially to those who belong to the family of believers.

Galatians 6:9–10

But while Christians are to definitely care for the material needs of their brothers and sisters within the Christian community, are they under obligation to care for their poor neighbors, the poor of the world? It is true that the social legislation of the Old Testament is largely about caring for the needy inside the believing community. Also most examples of generosity in the New Testament are of care for the poor within the church, such as the support for widows (Acts 6:1–7; 1 Tim. 5:3–16). Even Jesus' parable of the sheep and the goats uses the test of caring for those whom Jesus calls 'the least of these my brothers,' probably referring to poor believers. Some of this is common sense. Our first responsibility is to our own families and relations (1 Tim. 5:8), and our second responsibility is to other members of the community of faith (Gal. 6:10).

However, the Bible is clear that Christians' practical love, their generous justice, is not to be confined to only those who believe as we do. Galatians 6:10 strikes the balance when Paul says: 'Do good to all people, especially the family of faith.' Helping 'all people' is not optional, it is a command.

Generous Justice

Who is my neighbor?

'Which of these three do you think was a neighbour to the man who fell into the hands of the robbers?'

Luke 10:36

[... T]he text that most informs Christians' relationships with their neighbors is the parable of the Good Samaritan. [...] What was Jesus doing with this story? He was giving a radical answer to the question, what does it mean to love your neighbor? What is the definition of 'love'? Jesus answered that by depicting a man meeting material, physical, and economic needs through deeds. Caring for people's material and economic needs is not an option for Jesus. He refused to allow the law expert to limit the implications of this command to love. He said it meant being sacrificially involved with the vulnerable, just as the Samaritan risked his life by stopping on the road.

But Jesus refuses to let us limit not only how we love, but who we love. It is typical for us to think of our neighbors as people of the same social class and means (cf. Luke 14:12). We instinctively tend to limit for whom we exert ourselves. We do it for people like us, and for people whom we like. Jesus will have none of that. By depicting a Samaritan helping a Jew, Jesus could not have found a more forceful way to say that anyone at all in need—regardless of race, politics, class, and religion—is your neighbor. Not everyone is your brother or sister in the faith, but everyone is your neighbor, and you must love your neighbor.

Generous Justice

The great Samaritan

'A man was going down from Jerusalem to Jericho, when he was attacked by robbers. They stripped him of his clothes, beat him and went away, leaving him half dead.'

Luke 10:30

According to the Bible, we are all like that man, dying in the road. Spiritually, we are dead in trespasses and sins (Eph. 2:5). But when Jesus came into our dangerous world, he came down our road. And though we had been his enemies, he was moved with compassion by our plight (Rom. 5:10). He came to us and saved us, not merely at the risk of his life, as in the case of the Samaritan, but at the cost of his life. On the cross he paid a debt we could never have paid ourselves. Jesus is the Great Samaritan to whom the Good Samaritan points.

Before you can give this neighbor-love, you need to receive it. Only if you see that you have been saved graciously by someone who owes you the opposite will you go out into the world looking to help absolutely anyone in need. Once we receive this ultimate, radical neighbor-love through Jesus, we can start to be the neighbors that the Bible calls us to be.

Generous Justice

Honoring the image

So God created mankind in his own image, in the image of God he created them; male and female he created them.

Genesis 1:27

The Bible teaches that the sacredness of God has in some ways been imparted to humanity, so that every human life is sacred and every human being has dignity. When God put his image upon us, we became beings of infinite, inestimable value. In Genesis 9:5–6, we read the reason that God considered murder to be so heinous. 'For your lifeblood I will surely demand an accounting,' he said, '. . . for in the image of God has made mankind.' In James 3:9, the writer castigates sharp-tongued people. It is a considerably less serious evil than murder, and yet he forbids all verbal abuse because such miscreants 'curse human beings, who have been made in God's likeness.' There is something so valuable about human beings that not only may they not be murdered, but they can't even be cursed without failing to give them their due, based on the worth bestowed upon them by God. The image of God carries with it the right to not be mistreated or harmed.

All human beings have this right, this worth, according to the Bible. Notice that neither Genesis nor James limits the prohibition on abusive behavior to 'good' people. Regardless of their record or character, all human beings have an irreducible glory and significance to them, because God loves them, indeed, he 'has compassion on all he has made' (Ps. 145:9, 17). He loves even those who turn away from him (Ezek. 33:11; John 3:16).

Generous Justice

Justice in response to God's grace

For the LORD your God is God of gods and LORD of lords, the great God, mighty and awesome, who shows no partiality and accepts no bribes. He defends the cause of the fatherless and the widow, and loves the foreigner residing among you, giving them food and clothing. And you are to love those who are foreigners, for you yourselves were foreigners in Egypt.

Deuteronomy 10:17–9

The Israelites had been poor, racial outsiders in Egypt. How then, Moses asks, could they be callous to the poor, racial outsiders in their own midst? Through Moses, God said: 'Israel, you were liberated by me. You did not accomplish it—I performed it *for* you, by my grace. Now do the same for others. Untie the yoke, unlock the shackles, feed and clothe them, as I did for you.' Of particular interest is Moses' exhortation to 'circumcise your hearts' (verse 16). Circumcision was the external sign that a family had come into a covenant relationship with God. Heart circumcision was a passionate commitment to God on the inside. Meeting the needs of the orphan, the widow, and the poor immigrant was a sign that the Israelites' relationship with God was not just formal and external but internal as well.

The logic is clear. If a person has grasped the meaning of God's grace in his heart, he will do justice. If he doesn't live justly, then he may say with his lips that he is grateful for God's grace, but in his heart he is far from him. If he doesn't care about the poor, it reveals that at best he doesn't understand the grace he has experienced, and at worst he has not really encountered the saving mercy of God. Grace should make you just.

Generous Justice

Justification and justice

What good is it, my brothers and sisters, if someone claims to have faith but has no deeds? Can such faith save them? . . . In the same way, faith by itself, if it is not accompanied by action, is dead.

James 2:14, 17

When we come to the New Testament book of James, we find what at first appears to be a contradiction of Paul, who wrote that Christians are 'justified freely by his grace' (Rom. 3:24) and 'justified by faith apart from the works of the law . . . apart from works' (Rom. 3:28; 4:6).

The contradiction is only apparent. While a sinner can get into relationship with God by only faith (Paul), the ultimate proof that you have saving faith is the changed life that true faith inevitably produces (James). To bring Paul's and James' teaching together, we can say: 'We are saved by faith alone, but not by a faith that remains alone. True faith will always produce a changed life.'

However, James does not merely say that true faith will change one's life in general. [. . .] If you look at someone without adequate resources and do nothing about it, James teaches, your faith is 'dead,' it is not really saving faith. So what are the 'works' he is talking about? He is saying that a life poured out in deeds of service to the poor is the inevitable sign of any real, true, justifying, gospel-faith. Grace makes you just. If you are not just, you've not truly been justified by faith.

Generous Justice

A new attitude toward the poor

Believers in humble circumstances ought to take pride in their high position. But the rich should take pride in their humiliation – since they will pass away like a wild flower.

James 1:9–10

This is a wonderfully paradoxical statement. Every Christian in Christ is at the same time a sinner who deserves death *and* also an adopted child of God, fully accepted and loved. This is true of Christians regardless of their social status. But James proposes that the well-off person who becomes a believer would spiritually benefit by especially thinking about her sinfulness before God, since out in the world she gets nothing but acclaim. On the other hand, the poor person who becomes a believer would spiritually benefit by especially thinking about her new high spiritual status, since out in the world she gets nothing but disdain.

Here we see why later James can say that concern for the poor and generous sharing of wealth are the inevitable signs of someone who has understood the gospel of grace. The world makes social class into bottom-line identities. You *are* your social status and bank account—that is the basis for your self-regard. But in the gospel these things are demoted and made peripheral. Someone who does not show any signs of at least gradual identity transformation in this manner does not give evidence of having really grasped the gospel. Thus, James can say that faith without respect, love, and practical concern for the poor is dead. It's not justifying, gospel faith.

Generous Justice

Always thinking of justice

'I put on righteousness as my clothing; justice was my robe and turban.'

Job 29:14

When Job says [these words], he is speaking about a social consciousness that infused his daily life as completely as his clothing covered his body. He shared his money and food with the poor. He cared for the blind, the crippled, and the poor widow. He was also a legal advocate for the immigrant and the orphan.

The vision is comprehensive. Job says he *wears* justice, suggesting that it is always on his mind, he is always looking for ways to do it. Psalm 41:1 (ESV) says, 'Blessed is the one who considers the poor,' and the Hebrew word translated as 'considers' means to give sustained attention to a subject and then to act wisely and successfully with regard to it. God does not want us to merely give the poor perfunctory help, but to ponder long and hard about how to improve their entire situation.[33]

[...] Doing justice, then, requires constant, sustained reflection and circumspection. If you are a Christian, and you refrain from committing adultery or using profanity or missing church, but you don't do the hard work of thinking through how to do justice in every area of life—you are failing to live justly and righteously.

Generous Justice

The ascension

After [Jesus] said this, he was taken up before their very eyes, and a cloud hid him from their sight. [The apostles] were looking intently up into the sky as he was going, when suddenly two men dressed in white stood beside them. 'Men of Galilee,' they said, 'why do you stand here looking into the sky? This same Jesus, who has been taken from you into heaven, will come back in the same way you have seen him go into heaven.'

Acts 1:9–11

What is the ascension? It is not simply Jesus' return from the earth to heaven. It is a new enthronement for Jesus, ushering in a new relationship with us and with the whole world. [. . .]

When someone becomes a king or queen, there is a ceremony in which authority is officially transferred. The person literally walks up onto a podium and then goes up steps and sits on a throne, a higher chair. And we say, 'She ascended to the throne.' The word *ascended* gets across more than a change in elevation. She is not just physically higher than everyone else—she has a new relationship to others and has new powers and privileges to exercise authority. The steps and the higher chair are symbolic. [. . .]

Now, if Jesus merely wanted to return to the Father, he could have just vanished. There were other times in which he vanished immediately out of sight, as with the disciples on the road to Emmaus. But instead, at the ascension Jesus literally rises up into the clouds and disappears into the distance of the heavens. Why did he do it that way? We can only speculate, but it may have been for the same reason that we have a coronation ceremony. The elevation in space symbolized the elevation in authority and relationship. Jesus was tracing out physically what was happening cosmically and spiritually.

And what was that? He was going, now as the unique God-man—fully human and fully divine—to take his place as the new king and head of the human race.

Encounters with Jesus

At the right hand of the Father

The Son is the radiance of God's glory and the exact representation of his being, sustaining all things by his powerful word. After he had provided purification for sins, he sat down at the right hand of the Majesty in heaven.

Hebrews 1:3

In ancient times, whoever sat at the right hand of the throne was something like the king's prime minister, the one who executed his kingly authority and rule in actual laws and policies. And so this is saying that Jesus ascended to begin his reign. But this idea that the ascension is an enthronement requires some clarifications to be made. Jesus has always been king—he has always had authority over us because he is God.

But now, at the ascension, as the risen God-man, he begins his job as heavenly head of the church, and now he rules over all other rulers and powers—indeed 'over *everything* for the church' (Eph. 1:21–2). He does this especially through the work of the Holy Spirit, work that Jesus laid out in detail to his disciples the night before he died (John 14–17). It also means he is ruling over and controlling all of history toward its final goal, in which the church, the new people of God, are finally and fully liberated, and, along with them, the whole world is renewed (Rom. 8:18ff). And at that time there will be no more suffering, evil, or death, because Jesus' saving and restoring work will be complete.

To put it simply, Jesus is directing a cosmic transition plan— one that will bring about new heavens and a new earth (Isa. 65:17–25). As ascended Lord he is spreading the gospel and building up his church by working in the hearts of people while he guides all the events of history toward a glorious end.

Encounters with Jesus

Money as a master

'Watch out! Be on your guard against all kinds of greed; life does not consist in an abundance of possessions.'

Luke 12:15

Paul says greed is a form of idolatry (Col. 3:5; Eph. 5:5). Luke is teaching us the same thing in his gospel. [...] What is greed? In the surrounding passages of Luke 11 and 12, Jesus warned people about worrying over their possessions. For Jesus, greed is not only love of money, but excessive anxiety about it. He lays out the reason our emotions are so powerfully controlled by our bank account—'a man's life does not consist in the abundance of his possessions.' To 'consist' of your possessions is to be defined by what you own and consume. The term describes a personal identity based on money. It refers to people who, if they lose their wealth, do not have a 'self' left, for their personal worth is based on their financial worth. Later Jesus comes right out and calls this what it is.

'No servant can serve two masters; either he will hate the one and love the other, or he will be devoted to the one and despise the other. You cannot serve both God and money.' The Pharisees, who loved money, heard all this and were sneering at Jesus. He said to them, 'You are the ones who justify yourselves in the eyes of men, but God knows your hearts. What is highly valued among men is detestable in God's sight.'

Luke 16:13–15

Counterfeit Gods

Grace and money

But Zacchaeus stood up and said to the Lord, 'Look, Lord! Here and now
I give half of my possessions to the poor, and if I have cheated anybody
out of anything, I will pay back four times the amount.' Jesus said to him,
'Today salvation has come to this house, because this man, too, is a son
of Abraham. For the Son of Man came to seek and to save the lost.'

Luke 19:8–10

Zacchaeus wanted to follow Jesus, and immediately he realized that, if he was to do that, money was an issue. So he made two remarkable promises.

He promised to give away 50 percent of his income to the poor. This was far beyond the 10 percent giving that the Mosaic law required. [. . .] Zacchaeus knew that when he made this offer. His heart had been affected. Since he knew salvation was not through the law, but through grace, he did not aim to live by only fulfilling the letter of the law. He wanted to go beyond it.

Zacchaeus's second promise did not have to do so much with charity and mercy but with justice. He had made a great deal of money by cheating. There were many people from whom he had taken exorbitant revenues. Here again, the Mosaic law made a provision. Leviticus 5:16 and Numbers 5:7 directed that if you had stolen anything, you had to make restitution with interest. You had to give it back with 20 percent interest. However, Zacchaeus wanted to do far more. He would give back 'four times the amount' he had stolen. That's 300 percent interest.

In response to these promises, Jesus said, 'Salvation has come to this house.' Notice, he didn't say, 'If you live like this, salvation will come to this house.' No, it *has* come. God's salvation does not come in response to a changed life. A changed life comes in response to the salvation, offered as a free gift.

Counterfeit Gods

The poverty of Christ

For you know the grace of our Lord Jesus Christ, that though he was rich, yet for your sake he became poor, so that you through his poverty might become rich.

2 Corinthians 8:9

In 2 Corinthians 8 and 9 Paul asks a church to give an offering to the poor. Though he is an apostle with authority, he writes: 'I am not commanding you' (2 Cor. 8:8). He means: 'I don't want to order you. I don't want this offering to be simply the response to a demand.' He doesn't put pressure directly on the will and say, 'I'm an apostle, so do what I say.' Rather, he wants to see the 'genuineness of your love,' and then writes these famous words [about Christ's poverty].

Jesus, the God-Man, had infinite wealth, but if he had held on to it, we would have died in our spiritual poverty. That was the choice—if he stayed rich, we would die poor. If he died poor, we could become rich. Our sins would be forgiven, and we would be admitted into the family of God. Paul was not giving this church a mere ethical precept, exhorting them to stop loving money so much and become more generous. Rather, he recapitulated the gospel.

This is what Paul was saying. Jesus gave up all his treasure in heaven, in order to make you his treasure—for you are God's special possession (1 Pet. 2:9–10). When you see him dying to make you his treasure, that will make him yours. Money will cease to be the currency of your significance and security, and you will want to bless others with what you have. To the degree that you grasp the gospel, money will have no dominion over you. Think on his costly grace until it changes you into a generous people.

Counterfeit Gods

The idolatry of success

The idols of the nations are silver and gold, made by human hands.
They have mouths, but cannot speak, eyes, but cannot see.

Psalm 135:15–16

More than other idols, personal success and achievement lead to a sense that we ourselves are god, that our security and value rest in our own wisdom, strength, and performance. To be the very best at what you do, to be at the top of the heap, means no one is like you. You are supreme. [...]

If our entire culture strongly encourages us to adopt this counterfeit god, how can we escape it?

One of the most successful and powerful men in the world in his time was Naaman, whose story is told in the Bible, in 2 Kings 5. Naaman had what some might call 'a designer life.' He was commander of the army of Aram, which today we call Syria. He was also the equivalent of the prime minister of the nation, since the king of Syria 'leaned on his arm' at formal state occasions (2 Kings 5:18). He was a wealthy man and a valiant soldier, highly decorated and honored. However, all of these great accomplishments and abilities had met their match.

Counterfeit Gods

The successful dead man

Now Naaman was commander of the army of the king of Aram. He was a great man in the sight of his master and highly regarded, because through him the LORD had given victory to Aram. He was a valiant soldier, but he had leprosy.

2 Kings 5:1

Notice how the author of 2 Kings piles up the accolades and accomplishments, and suddenly adds that, despite all of them, he was a dead man walking. *Leprosy* in the Bible encompassed a variety of fatal, wasting skin diseases that slowly crippled, disfigured, and finally killed their victims. [...] Naaman had everything—wealth, athletic prowess, popular acclaim—but under it all he was literally falling apart.

[...] Naaman had success and money and power, but he was a leper. Success, wealth, and power are supposed to make you the consummate *in*sider, admitted to the most exclusive social circles and inner rings. However, his contagious skin disease had made him an outsider. All his success was useless, since it could not overcome his social alienation and emotional despair.

In this, the story of Naaman functions as a parable. Many people pursue success as a way to overcome the sense that they are somehow 'outsiders.' If they attain it, they believe, it will open the doors into the clubs, into the social sets, into relationships with the connected and the influential. Finally, they think, they will be accepted by all the people who really matter. Success promises to do that, but in the end it cannot deliver. Naaman's leprosy represents the reality that success can't deliver the satisfaction we are looking for.

Counterfeit Gods

Some great thing

So Naaman went with his horses and chariots and stopped at the door of Elisha's house. Elisha sent a messenger to say to him, 'Go, wash yourself seven times in the Jordan, and your flesh will be restored and you will be cleansed.' But Naaman went away angry . . .

2 Kings 5:9–11

Naaman expected that Elisha would take the money and perform some magic ritual. Or, he thought, if Elisha did not take the money, he would at least demand that Naaman do 'some great thing' to earn his healing. Instead he was asked to simply go and dip himself seven times in the Jordan River. At this he went off in a rage.

Why? Again, Naaman's entire worldview was being challenged. He had just learned that this God is not an extension of culture, but a transformer of culture, not a controllable but a sovereign Lord. Now he was being confronted with a God who in his dealings with human beings only operates on the basis of grace. These two go together. No one can control the true God because no one can earn, merit, or achieve their own blessing and salvation. Naaman was angry because he thought he was going to be asked to do a mighty thing, as it were; to bring back the broomstick of the Wicked Witch of the West, or to return the Ring of Power to Mount Doom. Those would have been requests in keeping with his self-image and worldview. But Elisha's message was an insult. 'Any idiot, any child, anyone can go down and paddle around in the Jordan,' he thought to himself. 'That takes no ability or attainment *at all!*' Exactly. That is a salvation for anyone, good or bad, weak or strong.

Counterfeit Gods

Two suffering servants

Now bands of raiders from Aram had gone out and had taken captive a young girl from Israel, and she served Naaman's wife. She said to her mistress, 'If only my master would see the prophet who is in Samaria! He would cure him of his leprosy.'

2 Kings 5:2–3

At every point in the Bible, the writers are at pains to stress that God's grace and forgiveness, while free to the recipient, are always costly for the giver. From the earliest parts of the Bible, it was understood that God could not forgive without sacrifice. [. . .]

In this story, too, someone had to bear her suffering with patience and love, in order for Naaman to receive his blessing. I'm referring to a character in the narrative who entered and exited so quickly that she is hardly noticed. Yet she was in some ways the most important character in the story. Who was she? The slave girl of Naaman's wife was captured by raiding bands of Syrians. [. . .]

She did not seek revenge, she trusted God to be the judge of all. She forgave him and became the vehicle for his healing and salvation. She trusted God and bore her suffering with patience. [. . .]

This biblical theme, that forgiveness always requires a suffering servant, finds its climax in Jesus, who fulfills the prophecies of a Suffering Servant who will come to save the world (Isaiah 53).

Counterfeit Gods

Be filled with the Spirit

Submit to one another out of reverence for Christ.

Ephesians 5:21

[This is] the introductory statement for Paul's famous paragraph on marriage in Ephesians [...] Modern Western readers immediately focus on (and often bristle at) the word 'submit,' because for us it touches the controversial issue of gender roles. But to start arguing about that is a mistake that will be fatal to any true grasp of Paul's introductory point. He is declaring that everything he is about to say about marriage assumes that the parties are being filled with God's Spirit. Only if you have learned to serve others by the power of the Holy Spirit will you have the power to face the challenges of marriage.

The first place in the New Testament that discusses the work of the Spirit at length is in the Gospel of John. Jesus considered the teaching so important that he devoted much time to it on the night before he died. When we hear of 'spiritual filledness,' we think of inner peace and power, and that may indeed be a result. Jesus, however, spoke of the Holy Spirit primarily as the 'Spirit of truth' who will 'remind you of everything I have said to you' (John 14:17, 26). The Holy Spirit 'will glorify me because it is from me that he will receive what he will make known to you' (John 16:14). What does this mean?

'Make known' translates a Greek word meaning a momentous announcement that rivets attention. The Holy Spirit's task, then, is to unfold the meaning of Jesus' person and work to believers in such a way that the glory of it—its infinite importance and beauty—is brought home to the mind and heart.

The Meaning of Marriage

Servants to one another

Do nothing out of selfish ambition or vain conceit. Rather, in humility value others above yourselves.

Philippians 2:3

All Christians who really understand the gospel undergo a radical change in the way they relate to people. [...] Notice that he doesn't say that we should unrealistically try to believe that all others are better than us in every way. That would be nonsense. Rather, we should *consider* and count the interests of others as more important than our own. Elsewhere he says that we should not 'please ourselves' but rather should 'please our neighbors for their own good, to build them up. For even Christ did not please himself' (Rom. 15:1–3). Paul goes so far as to tell Christians to be *douloi* of one another (Gal. 5:13)—literally bond-servants. Because Christ humbled himself and became a servant and met our needs even at the cost of his own life, now we are like servants—but to one another.

This is a radical, even distasteful image for modern people. Servant? When Paul uses this metaphor, he is not saying that we are to relate to one another in every way that literal bond-servants served their masters in ancient times. What he is saying is this: A servant puts someone else's needs ahead of his or her own. That is how all believers should live with each other.

The Meaning of Marriage

The antidote to self-centeredness

Love is patient and kind. It does not envy, it does not boast, it is not proud. It does not dishonor others, it is not self-seeking, it is not easily angered, it keeps no record of wrongs.

1 Corinthians 13:4–5

Repeatedly Paul shows that love is the very opposite of 'self-seeking,' which is literally pursuing one's own welfare before those of others. Self-centeredness is easily seen in the signs Paul lists: impatience, irritability, a lack of graciousness and kindness in speech, envious brooding on the better situations of others, and holding past injuries and hurts against others. [...] Self-centeredness by its very character makes you blind to your own while being hypersensitive, offended, and angered by that of others. The result is always a downward spiral into self-pity, anger, and despair, as the relationship gets eaten away to nothing.

But the gospel, brought home to your heart by the Spirit, can make you happy enough to be humble, giving you an internal fullness that frees you to be generous with the other even when you are not getting the satisfaction you want out of the relationship. Without the help of the Spirit, without a continual refilling of your soul's tank with the glory and love of the Lord, such submission to the interests of the other is virtually impossible to accomplish for any length of time without becoming resentful. [...] To have a marriage that sings requires a Spirit-created ability to serve, to take yourself out of the center, to put the needs of others ahead of your own. The Spirit's work of making the gospel real to the heart weakens the self-centeredness in the soul. It is impossible for us to make major headway against self-centeredness and move into a stance of service without some kind of supernatural help.

The Meaning of Marriage

The path to true happiness

For whoever wants to save their life will lose it, but whoever loses their life for me will find it.

Matthew 16:25

Today's culture of the 'Me-Marriage' finds [the idea] of putting the interests of your spouse ahead of your own oppressive. But that is because it does not look deeply enough into this crucial part of Christian teaching about the nature of reality. What is that teaching?

Christianity asserts, to begin with, that God is triune—that is, three persons within one God. And from John 17 and other passages we learn that from all eternity, each person—Father, Son, and Holy Spirit—has glorified, honored, and loved the other two. So there is an 'other-orientation' within the very being of God. When Jesus Christ went to the cross, he was simply acting in character. As C. S. Lewis wrote, when Jesus sacrificed himself for us, he did 'in the wild weather of his outlying provinces' that which from all eternity 'he had done at home in glory and gladness.'[34]

Then the Bible says that human beings were made in God's image. That means, among other things, that we were created to worship and live for God's glory, not our own. We were made to serve God and others. That means paradoxically that if we try to put our own happiness ahead of obedience to God, we violate our own nature and become, ultimately, miserable. Jesus restates the principle when he says, 'Whoever wants to save his life shall lose it, but whoever loses his life *for my sake* will find it' (Matt. 16:25). He is saying, 'If you seek happiness more than you seek me, you will have neither; if you seek to serve me more than serve happiness, you will have both.'

The Meaning of Marriage

The joyful fear of the Lord

And now, Israel, what does the LORD your God ask of you but to fear the LORD your God, to walk in obedience to him, to love him, to serve the LORD your God with all your heart and with all your soul.

Deuteronomy 10:12

Paul says [in Ephesians] that we should submit to one another 'out of reverence for Christ.' That's what many modern translations say, but literally Paul says we should do it out of the *fear of Christ*. The word 'reverence' is too weak to convey what Paul is talking about here, but the word 'fear' is also misleading, because to English readers it conveys the idea of fright and dread. What does it mean?

When we go to the Old Testament, where the term 'the fear of the Lord' is very common, we come upon some very puzzling usages. Often the fear of the Lord is linked with great joy. Proverbs 28:14 (KJV) tells us that 'Happy is the man that feareth always.' How can someone who is constantly in fear be filled with happiness?

Perhaps most surprising is Psalm 130:4 (ESV), where the Psalmist says, 'But with you there is forgiveness, that you may be feared.' Forgiveness and grace increase the fear of the Lord.

Other passages tell us that we can be instructed and grow in the fear of the Lord (2 Chron. 26:5; Ps. 34:11), that it is characterized by praise, wonder, and delight (Ps. 40:3; Isa. 11:3). How can that be? One commentator on Psalm 130 puts it like this: 'Servile fear [being scared] would have been diminished, not increased, by forgiveness ... The true sense of the "fear of the Lord" in the Old Testament [then] ... implies relationship.'

The Meaning of Marriage

The liberating fear of the Lord

Since, then, we know what it is to fear the Lord, we try to persuade others . . . For Christ's love compels us, because we are convinced that one died for all.

2 Corinthians 5:11, 14

Obviously, to be in the fear of the Lord is not to be scared of the Lord, even though the Hebrew word has overtones of respect and awe. 'Fear' in the Bible means to be overwhelmed, to be controlled by something. To fear the Lord is to be overwhelmed with wonder before the greatness of God and his love. It means that, because of his bright holiness and magnificent love, you find him 'fearfully beautiful.' That is why the more we experience God's grace and forgiveness, the more we experience a trembling awe and wonder before the greatness of all that he is and has done for us. Fearing him means bowing before him out of amazement at his glory and beauty.

Paul speaks of the love of Christ 'compelling' us (2 Cor. 5:14). What is it that most motivates and moves you? Is it the desire for success? The pursuit of some achievement? The need to prove yourself to your parents? The need for respect from your peers? Are you largely driven by anger against someone or some people who have wronged you? Paul says that if any of these things is a greater controlling influence on you than the reality of God's love for you, you will not be in a position to serve others unselfishly. Only out of the fear of the Lord Jesus will we be liberated to serve one another.

The Meaning of Marriage

Enjoying the triune God

Therefore go and make disciples of all nations, baptizing them in the name of the Father and of the Son and of the Holy Spirit.

Matthew 28:19

God has always had within himself a perfect friendship. The Father, the Son, and the Holy Spirit are adoring one another, giving glorifying love to one another, and delighting in one another. We know of no joy higher than being loved and loving in return, but a triune God would know that love and joy in unimaginable, infinite dimensions. God is, therefore, infinitely, profoundly *happy*, filled with perfect joy—not some abstract tranquility but the fierce happiness of dynamic loving relationships. Knowing this God is not to get beyond emotions or thoughts but to be filled with glorious love and joy.

If God did not need to create other beings in order to know love and happiness, then why did he do so? Jonathan Edwards argues, in *A Dissertation Concerning the End for Which God Created the World*, that the only reason God would have had for creating us was not to *get* the cosmic love and joy of relationship (because he already had that) but to *share* it.[35] Edwards shows how it is completely consistent for a triune God—who is 'other-oriented' in his very core, who seeks glory only to give it to others—to communicate happiness and delight in his own divine perfections and beauty to others.

As Augustine wrote in his great work *On the Trinity*, our ability to love other persons is just an image of the internal Trinitarian love that we were created to reflect.[36] We can see why a triune God would call us to converse with him, to know and relate to him. It is because he wants to share the joy he has. Prayer is our way of entering into the happiness of God himself.

Prayer

Encountering the Father

*God sent his Son, born of a woman, born under the law, to redeem
those under the law, that we might receive adoption to sonship.
Because you are his sons, God sent the Spirit of his Son into our hearts,
the Spirit who calls out, 'Abba, Father.'*

Galatians 4:4–6

While God was called Father only occasionally in the Old
Testament, it is when the Trinity becomes explicit in the
New Testament that the character of God's fatherhood also
becomes prominent and clear. The Father sends the Son to save us
from our sins so that we can become God's adopted sons and
daughters (Eph. 1:3–10). When we are born again through faith in
Christ, we receive the right to be his children and call on him as
father (John 1:12–13). [...]

To be adopted into a new family means a revolution in how
you live your life day to day. In Christ, therefore, believers are not
only legally but personally established in God's fatherly love. In a
remarkable passage, Jesus prays to the Father for his followers
'[that] the world will know that you sent me and have loved them
even as you have loved me' (John 17:23). To be adopted means that
now God loves us as if we had done all Jesus had done. This means
Christ, as one theologian said, 'has not merely paid the penalty' for
our sins but 'also he has positively merited for us eternal life ...
merited for [us] the reward by his perfect obedience to God's
law,'[37] so we can run to our Father without fear. We have the most
intimate and unbreakable relationship possible with the God of
the universe.

Prayer

Encountering the Spirit

In the same way, the Spirit helps us in our weakness. We do not know what we ought to pray for, but the Spirit himself intercedes for us through wordless groans. And he who searches our hearts knows the mind of the Spirit, because the Spirit intercedes for God's people in accordance with the will of God.

Romans 8:26–7

There has been debate over the meaning of 'the Spirit's groans.' Some believe this is the Spirit helping us when we are desperate and groaning, but it is unlikely that this is describing only times of depression. Rather, the 'weakness' referred to in verse 26 is the weakness described in the preceding verses, which refer not just to times of despondency but to our entire human situation of frustrated longings as we await the future glory (Rom. 8 vv. 18–25, especially v. 23). We know that God is working out all things for our good according to his will (v. 28), but seldom can we discern what that good actually is. In other words, most of the time, we don't know exactly what outcome we should pray for. The Spirit, however, makes our groaning *his* groaning, putting his prayers to the Father inside our prayers. He does so by placing within us a deep, inexpressible longing to do God's will and see his glory. This aspiration—this 'groaning' desire to please him—comes through in our petitions to God. In every specific request, then, the Father hears us praying for what is both truly best for us and pleasing to him, 'and the intercession of the Spirit is answered as God works all things for our good.'[38] The Spirit enables us to long for the future glory of God and his will, even though we don't know the specific thing we should pray for here and now.[39]

Prayer is the way to experience a powerful confidence that God is handling our lives well, that our bad things will turn out for good, our good things cannot be taken from us, and the best things are yet to come.

Prayer

Encountering the Son

For there is one God and one mediator between God and mankind, the man Christ Jesus.

1 Timothy 2:5

We come to the Father not only in the Spirit but through the Son. We can only be confident that God is our father if we come to him through the mediation of Christ, in Jesus' name. [. . .]

Jesus is the mediator between us and God (1 Tim. 2:5; cf. Heb. 8:6; 12:24). All ancient lands and cultures had temples, because human beings once knew innately that there was a gap, a yawning chasm, between us and the divine. [. . .]

Now, however, we have the ultimate mediator and priest to end all priests (Heb. 4:14–15). He eliminates the gap so that we can know God as friend (cf. Ex. 33:11). It is because the Son of God was 'made like them, fully human in every way, in order that he might become a merciful and faithful high priest' (Heb. 2:17). And because 'we do not have a high priest who is unable to empathize with our weaknesses, but . . . has been tempted in every way, just as we are—yet he did not sin,' we are able to 'approach God's throne of grace with confidence' (Heb. 4:15–16).

Here, then, is a claim that Aristotle—indeed, all the other philosophers and religious teachers of the world—would find outrageous. How could God be our intimate friend? How could we approach him with complete confidence? It is because God became like us, equally mortal and subject to suffering and death. He did it so we could be forgiven and justified by faith apart from our efforts and merits. That is why we can draw near.

Prayer

Doing justice and preaching grace

Because we loved you so much, we were delighted to share with you not only the gospel of God but our lives as well.

1 Thessalonians 2:8

Deeds of mercy and justice should be done out of love, not simply as a means to the end of evangelism. And yet there is no better way for Christians to lay a foundation for evangelism than by doing justice.

It is also impossible to separate word and deed ministry from each other in ministry because human beings are integrated wholes—body and soul. When some Christians say, 'Caring for physical needs will detract from evangelism,' they must be thinking only of doing evangelism among people who are comfortable and well-off. The London City Mission is a nearly two-hundred-year-old evangelical mission that seeks to do evangelism among the urban poor of London. Though evangelism is its central purpose, this is done through relationship, visitation, and friendship. Its mission is: *the same person, going to the same people, regularly, to become their friend for Jesus' sake.* Because of this mission, LCM missionaries run neither large-scale evangelism nor social programs. Instead 'word' and 'deed' are seamlessly integrated in their ministry. Helping their neighbors with their children's educational needs, or with finding jobs or learning English as a second language, goes hand-in-hand with sharing their faith verbally. On paper, we may ask, 'Should Christians do evangelism or social justice?' But in real life, these things go together.[40]

Generous Justice

God in the face of the poor

'For I was hungry and you gave me something to eat, I was thirsty and you gave me something to drink, I was a stranger and you invited me in, I needed clothes and you clothed me, I was sick and you looked after me, I was in prison and you came to visit me.'

Matthew 25:35–6

Many people say, 'I can't believe in God when I see all the injustice in the world.' But here is Jesus, the Son of God, who knows what it's like to be the victim of injustice, to stand up to power, to face a corrupt system and be killed for it. He knows what it is like to be lynched. I'm not sure how you believe in a God remote from injustice and oppression, but Christianity doesn't ask you to believe in that. [. . .]

On Judgment Day, don't say to the Lord, 'When did we see you thirsty, naked, and captive?' Because the answer is—on the cross! There we see how far God was willing to go to identify with the oppressed of the world. And he was doing it all for us! There Jesus, who deserved acquittal and freedom, got condemnation— so that we who deserve condemnation for our sins can receive acquittal (Gal. 3:10–14; 2 Cor. 5:21). This was the ultimate instance of God's identification with the poor. He not only became one of the actually poor and marginalized, he stood in the place of all those of us in spiritual poverty and bankruptcy (Matt. 5:3) and paid our debt.

Now *that* is a thing of beauty. To take *that* into the center of your life and heart will make you one of the just.

Generous Justice

Racial reconciliation

'From one man he made all the nations, that they should inhabit the whole earth; and he marked out their appointed times in history and the boundaries of their lands.'

Acts 17:26

The Bible provides deep resources for racial rapprochement. Its depiction of creation cuts the nerve of racism at its source. It insists that all human beings are 'of one blood' (Acts 17:26). The account of Adam's creation is crucial for an understanding of race. Here is a comment from the *Mishnah,* the first major commentary on the Bible compiled by Jewish Bible scholars. 'Why did God create only one human being? So that no one can say to a fellow human being: My father was better than yours.'[41] Because all are created in the image of God, no one race is inherently superior to any other.

Where does racism come from? In Genesis 11, the story of the Tower of Babel tells us that the people of the earth were marked by pride and a lust for power. As due punishment for this pride, we are told that God 'confused their speech.' They could not understand each other or work together and as a result they scattered into different nations. We must not miss the profound message of this account—that human pride and lust for power leads to racial and national division, strife, and hatred.

Generous Justice

Grace and race

When the day of Pentecost came, they were all together in one place ... All of them were filled with the Holy Spirit and began to speak in other tongues as the Spirit enabled them.

Acts 2:1, 4

In Acts 2, when the Holy Spirit descends on the church on the day of Pentecost, another miracle occurs. While at Babel people who spoke the same language couldn't understand each other, at Pentecost, everyone who spoke different languages could nonetheless all understand the preaching of the gospel by the apostles. It was a reversing of the curse of Babel. It was a declaration that the grace of Jesus can heal the wounds of racism. At Pentecost the first gospel preaching was in every language, showing that no one culture is *the* 'right' culture, and that in the Spirit we can have a unity that transcends all national, linguistic, and cultural barriers. The result, according to Ephesians 2:11–22, is a community of equal 'fellow-citizens' from all races. According to 1 Peter 2:9, Christians are a 'new ethnic.' Partnership and friendship across racial barriers within the church is one of the signs of the presence and power of the gospel. In Christ our racial and cultural identities, while not insignificant, are no longer primary to our self-understanding. [...]

In the final chapters of the Bible, a time is envisioned in which God's people are united from 'every tribe and language and people and nation' (Rev. 5:9; 7:9; 11:9; 14:6). At the climax of the world's history, brought about by the death and resurrection of Jesus, there will be the end of all racial division and hatred.

Generous Justice

Common grace cooperation

Learn to do right; seek justice. Defend the oppressed. Take up the cause of the fatherless; plead the case of the widow.

Isaiah 1:17

Why should Christians expect that many who do not share their biblical beliefs will nonetheless want to work for the same goals? The apostle Paul taught that human beings who have never read or known the Bible, nevertheless 'show that the requirements of [God's] law are written on their hearts, their consciences also bearing witness' (Rom. 2:15). Theologians have called this 'general revelation' as contrasted with the 'special revelation' of the Bible. God reveals much of his will to human consciences through what has been called 'the light of nature.' For example, even if someone does not believe the biblical teaching that God made man in his own image, nevertheless the sacredness and dignity of every human being can be known intuitively, without belief in the Bible.

As a result of this general revelation, Christians believe that there is much 'common grace' in every culture. The implication of James 1:17 is that God scatters gifts of wisdom, goodness, justice, and beauty across all the human race, regardless of people's beliefs. [...] In short, the Bible warns us not to think that only Bible-believing people care about justice or are willing to sacrifice in order to bring it about.

Generous Justice

Justice and Christian provocation

Your love, LORD, reaches to the heavens, your faithfulness to the skies. Your righteousness is like the highest mountains, your justice like the great deep.

Psalm 36:5–6

We have said that Christians should acknowledge 'common grace,' that non-Christians share with us common intuitions about the good, the true, and the just. We should appeal to those common values and work alongside our neighbors in an effort to improve justice in society. We should agree that, according to the Bible, all the various views of justice out there in our society are partly right.

But they are also partly wrong. Each of the theories [of justice current in our culture] makes one of these factors—virtue, rights, or the common good—into a 'bottom line' that trumps the other two. However, the biblical understanding of justice is not rooted in any one of these, but in the character and being of God himself. This means that no current political framework can fully convey the comprehensive biblical vision of justice, and Christians should never identify too closely with a particular political party or philosophy. [...]

So even as Christians practice humble cooperation with their allies, they should at the same time be respectfully provocative with them, arguing that their models of justice are reductionistic and incomplete.

Generous Justice

Two ways to 'love'

We love because he first loved us.

1 John 4:19

One of William Blake's 'Songs of Experience' shows in the most striking way that there are two ways to conduct a romantic relationship.

Love seeketh not itself to please,
Nor for itself hath any care,
But for another gives its ease,
And builds a heaven in hell's despair.

Love seeketh only self to please,
To bind another to its delight,
Joys in another's loss of ease,
And builds a hell in heaven's despite.

(from 'The Clod and the Pebble')

It is possible to feel you are 'madly in love' with someone, when it is really just an attraction to someone who can meet your needs and address the insecurities and doubts you have about yourself. In that kind of relationship, you will demand and control rather than serve and give. The only way to avoid sacrificing your partner's joy and freedom on the altar of your need is to turn to the ultimate lover of your soul. He voluntarily sacrificed himself on the cross, taking what you deserved for your sins against God and others. On the cross he was forsaken and experienced the lostness of hell, but he did it all for us. Because of the loving sacrifice of the Son, you can know the heaven of the Father's love through the work of the Spirit. Jesus truly 'built a heaven in hell's despair.' And fortified with the love of God in your soul, you likewise can now give yourself in loving service to your spouse.

The Meaning of Marriage

The character of friendship

A friend loves at all times, and a brother is born for a time of adversity.

Proverbs 17:17

What is friendship? The Bible, and particularly the book of Proverbs, spends much time describing and defining it. One of the prime qualities of a friend is constancy. Friends 'love at *all* times' and especially during 'adversity' (Prov. 17:17). The counterfeit is a 'fair-weather friend' who comes over when you are successful but goes away if prosperity, status, or influence wanes (Prov. 14:20; 19:4,6,7). True friends stick closer than a brother (Prov. 18:24). They are always there for you. Another of the essential characteristics of friendship is transparency and candor. Real friends encourage and affectionately affirm one another (Prov. 27:9; cf. 1 Sam. 23:16–18), yet real friends also offer bracing critiques: 'Faithful are the wounds of a friend' (Prov. 27:5–6). Like a surgeon, friends cut you in order to heal you. Friends become wiser together through a healthy clash of viewpoints. 'As iron sharpens iron, so friend sharpens friend' (Prov. 27:17).

There are two features of real friendship—constancy and transparency. Real friends always let you in, and they never let you down. [...] However, there is a third quality to friendship, and it is not as easy to put into a single word. The right word, literally, is 'sympathy'—*sym-pathos*, common passion. This means that friendships are discovered more than they are created at will. They arise between people who discover that they have common interests in and longings for the same things.

The Meaning of Marriage

Christian friendship

'A new command I give you: Love one another. As I have loved you, so you must love one another. By this everyone will know that you are my disciples, if you love one another.'

John 13:34–5

When we come to the New Testament, there is a new layer added to our understanding of friendship. Friendship is only possible when there is a common vision and passion—think of what that means for all Christians. For believers in Christ, despite enormous differences in class, temperament, culture, race, sensibility, and personal history, there is an underlying commonality that is more powerful than them all. This is not so much a 'thread' as an indestructible steel cable. Christians have all experienced the grace of God in the gospel of Jesus. We have all had our identity changed at the root, so now God's calling and love are more foundational to who we are than any other thing. And we also long for the same future, journey to the same horizon, what the Bible calls the 'new creation.' Paul speaks of 'the good work' God is doing in believers that will be complete at the end of time (Phil. 1:6). We will become our true selves, the persons we were created to be, freed from all flaws, imperfections, and weaknesses. He speaks of 'the glory that will be revealed in us,' a liberation from our 'bondage to decay ... the glorious freedom of the children of God' (Rom. 8:18, 20). We 'hope' and 'wait eagerly' for this final and full redemption (Rom. 8:23,24).

What does this mean? It means that any two Christians, with nothing else but a common faith in Christ, can have a robust friendship, helping each other on their journey toward the new creation, as well as doing ministry together in the world.

The Meaning of Marriage

Friendship in action

Perfume and incense bring joy to the heart, and the pleasantness of a friend springs from their heartfelt advice.

Proverbs 27:9

Christian friends support one another through spiritual transparency. [They] are not only to honestly confess their own sins to each other (James 5:16), but they are to lovingly point out their friend's sins if he or she is blind to them (Rom. 15:14). You should give your Christian friends 'hunting licenses' to confront you if you are failing to live in line with your commitments (Gal. 6:1). Christian friends are to stir one another up, even provoking one another to get them off dead center (Heb. 10:24). This isn't to happen infrequently but should happen at a very concrete level every day (Heb. 3:13). Christian friends admit wrongs, offer or ask forgiveness (Eph. 4:32), and take steps to reconcile when one disappoints another (Matt. 5:23ff; 18:15ff).

The other way is spiritual *constancy*. Christian friends bear each other's burdens (Gal. 6:2). They should be there for each other through thick and thin (1 Thess. 5:11,14–15), sharing their goods and their very lives with each other if there is need (Heb. 13:16; Phil. 4:14; 2 Cor. 9:13). Friends must encourage each other through honor and affirmation (Rom. 12:3–6,10; Prov. 27:2). They are to identify and call out one another's gifts, strengths, and abilities. They are to build up each other's faith through study and common worship (Col. 3:16; Eph. 5:19).

The Meaning of Marriage

Spiritual friendship

Dear friends, now we are children of God, and what we will be has not yet been made known. But we know that when Christ appears, we shall be like him, for we shall see him as he is. All who have this hope in him purify themselves, just as he is pure.

1 John 3:2–3

How does this supernatural friendship that can exist between any two Christians relate to [...] natural human friendship [...] which is based on the common thread of similar loves and passions? The answer is that they can overlap or coincide. A Christian can become great friends with a non-Christian who, for example, shares her enthusiasm for an author. They read the author's books and meet to talk enthusiastically and joyfully about what they loved in the books. If the two friends are also, say, young mothers, then they have another basis for friendship, and the friendship can become warm and close, despite the lack of common Christian faith. As we have shown, two Christians can have the spiritual friendship described in the 'one anothering' directives of the New Testament, even if temperamentally and in every other way the two are extremely different and, humanly speaking, incompatible. Perhaps the richest and best relationships, however, are those that combine both the natural and the supernatural elements. Marriage, of course, can add the power of romantic love to the natural and supernatural bonds of friendship, and this is what can make marriage the richest of all human relationships.

Friendship is a deep oneness that develops as two people, speaking the truth in love to each other, journey together to the same horizon. Spiritual friendship is the greatest journey of all, because the horizon is so high and far, yet sure—it is nothing less than 'the day of Jesus Christ' and what we will be like when we finally see him face to face.

The Meaning of Marriage

In the beginning, there was work

The LORD God took the man and put him in the Garden of Eden to work it and take care of it.

Genesis 2:15

The Bible begins talking about work as soon as it begins talking about anything—that is how important and basic it is. The author of the book of Genesis describes God's creation of the world as *work*. In fact, he depicts the magnificent project of cosmos invention within a regular workweek of seven days. And then he shows us human beings working in paradise. This view of work—connected with divine, orderly creation and human purpose—is distinct among the great faiths and belief systems of the world.

The creation narrative in the book of Genesis is unique among ancient accounts of origins. Many cultures had stories that depicted the beginning of the world and human history as the result of a struggle between warring cosmic forces. In the Babylonian creation story the *Enuma Elish*, the god Marduk overcomes the goddess Tiamat and forges the world out of her remains. In this and similar accounts, the visible universe was an uneasy balance of powers in tension with one another. In the Bible, however, creation is not the result of a conflict, for God has no rivals. Indeed, all the powers and beings of heaven and earth are created by him and dependent on him. Creation, then, is not the aftermath of a battle but the plan of a craftsman.

Every Good Endeavour

The forms of God's work

God saw all that he had made, and it was very good. [. . .] Thus the heavens and the earth were completed in all their vast array.

Genesis 1:31–2:1

It is remarkable that in Chapter 1 of Genesis, God not only works but finds delight in it. God finds what he has done beautiful. He stands back, takes in 'all that he has made,' and says, in effect, 'That's good!' Like all good and satisfying work, the worker sees himself in it. 'The harmony and perfection of the completed heavens and earth express more adequately the character of their creator than any of the separate components can,' said G. J. Wenham. The second chapter of Genesis goes on to show that God works not only to create but also to care for his creation. This is what theologians call the work of 'providence.' God creates human beings and then works for them as their Provider. He forms a man (Genesis 2:7), plants a garden for him and waters it (Genesis 2:6, 8), and fashions a wife for him (Genesis 2:21–2). The rest of the Bible tells us that God continues this work as Provider, caring for the world by watering and cultivating the ground (Psalm 104:10–22), giving food to all he has made, giving help to all who suffer, and caring for the needs of every living thing (Psalm 145:14–6). [...] As Martin Luther argued, Psalm 145 says that God feeds every living thing, meaning he is feeding us through the labor of farmers and others.

Every Good Endeavour

The goodness of our work

'My Father is always at his work to this very day, and I too am working.'
John 5:17

The book of Genesis leaves us with a striking truth—work was part of paradise. One biblical scholar summed it up: 'It is perfectly clear that God's good plan always included human beings working, or, more specifically, living in the constant cycle of work and rest.'[42] Again, the contrast with other religions and cultures could not be sharper. Work did not come in after a golden age of leisure. It was part of God's perfect design for human life, because we were made in God's image, and part of his glory and happiness is that he works, as does the Son of God, [as he said in] John 5:17.

The fact that God put work in paradise is startling to us because we so often think of work as a necessary evil or even punishment. Yet we do not see work brought into our human story after the fall of Adam, as part of the resulting brokenness and curse; it is part of the blessedness of the garden of God. Work is as much a basic human need as food, beauty, rest, friendship, prayer, and sexuality; it is not simply medicine but food for our soul. Without meaningful work we sense significant inner loss and emptiness. People who are cut off from work because of physical or other reasons quickly discover how much they need work to thrive emotionally, physically, and spiritually.

Every Good Endeavour

The limits of all work

By the seventh day God had finished the work he had been doing; so on the seventh day he rested from all his work.

Genesis 2:2

It is meaningful that God himself rested after work. Many people make the mistake of thinking that work is a curse and that something else (leisure, family, or even 'spiritual' pursuits) is the only way to find meaning in life. The Bible exposes the lie of this idea. But it also keeps us from falling into the opposite mistake, namely, that work is the only important human activity and that rest is a necessary evil—something we do strictly to 'recharge our batteries' in order to continue to work. We look to what we know about God to make this case. He did not need any restoration of his strength—and yet he rested on the seventh day (Genesis 2:1–3). As beings made in his image, then we can assume that rest, and the things you do as you rest, are good and life-giving in and of themselves. Work is not all there is to life. You will not have a meaningful life without work, but you cannot say that your work is *the* meaning of your life. If you make any work the purpose of your life—even if that work is church ministry—you create an idol that rivals God. Your relationship with God is the most important foundation for your life, and indeed it keeps all the other factors—work, friendships and family, leisure and pleasure—from becoming so important to you that they become addicting and distorted.

Every Good Endeavour

Work and human dignity

Then God said, 'Let us make mankind in our image, in our likeness, so that they may rule over the fish in the sea and the birds in the sky, over the livestock and all the wild animals, and over all the creatures that move along the ground.'

Genesis 1:26

Work of all kinds, whether with the hands or the mind, evidences our dignity as human beings—because it reflects the image of God the Creator in us. Biblical scholar Derek Kidner notices something profound in the creation of animals and human beings in Genesis chapter 1: Only man is set apart and given a job description, 'an *office* (1:26b, 28b; 2:19; cf. Ps.8:4–8; James 3:7)[43]...' In other words, while the plants and animals are called to simply 'teem' and 'reproduce,' only humans are explicitly given a job. They are called to 'subdue' and 'have dominion,' or rule the earth.

We are given specific work to do because we are made in God's image. What does this mean? 'The rulers of the ancient Near East set up images and statues of themselves in places where they exercised or claimed to exercise authority. The images represented the ruler himself as symbols of his presence and authority[44]...' The close connection of Genesis chapter 1, verse 26 with the mandate to 'rule' shows that this act of ruling is a defining aspect of what it means to be made in God's image. We are called to stand in for God here in the world, exercising stewardship over the rest of creation in his place as his vice-regents. We share in doing the things that God has done in creation—bringing order out of chaos, creatively building a civilization out of the material of physical and human nature, caring for all that God has made. This is a major part of what we were created to be.

Every Good Endeavour

Common grace at work

When a farmer plows for planting . . . when he has levelled the surface . . . does he not plant wheat in its place, barley in its plot, and spelt in its field? His God instructs him and teaches him the right way . . . Grain must be ground to make bread . . . all this also comes from the LORD Almighty, whose plan is wonderful, whose wisdom is magnificent.

Isaiah 28:24–9

This is remarkable. Isaiah tells us that anyone who becomes a skillful farmer, or who brings advancements in agriculture, is being taught by God. One commentator writes of this text, 'What appears as a discovery (the proper season and conditions for sowing, farm management, rotation of crops, etc.) is actually the Creator opening his book of creation and revealing his truth.'[45]

Remember that farming is an analogue to all culture making. So every advancement in learning, every work of art, every innovation in health care or technology or management or governance, is simply God 'opening his book of creation and revealing his truth' to us. Of course, the vast majority of farmers in the history of the world did not know that God was doing this, but Isaiah says that was what was happening. This is what theologians call 'general revelation,' an aspect of common grace in which God reveals himself to all people. [. . .] So through his common grace God blesses all people, so that Christians can benefit from, and cooperate with, non-Christians.

Every Good Endeavour

The creation mandate

God blessed them and said to them, 'Be fruitful and increase in number; fill the earth and subdue it. Rule over the fish in the sea and the birds in the sky and over every living creature that moves on the ground.'

Genesis 1:28

This command has been called the 'cultural mandate.' What does it mean?

First, we are called to 'fill the earth'—to increase in number. While God usually says of plants and animals 'let them' multiply (verses 11, 20a, 20b, 22, and 24), human beings are not only given a command to do so actively (verse 28a) but then receive a detailed job description (verses 28b–29). In other words, only humans are given multiplication as a task to fulfill with intention. But why would this be a job—isn't it just a natural process? Not exactly. Human beings 'filling the earth' means something more than plants and animals filling the earth. It means civilization, not just procreation. We get the sense that God does not want merely more individuals of the human species; he also wants the world to be filled with a human society. He could have just spoken the word and created millions of people in thousands of human settlements, but he didn't. He made it our job to develop and build this society.

Second, we are called to 'rule' the rest of creation and even to 'subdue' it. What does that mean? [. . .] There is no violent intent to 'subduing' the earth. Instead, 'ruling' the world as God's image bearers should be seen as stewardship or trusteeship. God owns the world, but he has put it under our care to cultivate it.

Every Good Endeavour

Called and assigned

Nevertheless, each person should live as a believer in whatever situation the Lord has assigned to them, just as God has called them. This is the rule I lay down in all the churches.

1 Corinthians 7:17

In 1 Corinthians 7, Paul counsels readers that when they become Christians it is unnecessary to change what they are currently doing in life—their marital state, job, or social station—in order to live their lives before God in a way that pleases him. [. . .]

Here Paul uses two religiously freighted words to describe ordinary work. Elsewhere, Paul has spoken of God *calling* people into a saving relationship with him, and *assigning* them spiritual gifts to do ministry and build up the Christian community (Rom. 12:3 and 2 Cor. 10:13). Paul uses these same two words here when he says that every Christian should remain in the work God has '*assigned* to him, and to which God has *called* him.' Yet Paul is not referring in this case to church ministries, but to common social and economic tasks—'secular jobs,' we might say—and naming them God's callings and assignments. The implication is clear: Just as God equips Christians for building up the Body of Christ, so he also equips all people with talents and gifts for various kinds of work, for the purpose of building up the human community.

Every Good Endeavour

Vocation and the Gospel

For in the Gospel the righteousness of God is revealed—a righteousness that is by faith from first to last, just as it is written: 'The righteous will live by faith.'

Romans 1:17

The doctrine of justification by faith alone—the foundational commitment of the Protestant Reformation—[...] profoundly shapes the Christian understanding of work. [...]

When [Protestant reformer Martin Luther] grasped that salvation was by grace rather than through any effort of his own, it made him rethink his whole understanding of Scripture, including his view of the meaning of work. Luther found two implications in particular. First, if religious works were crucial to achieving a good standing with God, then there would always be a fundamental difference between those in church ministry and everyone else. But if religious work did absolutely nothing to earn favor with God, it could no longer be seen as superior to other forms of labor.

The gospel of salvation through sheer grace holds a second implication for work. While ancient monks may have sought salvation through religious works, many modern people seek a kind of salvation—self-esteem and self-worth—from career success. This leads us to seek only high-paying, high-status jobs, and to 'worship' them in perverse ways. But the gospel frees us from the relentless pressure of having to prove ourselves and secure our identity through work, for we are already proven and secure. It also frees us from a condescending attitude toward less sophisticated labor and from envy over more exalted work. All work now becomes a way to love the God who saved us freely; and by extension, a way to love our neighbor.

Every Good Endeavour

The idolatry of power

'For all those who exalt themselves will be humbled, and those who humble themselves will be exalted.'

Luke 14:11

Reinhold Niebuhr was a prominent American theologian of the mid-twentieth century. He believed all humans struggle with a sense of being dependent and powerless. The original temptation in the Garden of Eden was to resent the limits God had put on us ('You shall not eat of the tree ...'; Genesis 2:17) and to seek to be 'as God' by taking power over our own destiny. We gave in to this temptation and now it is part of our nature. Rather than accept our finitude and dependence on God, we desperately seek ways to assure ourselves that we still have power over our own lives. But this is an illusion. Niebuhr believed this cosmic insecurity creates a 'will to power' that dominates our social and political relationships.

[...] In any culture in which God is largely absent, sex, money, and politics will fill the vacuum for different people. This is the reason that our political discourse is increasingly ideological and polarized. Many describe the current poisonous public discourse as a lack of bipartisanship, but the roots go much deeper than that. As Niebuhr taught, they go back to the beginning of the world, to our alienation from God, and to our frantic efforts to compensate for our feelings of cosmic nakedness and powerlessness. The only way to deal with all these things is to heal our relationship with God.

Counterfeit Gods

The insecure king

In the second year of his reign, Nebuchadnezzar had dreams; his mind was troubled and he could not sleep. So the king summoned the magicians, enchanters, sorcerers and astrologers to tell him what he had dreamed. When they came in and stood before the king, he said to them, 'I have had a dream that troubles me and I want to know what it means.'

Daniel 2:1–3

In the sixth century before Christ, the Babylonian empire rose to displace Assyria and Egypt as the dominant world power. Soon it invaded Judah and captured Jerusalem, exiling Israel's professional class, including military officers, artists, and scholars, to Babylon. Eventually most of the known world was under the sway of Babylon's king and general, Nebuchadnezzar. In the biblical book of Daniel, chapter 2, however, we learn that the most powerful man on earth slept uneasily.

Nebuchadnezzar was deeply troubled by the dream. His dream had been about a towering figure, and it may be that this is the vision he wanted the world to have of him—'an impregnable giant, towering over the world . . .' However,[46] the statue had 'feet of clay' and came crashing down. He woke up in a sweat. Did this mean his empire would fail? Or that someone would come and exploit hidden weaknesses?

Many people with a great drive for power are very anxious and fearful. Niebuhr believed that fear and anxiety are the reason that many seek political power.[47] However, even if fear is not a reason for seeking power, it almost always comes with having it. [. . .] Power, then, is often born of fear and in turn gives birth to more fear. The dream was forcing Nebuchadnezzer's insecurity to the surface, and it was exceedingly uncomfortable. Powerful people do not like to admit how weak they really feel.

Counterfeit Gods

The mad king

'This is the interpretation, Your Majesty, and this is the decree the Most High has issued against my lord the king: You will be driven away from people and will live with the wild animals; you will eat grass like the ox and be drenched with the dew of heaven. Seven times will pass by for you until you acknowledge that the Most High is sovereign over all kingdoms on earth and gives them to anyone he wishes.'

Daniel 4:24–5

Now God was going to teach [Nebuchadnezzar] what he needed to learn. But there was hope. The tree would be cut down, but the stump would be left in the ground to grow back. God was not after retribution, vengeance, or destruction. This was discipline—pain inflicted with the motive of correction and redemption.

What was, then, the lesson that God wanted to drive into Nebuchadnezzar's heart? It was this: 'The Most High is sovereign over all kingdoms on earth and gives them to anyone he wishes' (Dan. 4:25). This means that anyone who is successful is simply a recipient of God's unmerited favor. Even the people at the top of the world's hierarchy of power, wealth, and influence are really 'lowliest' —they are no better than anyone else. This is a rudimentary form of the gospel—that what we have is the result of grace, not of our 'works' or efforts.

God was saying something like this: 'King Nebuchadnezzar— you must understand that your power has been given to you by grace from God. If you knew that, you would be both more relaxed and secure *and* more humble and just. If you think you earned your position through your own merit and works, you will continue to be both scared and cruel.'

Counterfeit Gods

A resurrection from the death of pride

At the end of that time, I, Nebuchadnezzar, raised my eyes toward heaven, and my sanity was restored. Then I praised the Most High; I honoured and glorified him who lives forever. His dominion is an eternal dominion; his kingdom endures from generation to generation . . . At the same time that my sanity was restored, my honour and splendour were returned to me for the glory of my kingdom. My advisers and nobles sought me out, and I was restored to my throne and became even greater than before.

Daniel 4:34, 36

[. . .] Pride leads to death, to breakdown, to a loss of humanity. But if you let it humble you rather than embitter you, and turn to God instead of living for your own glory, then the death of your pride can lead to a resurrection. You can emerge, finally, fully human, with a tender heart instead of a hard heart.

Something like this happened to Nebuchadnezzar. When he 'raised his eyes toward heaven,' to look to God, the result was more than the restoration of his sanity. He had become 'greater than before' (Verse 36). This is a deep pattern of grace, which we see supremely in Jesus. Our hearts say, 'I will ascend, I will be as the Most High for my own sake,' but Jesus said, 'I will descend, I will go low, for their sakes.' He became human and went to the Cross to die for our sins (Phil. 2:4–10). Jesus *lost* all power and served, in order to save us. He died, but that led to redemption and resurrection. So if like Eustace, Nebuchadnezzar, and Jesus you fall into great weakness, but say, 'Father, into your hands, I commit my spirit' (Luke 23:46), there will be growth, a change, and a resurrection.

Counterfeit Gods

Nothing is more common

Who among the gods is like you, LORD? Who is like you—majestic in holiness, awesome in glory, working wonders?

Exodus 15:11

The seventeenth-century English minister David Clarkson preached one of the most comprehensive and searching sermons on counterfeit gods ever written.[48] About idolatry he said, 'Though few will own it, nothing is more common.' If we think of our soul as a house, he said, 'idols are set up in every room, in every faculty.' We prefer our own wisdom to God's wisdom, our own desires to God's will, and our own reputation to God's honor. Clarkson looked at human relationships and showed how we have a tendency to make them more influential and important to us than God. In fact, he showed that 'many make even their enemies their god ... when they are more troubled, disquieted, and perplexed at apprehensions of danger to their liberty, estates, and lives from men' than they are concerned about God's displeasure.[49] The human heart is indeed a factory that mass-produces idols.

Is there any hope? Yes, if we begin to realize that idols cannot simply be removed. They must be replaced. If you only try to uproot them, they grow back; but they can be supplanted. By what? By God himself, of course. But by *God* we do not mean a general belief in his existence. Most people have that, yet their souls are riddled with idols. What we need is a living encounter with God.

Counterfeit Gods

Blessing with a limp

So Jacob was left alone, and a man wrestled with him till daybreak. When the man saw that he could not overpower him, he touched the socket of Jacob's hip so that his hip was wrenched as he wrestled with the man. Then the man said, 'Let me go, for it is daybreak.' But Jacob replied, 'I will not let you go unless you bless me.'

Genesis 32:24–6

The blessing of God, promised to Abraham, 'comes ... through Christ Jesus, so that by faith we might receive the promise of the Spirit.' What was that 'promise of the Spirit'? Later in Galatians, Paul writes that 'God sent the Spirit of his Son into our hearts who cries out, "Abba, Father"'(Gal. 4:6). *Abba* was the Aramaic diminutive word for 'father,' roughly to be translated 'papa.' It is a term of trusting confidence that a little child has in a parent's love. Paul is saying that, if you believe the gospel, the Spirit will make God's love and blessing an existential reality in your heart.

Have you heard God's blessing in your inmost being? Are the words *'You are my beloved child, in whom I delight'* an endless source of joy and strength? Have you sensed, through the Holy Spirit, God speaking them to you? That blessing—the blessing through the Spirit that is ours through Christ—is what Jacob received, and it is the only remedy against idolatry. Only that blessing makes idols unnecessary. As with Jacob, we usually discover this only after a life of 'looking for blessing in all the wrong places.' It often takes an experience of crippling weakness for us to finally discover it. That is why so many of the most God-blessed people limp as they dance for joy.

Counterfeit Gods

173

The importance of discerning idols

For although they knew God, they neither glorified him as God nor gave thanks to him ... They exchanged the truth of God for a lie, and worshipped and served created things rather than the Creator.

Romans 1:21, 25

It is impossible to understand your heart or your culture if you do not discern the counterfeit gods that influence them. In Romans 1:21–25 Saint Paul shows that idolatry is not only one sin among many, but what is fundamentally wrong with the human heart.

Paul goes on to make a long list of sins that create misery and evil in the world, but they all find their roots in this soil, the inexorable human drive for 'god-making.'[50] In other words, *idolatry is always the reason we ever do anything wrong*. No one grasped this better than Martin Luther. In his *Large Catechism* (1529) and in his *Treatise on Good Works* he wrote that the Ten Commandments begin with a commandment against idolatry. Why does this come first? Because, he argued, the fundamental motivation behind lawbreaking is idolatry.[51] We never break the other commandments without breaking the first one. Why do we fail to love or keep promises or live unselfishly? Of course, the general answer is 'because we are weak and sinful,' but the specific answer in any actual circumstance is that there is something you feel you *must* have to be happy, something that is more important to your heart than God himself. We would not lie unless we first had made something—human approval, reputation, power over others, financial advantage—more important and valuable to our hearts than the grace and favor of God. The secret to change is to identify and dismantle the counterfeit gods of your heart.

Counterfeit Gods

Replacing idols

Since, then, you have been raised with Christ, set your hearts on things above, where Christ is, seated at the right hand of God. Set your minds on things above, not on earthly things. For you died, and your life is now hidden with Christ in God. When Christ, who is your life, appears, then you also will appear with him in glory.

Colossians 3:1–5

Rejoicing and repentance must go together. Repentance without rejoicing will lead to despair. Rejoicing without repentance is shallow and will only provide passing inspiration instead of deep change. Indeed, it is when we rejoice over Jesus' sacrificial love for us most fully that, paradoxically, we are most truly convicted of our sin. When we repent out of fear of consequences, we are not really sorry for the sin, but for ourselves. Fear-based repentance ('I'd better change or God will get me') is really self-pity. In fear-based repentance, we don't learn to hate the sin for itself, and it doesn't lose its attractive power. We learn only to refrain from it for our own sake. But when we rejoice over God's sacrificial, suffering love for us—seeing what it cost him to save us from sin—we learn to hate the sin for what it is. We see what the sin cost God. What most assures us of God's unconditional love (Jesus' costly death) is what most convicts us of the evil of sin. Fear-based repentance makes us hate ourselves. Joy-based repentance makes us hate the sin.

Counterfeit Gods

The ministry of competence

Nevertheless, each person should live as a believer in whatever situation the Lord has assigned to them, just as God has called them. This is the rule I lay down in all the churches.

1 Corinthians 7:17

One of the main ways that you love others in your work is through the 'ministry of competence.' If God's purpose for your job is that you serve the human community, then the way to serve God best is to do the job as well as it can be done. [...]

So how do we connect what we do on Sunday morning with what we do during the rest of the week? How can we 'touch God in the world' through our work? [... T]he very first way to be sure you are serving God in your work is to be competent.

When United Airlines Flight 811 got into trouble, the greatest gift Captain Cronin had for his passengers was his experience and good judgment. In those moments of peril, it mattered not to the passengers how Captain Cronin related to his co-workers or how he communicated his faith to others ... The critical issue was this: was he competent enough as a pilot to bring that badly damaged plane in safely ... Through our work we can touch God in a variety of ways ... but if the call of the Christian is to participate in God's ongoing creative process, the bedrock of our ministry has to be *competency*. We must use our talents in as competent a manner as possible.

[...] It means that all jobs—not merely so-called helping professions—are fundamentally ways of loving your neighbor. Christians do not have to do direct ministry or nonprofit charitable work in order to love others through their jobs.

Every Good Endeavour

Paradise lost

When the woman saw that the fruit of the tree was good for food and pleasing to the eye, and also desirable for gaining wisdom, she took some and ate it. She also gave some to her husband, who was with her, and he ate it.

Genesis 3:6

We have surveyed the rich biblical view of God's perfect design for work. But that is not how we experience it. Everyone knows that this is a broken, troubled world—shot through with sickness and death, injustice and selfishness, natural disasters, and chaos. Since the beginning of time there has been a wide variety of explanations for why this is so and what to do about it.

At the heart of the Bible's account is the concept of sin: man's rebellion against God and our resulting alienation from him. The fall of Adam and Eve (and therefore the rest of the human race) into sin has been disastrous. It has unraveled the fabric of the entire world—and in no area as profoundly as our work. The story presented in the Bible is that while God blessed work to be a glorious use of our gifts and his resources to prosper the world, it is now also cursed because of mankind's fall. Work exists now in a world sustained by God but disordered by sin.

Only if we have some understanding of how sin distorts work can we hope to counteract its effects and salvage some of the satisfaction God planned for our work.

Every Good Endeavour

Painful labor

To Adam he said, 'Because you listened to your wife and ate fruit from the tree about which I commanded you, "You must not eat from it," Cursed is the ground because of you; through painful toil you will eat food from it all the days of your life.'

Genesis 3:17

Genesis 3 is an ancient text, filled with rich theology in narrative form. But it could not be more relevant and practical to life today. It goes for the jugular, as if to say, 'Do you find the two great tasks in life—love and work—to be excruciatingly hard? This explains why.'

God ties the pain of love and marriage and the pain of work very closely together in [Genesis 3:14–19]. Both child-bearing and farming are now called 'painful labor.' Theologian W. R. Forrester writes, 'in language after language the same word is used for toil and child-bearing, e.g. "labor" and "travail."'[52] So companies assemble teams to work furiously for months or years to 'give birth' to new products or ventures, which may die a quick death in the marketplace. Star football players often suffer the effects of injuries throughout their lives. Brilliant entrepreneurs like Steve Jobs get thrown out of companies when times get tough. (Few get invited back, like Jobs was.) The weeds, or the computer viruses, or the corruption scandals, come back with a vengeance. Research into the properties of the atom becomes the basis for the atomic bomb. In other words, work, even when it bears fruit, is always painful, often miscarries, and sometimes kills us.

Every Good Endeavour

Deep consolation

For the creation was subjected to frustration, not by its own choice, but by the will of the one who subjected it, in hope that the creation itself will be liberated from its bondage to decay and brought into the freedom and glory of the children of God.

Romans 8:20–1

Because of the nature of God's creation, we need work for our happiness. And because of God's intentions for our work—to contribute to the flourishing of the world—we have glimpses of what we could accomplish. But because of the fall of the human race, our work is also profoundly frustrating, never as fruitful as we want, and often a complete failure. This is why so many people inhabit the extremes of idealism and cynicism—or even ricochet back and forth between those poles. Idealism says, 'Through my work I am going to change things, make a difference, accomplish something new, bring justice to the world.' Cynicism says, 'Nothing really changes. Don't get your hopes up. Do what it takes to make a living. Don't let yourself care too much. Get out of it whatever you can.'

Genesis 3, verse 18 tells us not only that 'thorns and thistles' will come out of the ground but also that 'you will eat the plants of the field.' Thorns and food. Work will still bear some fruit, though it will always fall short of its promise. Work will be both frustrating and fulfilling, and sometimes—just often enough—human work gives us a glimpse of the beauty and genius that might have been the routine characteristic of all our work, and what, by the grace of God, it will be again in the new heavens and new earth.

Every Good Endeavour

Under the sun

*So I hated life, because the work that is done under the sun was griev-
ous to me. All of it is meaningless, a chasing after the wind.*

Ecclesiastes 2:17

Some books of the Bible are like listening to a pastor giving
counsel on how to live (the book of James in the New
Testament, for example, or Proverbs in the Old Testament). But
reading Ecclesiastes is like sitting in a philosophy class with a
professor who provokes you with thorny Socratic questions and
strange case studies, who pulls you into a dialogue to lead you to
discover truth for yourself. The Philosopher pushes you to look at
the foundations of your life and to ask the basic questions that we
might otherwise avoid: 'Is there any meaning to your life? What
are you really doing it all for? Why is there so much wrong with
the world? How will you cope with it?'

The author of Ecclesiastes is using the character of the
Philosopher to push readers toward an understanding of the transcendent uniqueness and necessity of God. Nothing within this
world is sufficient basis for a meaningful life here. If we base our
lives on work and achievement, on love and pleasure, or on knowledge and learning, our existence becomes anxious and fragile—
because circumstances in life are always threatening the very
foundation of our lives, and death inevitably strips us of everything we hold dear. Ecclesiastes is an argument that existential
dependence on a gracious Creator God—not only abstract
belief—is a precondition for an unshakeable, purposeful life.

Every Good Endeavour

The meaninglessness of work

*I hated all the things I had toiled for under the sun, because I must
leave them to the one who comes after me. And who knows whether
that person will be wise or foolish? Yet they will have control over all
the fruit of my toil into which I have poured my effort and skill under
the sun. This too is meaningless. So my heart began to despair over all
my toilsome labour under the sun.*

Ecclesiastes 2:18–20

When we work, we want to make an impact. That can mean
getting personal recognition for our work, or making a
difference in our field, or doing something to make the world a
better place. Nothing is more satisfying than a sense that through
our work we have accomplished some lasting achievement. But the
Philosopher startles us by arguing that even if you are one of the
few people who breaks through and accomplishes all you hope for,
it's all for nothing, for in the end there *are* no lasting achievements.

Whether quickly or slowly, all the results of our toil will be
wiped away by history. The person who takes the business after
you, or who picks up the cause or organization after you, may
undo all you have done. Of course, some history makers have
brought inventions or innovations that stay with the human race
for a long time, but those persons are very rare, and of course
eventually even the most famous 'will not be long remembered'
(Eccles. 2:16) since everything and every accomplishment under
the sun will be ground to dust in the end—even civilization itself.
All work, even the most historic, will eventually be forgotten and
its impact totally neutralized (1:3–11).

In short even if your work is not fruitless, it is ultimately pointless if life 'under the sun' is all there is.

Every Good Endeavour

A handful of quietness

There is nothing better for a person than to enjoy their work, because that is their lot.

Ecclesiastes 3:22

In the midst of Qoheleth's gloom regarding the pointlessness of work, a couple of gleams shine through. Yes, work is our inescapable 'lot,' and so satisfaction in that realm is essential to a satisfactory life. But how do we get that satisfaction in light of all that we have against us? The answer: 'to . . . find satisfaction in all their toil—this is the gift of God' (Eccles. 3:13). How can we secure this gift? Qoheleth provides a hint.

Fools fold their hands and ruin themselves. Better one handful with tranquility than two handfuls with toil and chasing after the wind.

Ecclesiastes 4:5–6

Qoheleth commends, literally, 'one handful of quietness'—by contrast with two alternatives. One is the 'two handfuls' of wealth that come from 'toil and chasing after the wind' (verse 6b). The other is the 'empty handful' of wealth that comes from the idleness of the fool who does not toil at all (verse 5). Qoheleth concedes that satisfaction in work in a fallen world is always a miraculous gift of God—and yet we have a responsibility to pursue this gift through a particular balance. Tranquility without toil will not bring us satisfaction; neither will toil without tranquility. There will be both toil *and* tranquility.

Every Good Endeavour

Rest for your soul

'Come to me, all you who are weary and burdened, and I will give you rest. Take my yoke upon you and learn from me, for I am gentle and humble in heart, and you will find rest for your souls. For my yoke is easy and my burden is light.'

Matthew 11:28–30

How we attain such a balanced life [of toil and tranquility] is one of the main themes of Scripture. First, it means recognizing and renouncing our tendency to make idols of money and power (see Ecclesiastes 4:4—'I saw that all toil and all achievement spring from one person's envy of another. This too is meaningless, a chasing after the wind'). Second, it means putting relationships in their proper place (see Ecclesiastes 4:8—'There was a man all alone; he had neither son nor brother'), even though it probably means making less money ('one handful' rather than two).

But most of all, it will mean pursuing something that is beyond the scope of Ecclesiastes to identify. The New Testament reveals that the ultimate source of the tranquility we seek is Jesus Christ, who—because he has toiled for us on the cross—can offer us the true rest for our souls. Without the gospel of Jesus, we will have to toil not for the joy of serving others, nor the satisfaction of a job well done, but to make a name for ourselves.

Every Good Endeavour

A new story for work

So whether you eat or drink or whatever you do, do it all for the glory of God.

1 Corinthians 10:31

The Christian storyline works beautifully to make sense of things and even to help us appreciate the truth embedded in stories that clearly come from another worldview. The Christian storyline, or worldview, is: creation (plan), fall (problem), redemption and restoration (solution):

The whole world is good. God made the world and everything in it was good. There are no intrinsically evil parts of the world. Nothing is evil in its origin. As Tolkien explained about his archvillain in the *Lord of the Rings* trilogy, in the beginning 'even Sauron was not so.' You can find this 'creational good' in anything.

The whole world is fallen. There is no aspect of the world affected by sin more or less than any other. For example, are emotion and passions untrustworthy and reason infallible? Is the physical bad and the spiritual good? Is the day-to-day world profane but religious observances good? None of these are true; but non-Christian storylines must adopt some variations of these in order to villainize and even demonize some created thing instead of sin.

The whole world is going to be redeemed. Jesus is going to redeem spirit and body, reason and emotion, people and nature. There is no part of reality for which there is no hope.

Every Good Endeavour

Transforming work

Whatever you do, work at it with all your heart, as working for the Lord, not for human masters, since you know that you will receive an inheritance from the Lord as a reward. It is the Lord Christ you are serving.

Colossians 3:23, 24

The gospel is the true story that God made a good world that was marred by sin and evil, but through Jesus Christ he redeemed it at infinite cost to himself, so that someday he will return to renew all creation; end all suffering and death; and restore absolute peace, justice, and joy in the world forever. The vast implications of this gospel worldview [. . .] affect everything, and especially our work.

Here's an example. Early in his career as a school administrator, our friend Bill Kurtz started to see that this gospel storyline—what the world should be, how it had gone wrong, and the hope for the future—gave him a better vision for education in poor inner-city schools. [. . .] Bill found that the gospel gave him a more comprehensive understanding of the problems facing the schools and a hope for redemption that incorporated some of the best practices of his field but did not idolize them.

His approach has been holistic, with the recognition that the gospel could actually shape the culture of a school community. In 2004 he launched a public charter high school in Denver to serve a very diverse student population. [. . .] The school has seen amazing success—every single senior in the school's history has earned a four-year college acceptance. This first school has grown into a network of six top-performing schools across Denver.

Every Good Endeavour

The power of deep rest

'Remember the Sabbath day by keeping it holy. Six days you shall labour and do all your work, but the seventh day is a sabbath to the LORD your God. On it you shall not do any work, neither you, nor your son or daughter, nor your male or female servant, nor your animals, nor any foreigner residing in your towns. For in six days the LORD made the heavens and the earth, the sea, and all that is in them, but he rested on the seventh day. Therefore the LORD blessed the Sabbath day and made it holy.'

Exodus 20:8–11

What does this mean practically? Since God rested after his creation, we must also rest after ours. This rhythm of work and rest is not only for believers; it is for everyone, as part of our created nature. Overwork or underwork violates that nature and leads to breakdown. To rest is actually a way to enjoy and honor the goodness of God's creation and our own. To violate the rhythm of work and rest (in either direction) leads to chaos in our life and in the world around us. Sabbath is therefore a *celebration of our design*.

Deuteronomy 5 goes on to tie the observance of Sabbath to God's redemption. Verse 15 says, 'Remember that you were slaves in Egypt and that the LORD your God brought you out of there with a mighty hand and an outstretched arm. Therefore the LORD your God has commanded you to observe the Sabbath day.' God portrays the Sabbath day as a re-enactment of emancipation from slavery. It reminds us how he delivered his people from a condition in which they were not human beings, but simply units of capacity in Pharaoh's brick production system. Anyone who cannot obey God's command to observe the Sabbath is a slave, even a self-imposed one. Your own heart, or our materialistic culture, or an exploitative organization, or all of the above, will be abusing you if you don't have the ability to be disciplined in your practice of Sabbath. Sabbath is therefore a *declaration of our freedom*.

Every Good Endeavour

Every good endeavour

Always give yourselves fully to the work of the Lord, because you know that your labour in the Lord is not in vain.

1 Corinthians 15:58

Everyone imagines accomplishing things, and everyone finds him- or herself largely incapable of producing them. Everyone wants to be successful rather than forgotten, and everyone wants to make a difference in life. But that is beyond the control of any of us. If this life is all there is, then everything will eventually burn up in the death of the sun and no one will even be around to remember anything that has ever happened. Everyone will be forgotten, nothing we do will make any difference, and all good endeavors, even the best, will come to naught.

Unless there is God. If the God of the Bible exists, and there is a True Reality beneath and behind this one, and this life is not the only life, then every good endeavor, even the simplest ones, pursued in response to God's calling, can matter forever. That is what the Christian faith promises. [...]

What about you? Let's say that you go into city planning as a young person. Why? You are excited about cities, and you have a vision about how a real city ought to be. You are likely to be discouraged because throughout your life you probably will not get more than a leaf or a branch done [of the Tree you imagine]. But there really is a New Jerusalem, a heavenly city, which will come down to earth like a bride dressed for her husband (Revelation 21–2).

Every Good Endeavour

Seeking the good of the city

Seek the peace and prosperity of the city to which I have carried you into exile. Pray to the LORD for it, because if it prospers, you too will prosper.

Jeremiah 29:7

Redeemer Presbyterian Church has made vocational discipleship—helping people integrate their faith and work—a major focus of its overall ministry for almost ten years. [...] We've sought to help our congregation live out the gospel in all spheres of culture in a way that seeks 'the peace and prosperity' (Jer. 29:7) of the city in which God has placed us.

The letter that Jeremiah sent from Jerusalem to the elders, priests, and people of Israel who had been carried into exile in Babylon has been influential in establishing the purpose and the tone of our ministry. First of all, the letter makes it clear that the Lord God claims responsibility for carrying his people into exile in the first place. When facing the trials of life in the big city and the demands of a high-pressure career it helps to remember God's sovereignty so that, by definition, we can be sure we are where he wants us to be. Second, he asks his people to seek the peace and prosperity of Babylon 'because if it prospers, you too will prosper.' As a congregation, we understand ourselves to be a small minority whom God has called to love and serve the city, our professions, our workplaces, and our neighborhoods. [...]

Redeemer also has been shaped by a deep commitment to the promise that the gospel changes everything—in our hearts, our community, and our world. In the words of Abraham Kuyper, 'There is not a square inch in the whole domain of our human existence over which Christ, who is Sovereign over all, does not cry: "Mine!"'[53]

Every Good Endeavour

Reach out to the outcast

When a Samaritan woman came to draw water, Jesus said to her, 'Will you give me a drink?' . . . The Samaritan woman said to him, 'You are a Jew and I am a Samaritan woman. How can you ask me for a drink?' (For Jews do not associate with Samaritans.)

John 4:7, 9

The first striking feature of this story is the radical move Jesus makes by initiating a conversation. It doesn't seem unusual to us to see these two talking, but it should. Notice her shock that he is even speaking to her, for the Jews and Samaritans were bitter enemies. [. . .] the Jews considered the Samaritans racially inferior *and* heretics. That's the first reason she is surprised he is even speaking to her. But on top of that, it was scandalous for a Jewish man to speak to any strange woman in public.

What's more, she had come to draw water at noon. Many biblical scholars have pointed out that this is not when women ordinarily came to draw water. They came early in the day when it wasn't hot yet, so they could have water for the housekeeping chores for the entire day. So why was she there alone, in the middle of the day? The answer is, she was a moral outcast, a complete outsider—even within her own marginalized part of society.

And so when Jesus begins to speak to her, he is deliberately reaching across almost every significant barrier that people can put up between themselves. In this case, a racial barrier, a cultural barrier, a gender barrier, and a moral barrier—and every convention of the time—that he, a religious Jewish male, should have nothing whatsoever to do with her. But he doesn't care. Do you see how radical that is? He reaches right across all the human divides in order to connect to her. She is amazed, and we should be amazed, too.

Encounters with Jesus

True satisfaction

Jesus answered her, 'If you knew the gift of God and who it is that asks you for a drink, you would have asked him and he would have given you living water.'

John 4:10

The second interesting feature about this encounter is that, though he is clearly open and warm to her, he still confronts her. But he does so in a gentle and artful way.

What on earth is Jesus talking about? He is speaking metaphorically, referring to 'living water,' which he calls 'eternal life.' The image is a little lost on us. Almost everywhere [...] we have ready access to drinking water. Most of us know very little about real thirst, but those who lived in an arid climate next to a desert knew a lot about it. Because our bodies contain so much water, to be in profound thirst is to be in agony. And then to taste water after you have been truly thirsty is about the most satisfying experience possible.

So what is Jesus saying to this outcast? He's saying this: 'I've got something for you that is as basic and necessary to you *spiritually* as water is to you *physically*. Something without which you are absolutely lost.'

But the metaphor of the living water means even more than that. Jesus is not just telling us that what he has to offer is life-saving—he's also revealing that it satisfies from the *inside*. He says, 'My water, if you get it, will become in you a spring of water welling up to eternal life.' He's talking about deep soul satisfaction, about incredible satisfaction and contentment that doesn't depend on what is happening outside of us. So I ask you, what will make you happy? What will really give you a satisfying life?

Encounters with Jesus

The search for living water

The woman said to him, 'Sir, give me this water so that I won't get thirsty and have to keep coming here to draw water.'

He told her, 'Go, call your husband and come back.'

'I have no husband,' she replied.

Jesus said to her, 'You are right when you say you have no husband. The fact is, you have had five husbands, and the man you now have is not your husband. What you have just said is quite true.'

John 4:15–18

[...] we often forget how thirsty we are because we believe we will fulfill our dreams. And when that happens, it's easy to walk past Jesus. But this woman at the well has no such illusions; and so the hook is set. She immediately says to Jesus, 'What is this living water? Would you give it to me?' And then he turns the tables on her [...]

What is Jesus doing? Surely here in this woman with her long and sordid sexual history we have someone who fits the traditional understanding of a 'sinner.' Is he trying to humiliate her? No; if that were the case, he would never have broken the social barriers of respectability and opened up the conversation with her in the gentle way he did.

Why does Jesus seem to suddenly change the subject from seeking living water to her history with men? The answer is—he isn't changing the subject. He's nudging her, saying, 'If you want to understand the nature of this living water I offer, you need to first understand how you've been seeking it in your own life. You've been trying to get it through men, and it's not working, is it? Your need for men is eating you alive, and it will never stop.'

Encounters with Jesus

The insider

Now there was a Pharisee, a man named Nicodemus who was a member of the Jewish ruling council. He came to Jesus at night and said, 'Rabbi, we know that you are a teacher who has come from God. For no one could perform the signs you are doing if God were not with him.'

Jesus replied, 'Very truly I tell you, no one can see the kingdom of God unless they are born again.'

John 3:1–3

Now let us turn to the encounter Jesus had just before this one with the Outcast. In John 3, Jesus meets a very important man, a Pharisee, a religious and civic leader. [. . .]

Did you notice that this is almost the opposite of how Jesus treated the woman at the well? He started off very gently with her, surprising her with his openness, and then slowly confronted her with her spiritual need. In his encounter with this Insider, however, Jesus is more forceful and direct. Nicodemus begins with courtesy: 'Ah, Rabbi, I've heard many wonderful things about you. People say you have a lot of wisdom that God has given you.' But Jesus confronts Nicodemus right up front, saying, 'You must be born again.' I suppose Nicodemus, who has spent his life worshiping God according to strict Jewish tradition, must have been offended by this strange pronouncement. [. . .]

He uses a different metaphor with the Insider than the one he used with the Outcast. Rather than pressing him on his lack of satisfaction ('I can give you living water'), he's pressing him on his smug *self*-satisfaction ('You must be born again'). What did you have to do, Jesus is asking, with being born? Did you work hard to earn the privilege of being born? Did it happen due to your skillful planning? Not at all. You don't earn or contribute *anything* to being born. It is a free gift of life. And so it is with the new birth. Salvation is by grace—there are no moral efforts that can earn or merit it. You must be born again.

Encounters with Jesus

Religious sin

'How can someone be born when they are old?' Nicodemus asked. 'Surely they cannot enter a second time into their mother's womb to be born!'

Jesus answered, 'Very truly I tell you, no one can enter the kingdom of God unless they are born of water and the Spirit.'

John 3:4–5

This is an astonishing thing to say to a man like Nicodemus. Jesus is saying that the pimps and the prostitutes outside on the street are in the same position, spiritually, as he is. There is Nicodemus, flush with his moral and spiritual accomplishments, and there is someone out on the street who is homeless and addicted, and as far as God is concerned they are equally lost. They both have to start from scratch. They both have to be born again. They both need eternal spiritual life or something will eat them alive. And that life is going to have to be a free gift.

How dare Jesus say that?

Jesus can say it because he is working on a deeper understanding of sin than most people have. [. . .] Sin is looking to something else besides God for your salvation. It is putting yourself in the place of God, becoming your own savior and lord, as it were. That's the biblical definition of sin, the first of the Ten Commandments. One way to do this is to break all the moral rules in your pursuit of pleasure and happiness, like the woman in the well. This makes sex or money or power into a kind of salvation. But then there is the religious way to be your own savior and lord. That is to act as if your good life and moral achievement will essentially require God to bless you and answer your prayers the way you want.

Encounters with Jesus

The only real savior

'Flesh gives birth to flesh, but the Spirit gives birth to spirit. You should not be surprised at my saying, "You must be born again."'

John 3:6–7

So you see, Nicodemus and the Samaritan woman are equal sinners in need of grace. And so are we all. In every case, you are trying to be your own savior and lord, trying to put God in your debt, or at least trying to tilt the odds of the universe in your favor. Either way, Jesus calls it sin. He says that you need living water and that you need to be born again to get it. You need to repent, admit your need, ask God to receive you for Jesus' sake, and be converted.

[...] if there is a God, you owe him literally everything. If there is a God, you owe him far more than a morally decent life. He deserves to be at the center of your life. Even if you are a good person but you are not letting God be God to you, you are just as guilty of sin as Nicodemus or the Samaritan woman. You are being your own savior and lord.

What is the solution? We need to stop looking to false forms of salvation, to pseudo-saviors. If you build your life on your career, or your spouse, or your money, or your morality, and it fails, there is no hope for you. Do you know why? Because every other savior but Jesus Christ is not really a savior. If your career fails, it won't forgive you. It can only punish you with self-loathing and shame. Jesus is the only savior who if you gain him will satisfy you, and if you fail him will forgive you. Your career and your moral performance, by contrast, cannot die for your sins.

Encounters with Jesus

Jesus' thirst

Then, leaving her water jar, the woman went back to the town and said to the people, 'Come, see a man who told me everything I've ever done. Could this be the Messiah?'

John 4:28-9

If you keep reading the fourth chapter of John, you'll see that the Samaritan woman tells her friends about the living water she has found. She testifies to meeting the Messiah and invites everyone to go meet him, too.

Why did she find salvation? I'll tell you: It was because Jesus was thirsty. If he had not been thirsty, he would not have gone to the well, and she would not have found the living water. But why was Jesus thirsty? It was because the divine Son of God, the maker of heaven and earth, had emptied himself of his glory and descended into the world as a vulnerable mortal, subject to becoming weary and thirsty. In other words, she found the living water because Jesus Christ said, 'I thirst.'

That is not the last time Jesus Christ said, 'I thirst,' in the book of John. On the cross just before he died, he said, 'I thirst,' and he meant more than just physical thirst. There Jesus was experiencing the loss of the relationship with his father because he was taking the punishment we deserved for our sins. [...] It is because Jesus Christ experienced cosmic thirst on the cross that you and I can have our spiritual thirst satisfied. It is because he died that we can be born again. And he did it gladly. Seeing what he did and why he did it will turn our hearts away from the things that enslave us and toward him in worship. That is the gospel, and it is the same for skeptics, believers, insiders, outcasts, and everyone in between.

Encounters with Jesus

Conversation and encounter

Rejoice always, pray continually, give thanks in all circumstances; for this is God's will for you in Christ Jesus.

1 Thessalonians 5:16–18

Prayer is both conversation *and* encounter with God. These two concepts give us a definition of prayer and a set of tools for deepening our prayer lives. The traditional forms of prayer—adoration, confession, thanksgiving, and supplication—are concrete practices as well as profound experiences. We must know the awe of praising his glory, the intimacy of finding his grace, and the struggle of asking his help, all of which can lead us to know the spiritual reality of his presence. Prayer, then, is both awe *and* intimacy, struggle *and* reality. These will not happen every time we pray, but each should be a major component of our prayer over the course of our lives.

We should not drive a wedge between seeking personal communion with God and seeking the advance of his kingdom in hearts and in the world. And if they are kept together, then communion will not be just wordless mystical awareness on the one hand, and our petitions will not be a way of procuring God's favor 'for our many words' (Matt 6:7) on the other.

J. I. Packer and Carolyn Nystrom's book on prayer has a subtitle that sums all this up nicely. Prayer is 'Finding Our Way through Duty to Delight.' That is the journey of prayer.

Prayer

The necessity of prayer

*The Spirit you received does not make you slaves, so that you live in
fear again; rather, the Spirit you received brought about your adoption
to sonship. And by him we cry, 'Abba, Father.' The Spirit himself testifies
with our spirit that we are God's children.*

Romans 8:15–16

In the second half of my adult life, I discovered prayer. I had to.
In the fall of 1999, I taught a Bible study course on the
Psalms. It became clear to me that I was barely scratching the
surface of what the Bible commanded and promised regarding
prayer. Then came the dark weeks in New York after 9/11, when
our whole city sank into a kind of corporate clinical depression,
even as it rallied. For my family the shadow was intensified as my
wife, Kathy, struggled with the effects of Crohn's disease. Finally, I
was diagnosed with thyroid cancer.

At one point during all this, my wife urged me to do something with her we had never been able to muster the self-
discipline to do regularly. She asked me to pray with her every
night. *Every* night. She used an illustration that crystallized her
feelings very well. As we remember it, she said something like this:

Imagine you were diagnosed with such a lethal condition that
the doctor told you that you would die within hours unless you
took a particular medicine—a pill every night before going to
sleep. Imagine that you were told that you could never miss it or
you would die. Would you forget? Would you not get around to it
some nights? No—it would be so crucial that you wouldn't forget,
you would never miss. Well, if we don't pray together to God,
we're not going to make it because of all we are facing. I'm
certainly not. We *have* to pray, we can't let it just slip our minds.

Prayer

The testimony of the Spirit

And pray in the Spirit on all occasions with all kinds of prayers and requests.
With this in mind, be alert and always keep on praying for all the Lord's people.

Ephesians 6:18

The Spirit of God assures us of God's love. First, the Spirit enables us to approach and cry to the great God as our loving father. Then he comes alongside our spirit and adds a more direct testimony.

I first came to grips with these verses by reading the sermons of D. Martyn Lloyd-Jones, a British preacher and author of the mid-twentieth century. He made the case that Paul was writing about a profound experience of God's reality.[54] Eventually I found that most modern biblical commentators generally agreed that these verses describe, as one New Testament scholar put it, 'a religious experience that is ineffable' because the assurance of secure love in God is 'mystical in the best sense of the word.' [...]

Lloyd-Jones's exposition also pointed me back to writers I had read in seminary, such as Martin Luther, John Calvin, the seventeenth-century British theologian John Owen, and the eighteenth-century American philosopher and theologian Jonathan Edwards. There I discovered no choice offered between truth *or* Spirit, between doctrine *or* experience. One of the most accomplished of the older theologians—John Owen—was especially helpful to me at this point. In a sermon on the gospel, Owen gave due diligence to laying the doctrinal foundation of Christian salvation. Then, however, he exhorted his hearers to 'get an *experience* of the power of the gospel ... in and upon your own hearts, or all your profession is an expiring thing.'[55]

This heart experience of the gospel's power can happen only through prayer—both publicly in the gathered Christian assembly and privately in meditation.

Prayer

'An intelligent mysticism'

Though you have not seen him, you love him; and even though you do not see him now, you believe in him and are filled with an inexpressible and glorious joy.

1 Peter 1:8

In my pursuit of a deeper prayer life, I chose a counterintuitive course. I deliberately avoided reading any new books on prayer at all. [...] One I consulted was the Scottish theologian John Murray, who provided one of the most helpful insights of all:

It is necessary for us to recognize that there is an intelligent mysticism *in the life of faith ... of living union and communion with the exalted and ever-present Redeemer ... He communes with his people and his people commune with him in conscious reciprocal love ... The life of true faith cannot be that of cold metallic assent. It must have the passion and warmth of love and communion because communion with God is the crown and apex of true religion.*[56]

Murray was not a writer given to lyrical passages. Yet when he speaks of 'mysticism' and 'communion' with the one who died and ever lives for us, he is assuming that Christians will have a palpable love relationship with him and do have a potential for a personal knowledge and experience of God that beggars the imagination. Which, of course, means prayer—but what prayer! In the midst of the paragraph, Murray quotes Peter's first epistle [...] the older King James version calls it 'joy unspeakable and full of glory.' Some translate it 'glorified joy beyond words.' [...]

We are not called to choose between a Christian life based on truth and doctrine *or* a life filled with spiritual power and experience. They go together. I was not being called to leave behind my theology and launch out to look for 'something more,' for experience. Rather, I was meant to ask the Holy Spirit to help me experience my theology.

Prayer

Learning to pray

Devote yourselves to prayer, being watchful and thankful.

Colossians 4:2

In the summer after I was treated successfully for thyroid cancer, I made four practical changes to my life of private devotion. First, I took several months to go through the Psalms, summarizing each one. That enabled me to begin praying through the Psalms regularly, getting through all of them several times a year. The second thing I did was always to put in a time of meditation as a transitional discipline between my Bible reading and my time of prayer. Third, I did all I could to pray morning and evening rather than only in the morning. Fourth, I began praying with greater expectation.

The changes took some time to bear fruit, but after sustaining these practices for about two years, I began to have some breakthroughs. Despite ups and downs since then, I have found new sweetness in Christ *and* new bitterness too, because I could now see my heart more clearly in the new light of vital prayer. In other words, there were more restful experiences of love as well as more wrestling to see God triumph over evil, both in my own heart and in the world. [. . .]

Prayer is the only entryway into genuine self-knowledge. It is also the main way we experience deep change—the reordering of our loves. Prayer is how God gives us so many of the unimaginable things he has for us. Indeed, prayer makes it safe for God to give us many of the things we most desire. It is the way we know God, the way we finally treat God *as* God. Prayer is simply the key to everything we need to do and be in life.

We must learn to pray. We have to.

Prayer

Knowing God better

I keep asking that the God of our Lord Jesus Christ, the glorious Father, may give you the Spirit of wisdom and revelation, so that you may know him better.

Ephesians 1:17

It is remarkable that in all of his writings Paul's prayers for his friends contain no appeals for changes in their circumstances. It is certain that they lived in the midst of many dangers and hardships. They faced persecution, death from disease, oppression by powerful forces, and separation from loved ones. Their existence was far less secure than ours is today. Yet in these prayers you see not one petition for a better emperor, for protection from marauding armies, or even for bread for the next meal. Paul does not pray for the goods we would usually have near the top of our lists of requests.

Does that mean it would have been wrong to pray for such things? Not at all. As Paul knew, Jesus himself invites us to ask for our 'daily bread' and that God would 'deliver us from evil.' In 1 Timothy 2, Paul directs his readers to pray for peace, for good government, and for the needs of the world. In his own prayers, then, Paul is not giving us a universal model for prayer in the same way Jesus did. Rather, in them he reveals what he asked most frequently for his friends—what he believed was the most important thing God could give them.

What is that? It is—to *know him better*.

Prayer

Open the eyes of our hearts

I pray that the eyes of your heart may be enlightened in order that you may know the hope to which he has called you, the riches of his glorious inheritance in his holy people.

Ephesians 1:18

Biblically, the heart is the control center of the entire self. It is the repository of one's core commitments, deepest loves, and most foundational hopes that control our feeling, thinking, and behavior. To have the 'eyes of the heart enlightened' with a particular truth means to have it penetrate and grip us so deeply that it changes the whole person.

In other words, we may know that God is holy, but when our hearts' eyes are enlightened to that truth, then we not only understand it cognitively, but emotionally we find God's holiness wondrous and beautiful, and volitionally we avoid attitudes and behavior that would displease or dishonor him. In Ephesians 3:18, Paul says he wants the Spirit to give them 'power ... to grasp' all the past, present, and future benefits they received when they believed in Christ. Of course, all Christians know about these benefits in their minds, but the prayer is for something beyond that—it is to have a more vivid sense of the reality of God's presence and of shared life with him.

Paul sees this fuller knowledge of God as a more critical thing to receive than a change of circumstances. Without this powerful sense of God's reality, good circumstances can lead to overconfidence and spiritual indifference. Who needs God, our hearts would conclude, when matters seem to be so in hand? Then again, without this enlightened heart, bad circumstances can lead to discouragement and despair, because the love of God would be an abstraction rather than the infinitely consoling presence it should be. Therefore, knowing God better is what we must have above all if we are to face life in any circumstances.

Prayer

Blessing then trial

As soon as Jesus was baptised, he went up out of the water. At that moment heaven was opened, and he saw the Spirit of God descending like a dove and alighting on him. And a voice from heaven said, 'This is my Son, whom I love; with him I am well pleased.' Then Jesus was led by the Spirit into the wilderness to be tempted by the devil.

Matthew 3:16–4:1

Outside of the crucifixion itself, the baptism is the only event of Jesus' life mentioned in all four Gospels. It is crucial. But only here in Matthew is the temptation scene recorded in detail. And it is important to recognize how the baptism and temptation are connected tightly by the single word *then*. God spoke words of powerful assurance: 'This is my Son, whom I love; with him I am well pleased.' *Then* Jesus was led by the Spirit into the desert to be tempted by the devil. *Then* is almost *therefore*. After great blessing and success came trial and temptation.

[... But] what if you could have faith in God without wavering? What if your life were perfectly pleasing to God? Then—surely! God would protect you, and your own holiness and wisdom would guard you as well, and your life would always go well. Right?

Wrong. Because here stands the one who did it. God the Father has just said that Jesus' life is perfectly pleasing to him. And the Spirit of God has descended on him to guide him. And look what happens. He is loved and affirmed and empowered by God, and then ... *then!* He is ushered into the clutches of the devil. So here's the order: God's love and power, then evil, temptation, wilderness, terrible hunger and thirst. That little word *then* is an amazing word. It is almost like Matthew is trying to tell us, 'Read my lips: No one is exempt from trials and tribulations. In fact, this is often what happens to people God loves very much, for it is part of God's often mysterious and good plan for turning us into something great.'

Encounters with Jesus

If you are the Son of God . . .

The tempter came to him and said, 'If you are the Son of God, tell these stones to become bread.' Jesus answered, 'It is written: "Man shall not live on bread alone, but on every word that comes from the mouth of God."'

Matthew 4:3–4

Notice that several times the devil says, 'If you are the Son of God ...' That is his main attack, not only against Jesus but against us as well. God has just assured Jesus that he is God's beloved Son, and Satan immediately and directly assaults Jesus at that very spot. He asks Jesus, essentially, to make God prove that he loves him and empowers him. But you don't need to ask someone for demonstrations and assurances and proofs unless you doubt. And that's Satan's main military goal—he wants Jesus to lose the certainty, the assurance of God's full acceptance, of his unconditional fatherly love.

Now, if that is Satan's main front of attack, how does he seek to accomplish this with us? To begin with, he wants to keep you from believing Jesus is really the Son of God and Savior of the world. Notice carefully what God said from heaven in the baptism. First he says, 'This is my Son, whom I love'—a quote from Psalm 2, a song about God's messianic king who is going to put down all rebellion and evil in the world. But then God says, 'with him I am well pleased.' That is a quote from Isaiah 53, where it describes the figure of the Suffering Servant, a mysterious person who Isaiah says will someday suffer and die for the transgressions of the people. [...]

God was trying to get us to understand this: Jesus is not just a good man who by word and example tells us how to live. Nor is he merely a heavenly king who came to destroy all evil in one stroke. As we have seen, evil is deep within us. And if he had come to end all evil on the spot, he would have ended us. Instead, he is a king who comes not to a throne but to a cross.

Encounters with Jesus

It is written

Then the devil took him to the holy city and set him on the highest point of the temple. 'If you are the Son of God,' he said, 'throw yourself down. For it is written: "He will command his angels concerning you, and they will lift you up in their hands, so that you will not strike your foot against a stone."'

Jesus answered him, 'It is also written: "Do not put the Lord your God to the test."'

Matthew 4:5–7

Jesus uses the Scripture *every time* he is assaulted by the devil. [...] Satan wants to destroy our grasp on the truth. But even more, he wants to affect the beliefs of our heart. According to the Bible, the heart is not just the seat of the emotions but also the source of our fundamental commitments, hopes, and trust. And from the heart flow our thinking, feelings, and actions. What the heart trusts, the mind justifies, the emotions desire, and the will carries out. If Satan can get you to consent with your mind to a God of loving grace but get your heart to believe that you must do X, Y, and Z in order to be a worthy, lovable, and valuable person, he will be most satisfied. [...]

Now I have to ask you: If Jesus Christ, the Son of God, did not presume to face the forces of evil in the world without a profound knowledge of the Bible in mind and heart, how could we try to face life any other way? It's true that this takes a great deal of time and effort. Worship, daily reading, meditation and memorization, singing, listening to teaching—all of these are necessary to become as acquainted with the Scripture as we must be. And when we are under attack—tempted to sin, or to be discouraged, or to just give up altogether—it is then that we must wrestle the words and promises of the Bible into the center of our being, to 'let the message of Christ dwell among you richly' (Col. 3:16). It will feel very much like a fight indeed.

Encounters with Jesus

Spiritual warfare

*Again, the devil took him to a very high mountain and showed him all
the kingdoms of the world and their splendour. 'All this I will give you,'
he said, 'if you will bow down and worship me.'*

*Jesus said to him, 'Away from me, Satan! For it is written: "Worship
the Lord your God, and serve him only."'*

Then the devil left him, and angels came and attended him.

Matthew 4:8–11

Like Jesus, we battle with Satan not merely in our hearts but
out in the world when we seek to undo his work. When we
seek to help a person find faith in Christ, or when we love our
poor neighbor through deeds of compassion and service, we are
fighting him on that front, too. [. . .]

We have one more resource for this spiritual warfare. And it is
right before us in this passage—it is Jesus himself. Hebrews 4:15
tells us he is our great high priest. Priests were counselors and
healers, and we are told that Jesus can 'empathize with our weaknesses' and can give us 'mercy and . . . grace to help us in our time
of need' (Heb. 4:16). Why? Because he was 'tempted in every way,
just as we are—yet he did not sin' (v. 15). He is there to help us
face the reality of evil, both inside and outside ourselves, having
done it himself as a man. So as we fight Satan's lies in our hearts,
and his works in our world, let's rely not only on the Word of the
Lord, but also on the Lord of the Word. We don't simply have a
book, as perfect as it is—we have Jesus himself, who has been
through fiery trials so intense that we can't imagine them. And he
has done it all for us. Now, strengthened with his deep empathy
and tender power, we can come through it all at his side.

Encounters with Jesus

The advocate

I will ask the Father, and he will give you another advocate to help you and be with you for ever—the Spirit of truth. The world cannot accept him, because it neither sees him nor knows him. But you know him, for he lives with you and will be in you.

John 14:16–7

Here Jesus says several remarkable things. He is talking about God's Spirit coming to the disciples, and anyone who has read the Hebrew Scriptures knows that the Spirit of God is a force in the world that proceeds from the Father. But Jesus speaks of the Spirit in certain ways that would have been extraordinary to them.

First, he says that the Spirit is not merely a force, but a person [...] Who is this person? Jesus calls this person 'another Advocate.' This name is different in nearly every translation. The old King James Version calls him 'Comforter,' while other translations render it 'Helper' or 'Counselor.' [...] When you and I think of [the word 'counselor'] in our time, we almost immediately think of a therapist. But this term would be better understood when we think of 'a counselor at law,' a defense attorney. Your defense attorney is sympathetically on and at your side, to be sure. But he or she is not there merely to comfort you. Indeed, your defense lawyer may have hard and challenging things to say to you, yet always in order to help your case and cause. And he or she does not merely speak to you—but also speaks to the powers that be *for* you.

Encounters with Jesus

Just to forgive

If anyone does sin, we have an advocate with the Father—Jesus Christ, the Righteous One. He is the atoning sacrifice for our sins.

1 John 2:1–2

But we must notice also [in John 14] that Jesus calls the Spirit *another* Advocate or counselor. Who, then, is the first Advocate? The only other place in the New Testament where the word *paraklete* is used is in 1 John 2:1–2 [...] So Jesus is the first Advocate, and the Spirit is the second. [...]

When Jesus goes before the Father, he is not actually asking for mercy for us. Of course it was infinitely merciful of God to send Christ to die for us, but that mercy has now been granted, so Jesus does not need to beg for it. 1 John 1:9 says that 'if we confess our sins, he is faithful and *just* and will forgive us our sins.' [...]

The best way for you to get an acquittal for your legal client is not to hope you can get some sympathy from the court. The best way is to show that your client *must* be acquitted under the law. You want to be able to say with integrity and conviction, 'This is the law, and the law demands my client's acquittal.' You want to make a case that is not based on how the court feels at the time but is open and shut according to the law. And Jesus has one! Jesus Christ can say, in effect, 'Father, my people have sinned, and the law demands that the wages of sin be death. But I have paid for those sins. See, here is my blood, the token of my death! On the cross I have paid the penalty for these sins completely. Now, if anyone were to exact two payments for the same sin, it would be unjust. And so—I am not asking for mercy for them; I'm asking for justice.'

Encounters with Jesus

The second advocate

But the Advocate, the Holy Spirit, whom the Father will send in my name, will teach you all things and will remind you of everything I have said to you. Peace I leave with you; my peace I give you. I do not give to you as the world gives. Do not let your hearts be troubled and do not be afraid.

John 14:26–7

If Jesus is your Advocate, the law of God is now completely *for* you. It's on your side of the scale. When you put your faith in Jesus, when you say from the heart, 'Father, accept me because of what Jesus did,' then Jesus' work on the cross is transferred to your account. Now the law of God demands your acquittal. That is why when John calls Jesus our Advocate, he also calls him 'the Righteous One.' This phrase suggests that when God looks at you, if you are a Christian, he sees you 'in Christ.' In yourself, alone on your side of the scale, you are a sinner; but in him you are perfect, just, beautiful, righteous. You're lost in your Advocate.

So what is the job of the first Advocate? It is to say before the Father, 'Look at what I've done. And now, accept them in me.' Then what is the job of the other Advocate, whom Jesus promises to send them—the Holy Spirit? [. . .]

The first Advocate is speaking to God for you, but the second Advocate is speaking to *you* for you. Throughout the Farewell Discourse, Jesus keeps saying that the job of the Spirit is to take all the things Jesus has done on our behalf—all the things that the apostles had still not yet grasped—and to 'teach you' and 'remind you' and enable the apostles to finally understand all that Jesus had taught them about his saving work. [. . .] he will not merely hold their hand or give them energy—he will teach them deep, life-changing truth.

Encounters with Jesus

209

The integrity of prayer

When you pray, do not be like the hypocrites, for they love to pray standing in the synagogues and on the street corners to be seen by others . . . But when you pray, go into your room, close the door and pray to your Father, who is unseen . . . in secret.

Matthew 6:5–6

The infallible test of spiritual integrity, Jesus says, is your private prayer life. Many people will pray when they are required by cultural or social expectations, or perhaps by the anxiety caused by troubling circumstances. Those with a genuinely lived relationship with God as Father, however, will inwardly *want* to pray and therefore will pray even though nothing on the outside is pressing them to do so. They pursue it even during times of spiritual dryness, when there is no social or experiential payoff.

Giving priority to the inner life doesn't mean an individualistic life. Knowing the God of the Bible better can't be achieved all by yourself. It entails the community of the church, participation in corporate worship as well as private devotion, and instruction in the Bible as well as silent meditation. At the heart of all the various ways of knowing God is both public and private prayer.

A pastor and friend of mine, Jack Miller, once said he could tell a great deal about a person's relationship with God by listening to him or her pray. 'You can tell if a man or woman is really on speaking terms with God,' he said. My first response was to make a mental note never to pray aloud near Jack again. I've had years to test out Jack's thesis. It is quite possible to become florid, theologically sound, and earnest in your public prayers without cultivating a rich, private prayer life. You can't manufacture the unmistakable note of reality that only comes from speaking not toward God but with him. The depths of private prayer and public prayer grow together.

Prayer

The hardness of prayer

'Even today my complaint is bitter; his hand is heavy in spite of my groaning. If only I knew where to find him; if only I could go to his dwelling!'

Job 23:2–3

I can think of nothing great that is also easy. Prayer must be, then, one of the hardest things in the world. To admit that prayer is very hard, however, can be encouraging. If you struggle greatly in this, you are not alone.

The Still Hour, a classic book on prayer by nineteenth-century American theologian Austin Phelps, starts with the chapter 'Absence of God, in Prayer' and the verse from Job 23:3—'Oh that I knew where I might find him!' Phelps's book begins with the premise that 'a consciousness of the *absence of God* is one of the standing incidents of religious life. Even when the forms of devotion are observed conscientiously, the sense of the presence of God, as an invisible Friend, whose society is a joy, is by no means unintermittent.'[57]

Phelps goes on to explain the numerous reasons why there is such dryness in prayer and how to endure through that sense of God's unreality. The first thing we learn in attempting to pray is our spiritual emptiness—and this lesson is crucial. We are so used to being empty that we do not recognize the emptiness as such until we start to try to pray. We don't feel it until we begin to read what the Bible and others have said about the greatness and promise of prayer. Then we finally begin to feel lonely and hungry. It's an important first step to fellowship with God, but it is a disorienting one. [. . .] Nevertheless, the pursuit of God in prayer eventually bears fruit, because God seeks for us to worship him (John 4:23) and because prayer is so infinitely rich and wondrous.

Prayer

211

Knowing God

For now we see only a reflection as in a mirror; then we shall see face to face. Now I know in part; then I shall know fully, even as I am fully known.

1 Corinthians 13:12

Prayer as a spiritual gift is a genuine, personal conversation in reply to God's specific, verbal revelation.

Yet prayer can be even more than that. Many or perhaps most of our conversations are relatively superficial. Persons can exchange information without much self-disclosure. Some conversations, however, go deep and we sense that both of us are revealing not just information but our very selves. The conversation then becomes a personal encounter, a true connection. [...]

The Bible speaks of our relationship with God as knowing and being known (Gal 4:9; 1 Cor 13:12). The goal is not just the sharing of ideas but also of ourselves. Communication can lead to two-way personal revelation that produces what can only be called a dynamic experience. J. I. Packer, in his famous work *Knowing God*, writes:

Knowing God is a matter of personal dealing . . . Knowing God is more than knowing about him; it is a matter of dealing with him as he opens up to you, and being dealt with by him . . . Friends . . . open their hearts to each other by what they say and do . . . We must not lose sight of the fact that knowing God is an emotional relationship, as well as an intellectual and volitional one, and could not indeed be a deep relationship between persons if it were not so.[58]

What is prayer, then, in the fullest sense? Prayer is continuing a conversation that God has started through his Word and his grace, which eventually becomes a full encounter with him.

Prayer

Prayer in Jesus' name

And I will do whatever you ask in my name, so that the Father may be glorified in the Son. You may ask me for anything in my name, and I will do it.

John 14:13–14

J esus taught his disciples that they must always pray in his name ([see also] John 15:16; 16:23–4). 'Prayers in his name are prayers ... in recognition that the only approach to God ... the only *way* to God is Jesus himself.'[59]

This is essentially about qualification and access. I remember how as a student in graduate school, I anxiously approached a well-known speaker after a lecture. He seemed distracted as he greeted other students with perfunctory pleasantries. I, however, was able to mention that I knew a friend of his. When I said the name, he immediately snapped to attention and spoke to me with warmth and interest. I got this kind of access to him not in my own name but in the name of our mutual friend. That is a very dim hint of how we have access to God the Father.

Because we know Jesus, because we are 'in Christ,' God focuses his almighty love and attention on us when we pray.

Prayer

The prayer of prayers

One day Jesus was praying in a certain place. When he finished, one of his disciples said to him, 'Lord, teach us to pray, just as John taught his disciples.'

Luke 11:1

Imagine you are, for the first time, visiting someone who has a home or an apartment near train tracks. You are sitting there in conversation, when suddenly the train comes roaring by, just a few feet from where you are sitting, and you jump to your feet in alarm. 'What's that?' you cry. Your friend, the resident of the house, responds, 'What was what?' You answer, 'That sound! I thought something was coming through the wall.' 'Oh, that,' she says. 'That's just the train. You know, I guess I've gotten so used to it that I don't even notice it anymore.' With wide eyes you say, 'I don't see how that is possible.' But it is.

It is the same with the Lord's Prayer. The whole world is starving for spiritual experience, and Jesus gives us the means to it in a few words. Jesus is saying, as it were, 'Wouldn't you like to be able to come face to face with the Father and king of the universe every day, to pour out your heart to him, and to sense him listening to and loving you?' We say, of course, *yes.*

Jesus responds, 'It's all in the Lord's Prayer,' and we say, 'In the *what*?' It's so familiar we can no longer hear it. Yet everything we need is within it. How do we overcome the deadly peril of familiarity?

Prayer

214

Trusting God's fatherly love

'Our Father in heaven . . .'

Matthew 6:9b

One of the best ways [to shake our overfamiliarity] is to listen to three great mentors, [Augustine, Luther and Calvin], who plumbed the depths of the prayer through years of reflection and practice. What did they believe the Lord's Prayer to be saying?

['Our Father in heaven'] is called the address, not actually one of the petitions. Calvin explains that to call God 'Father' *is* to pray in Jesus' name. 'Who would break forth into such rashness as to claim for himself the honor of a son of God unless we had been adopted as children of grace in Christ?'[60] Luther also believed the address was a call to not plunge right into talking to God but to first recollect our situation and realize our standing in Christ before we proceed into prayer. We are to say to God, 'You have taught us to regard you and call upon you as one Father of us all ... although ... you could rightly and properly be a severe judge over us.' Therefore, we should start by asking God to 'implant in our hearts a comforting trust in your fatherly love.'[61] Calvin agrees that 'by the great sweetness of this name [Father] he frees us from all distrust.'

Prayer

Honoring God's holy name

'Hallowed be your name ...'

Matthew 6:9c

This first petition is somewhat opaque to contemporary English speakers. One reason is that the word *hallowed* is seldom used today, and another is that the idea of holiness (the basic meaning of the older English word *hallowed*) is alien in our secularized society. The third is a seeming problem of logic, expressed by Luther. 'What are we praying for when we ask that His name become holy? Is it not holy already?' He immediately answers that of course it is holy, but that 'in our use of it his name is not kept holy.'[62] Luther points to the fact that all baptized Christians have God's name put upon them. As name bearers they represent a good and holy God, and so we are praying that God keep us from dishonoring the name by which we are called, that he would empower us to become ourselves good and holy. This petition, however, has a second meaning for Luther, who joins Augustine when he says it is a prayer that God 'be glorified among all nations as you are glorified among us.'[63] It is a request that faith in God would spread throughout the world, that Christians would honor God with the Christ-likeness or holiness of their lives, and that more and more people would honor God and call on his name.

Calvin agrees but adds a thought that goes deep into the heart. 'What is more unworthy than for God's glory to be obscured partly by our ungratefulness?' In other words, ingratitude and an indifferent attitude toward God fails to honor his name. To 'hallow' God's name is not merely to live righteous lives but to have a heart of grateful joy toward God—and even more, a wondrous sense of his beauty.

Prayer

Yearning for a future of justice and peace

'Your kingdom come . . .'

Matthew 6:10a

Augustine says God is reigning now, but just as a light is absent to those refusing to open their eyes, so it is possible to refuse God's rule.[64] This is the cause of all our human problems, since we were created to serve him, and when we serve other things in God's place, all spiritual, psychological, cultural, and even material problems ensue. Therefore, we need his kingdom to 'come.' Calvin believed there were two ways God's kingdom comes—through the Spirit, who 'corrects our desires,' and through the Word of God, which 'shapes our thoughts.'[65] This, then, is a 'Lordship' petition: It is asking God to extend his royal power over every part of our lives—emotions, desires, thoughts, and commitments. It is reminiscent of Thomas Cranmer's 'collect' for the fourteenth Sunday after Trinity, 'that we may obtain that which thou dost promise, make us to love that which thou dost command.' We are asking God to so fully rule us that we *want* to obey him with all our hearts and with joy.

Luther adds also an outward and a future dimension. The reign of God on earth is only partial now, but the fullness of the future kingdom is unimaginable. All suffering, injustice, poverty, and death will be ended. To pray 'thy kingdom come' is to 'yearn for that future life' of justice and peace, and to ask that 'your future kingdom may be the end and consummation of the kingdom you have begun in us.'[66]

Prayer

217

Submitting our wills to God's perfect will

'Your will be done, on earth as it is in heaven.'

Matthew 6:10b

Luther is the most vivid and forthright about the meaning of the third petition. He paraphrases like this: 'Grant us grace to bear willingly all sorts of sickness, poverty, disgrace, suffering, and adversity and to recognize that in this your divine will is crucifying our will.'[67] We may be reticent to make such a bold statement, but now we can discern the importance of the initial address. Unless we are profoundly certain God is our Father, we will never be able to say 'thy will be done.' Fathers are often inscrutable to little children. A four-year-old cannot understand many of his father's prohibitions—but he trusts him. Only if we trust God as Father can we ask for grace to bear our troubles with patience and grace.

Well, someone asks, how can we be sure God is trustworthy? The answer is that this is the one part of the Lord's Prayer Jesus himself prayed in the Garden of Gethsemane, under circumstances far more crushing than any of us will ever face. He submitted to his Father's will rather than following his own desires, and it saved us. That's why we can trust him. Jesus is not asking us to do anything for him that he hasn't already done for us, under conditions of difficulty beyond our comprehension. [...]

We have considered the first three petitions of the Lord's Prayer. All our teachers observe the significance of their place in the order—that these petitions come first in prayer. The beginning of prayer is all about God. [...] Now that the prayer is nearly half over, and our vision is reframed and clarified by the greatness of God, we can turn to our own needs and those of the world.

Prayer

Seeking provision and justice

'Give us today our daily bread.'

Matthew 6:11

Augustine reminds us that 'daily bread' is a metaphor for necessities rather than luxuries. Since we have just spent the first three petitions of prayer recognizing God as our true food, wealth, and happiness, Jesus is charging us to now bring our 'prayer list' of needs into line with this new frame of heart. As we have seen, Augustine believes the full petition should be Proverbs 30:8, 'Give me neither poverty (lest I resent you) or riches (lest I forget you).'[68] Calvin follows Augustine's reasoning when he says that, in speaking of our daily bread, 'we do not . . . bid farewell to God's glory . . . [but we] ask only what is expedient for him.'[69] We come with our needs expectant of positive response, but we do so changed by our satisfaction in him and our trust of him. We do not come arrogantly and anxiously telling him what *has* to happen. Many things we would have otherwise agonized over, we can now ask for without desperation.

Luther sees a social dimension to this prayer as well. For all to get daily bread, there must be a thriving economy, good employment, and a just society. Therefore, to pray 'give us—all the people of our land—daily bread' is to pray against 'wanton exploitation' in business, trade, and labor, which 'crushes the poor and deprives them of their daily bread.' Ominously he warns those who do injustice about the power of this petition. 'Let them beware of . . . the intercession of the church, and let them take care that this petition of the Lord's Prayer does not turn against them.'[70] For Luther, then, to pray for our daily bread is to pray for a prosperous and just social order.

Prayer

Receiving grace, showing grace

'And forgive us our debts, as we also have forgiven our debtors.'

Matthew 6:12

The fifth petition concerns our relationships, both with God and others. Luther, who for years struggled mightily and personally with the issues of guilt and pardon, gives a clarion call to seek God's forgiveness every day in prayer:

If anyone insists on his own goodness and despises others ... let him look into himself when this petition confronts him. He will find he is no better than others and that in the presence of God everyone must duck his head and come into the joy of forgiveness only through the low door of humility.[71]

Luther adds that this petition is not only a challenge to our pride but a test of spiritual reality. If we find confession and repentance intolerably traumatic or demeaning, it means 'the heart is not right with God and cannot draw ... confidence from his Gospel.' If regular confession does not produce an *increased* confidence and joy in your life, then you do not understand the salvation by grace, the essence of the faith.

Jesus tightly links our relationship with God to our relationship with others. It works two ways. If we have not seen our sin and sought radical forgiveness from God, we will be unable to forgive and to seek the good of those who have wronged us. So unresolved bitterness is a sign that we are not right with God. It also means that if we are holding a grudge, we should see the hypocrisy of seeking forgiveness from God for sins of our own.

Prayer

From temptation to trust

'And lead us not into temptation . . .'

Matthew 6:13a

With this petition Augustine makes an important distinction. He says, 'The prayer is not that we should not be tempted, but that we should not be brought [or led] *in*to temptation.'[72] Temptation in the sense of being tried and tested is not only inevitable but desirable. The Bible talks of suffering and difficulty as a furnace in which many impurities of soul are 'burned off' and we come to greater self-knowledge, humility, durability, faith, and love.

However, to '*enter in*to temptation,' as Jesus termed it (Matt. 26:41), is to entertain and consider the prospect of giving in to sin. Calvin lists two categories of temptations from the 'right' and from the 'left.' From the right comes 'riches, power, and honors,' which tempt us into the sin of thinking we do not need God. From the left comes 'poverty, disgrace, contempt, and afflictions,' which tempt us to despair, to lose all hope, and to become angrily estranged from God.[73]

Both prosperity and adversity, then, are sore tests, and each one brings its own set of enticements away from trusting in God and toward centering your life on yourself and on 'inordinate desires' for other things.[74]

Prayer

221

Calling on God's victory over evil

'But deliver us from the evil one. [Some early manuscripts: For yours is the kingdom and the power and the glory for ever. Amen.]'

Matthew 6:13b

Calvin combined this phrase with 'lead us not into temptation' and called it the sixth and last petition. Augustine and Luther, however, viewed 'deliver us from evil' as a separate, seventh petition. It can also be translated 'deliver us from the Evil One,' that is, the devil. Luther writes that this petition is 'directed against specific evils that emanate from the devil's kingdom ... poverty, dishonor, death, in short ... everything that threatens our bodily welfare.'[75] Augustine indicates that while the sixth petition is for deliverance from the remaining evil inside us, this seventh petition is for protection from evil outside us, from malignant forces in the world, especially our enemies who wish to do us harm.[76] [...]

Finally, there is what is called the ascription: 'For thine is the kingdom, the power, and the glory, forever. Amen.' Augustine does not mention it because it was not in most earlier manuscripts of the Bible or in the Latin Vulgate. Luther does not treat it. However, Calvin, while noting that 'this is not extant in the Latin versions,' believes that 'it is so appropriate to this place that it ought not to be omitted.'

After descending into our needs, troubles, and limitations, we return to the truth of God's complete sufficiency. Here our hearts can end with 'tranquil repose' in the remembrance that nothing can ever snatch away the kingdom, power, and glory from our heavenly, loving Father.

Prayer

Praying with one another

And they were calling to one another: 'Holy, holy, holy is the LORD Almighty; the whole earth is full of his glory.'

Isaiah 6:3

An [...] important insight is a reminder that the Lord's Prayer was given to us in plural form. [...] Prayer is therefore not a strictly private thing. As much as we can, we should pray with others both formally in gathered worship and informally. Why? If the substance of prayer is to continue a conversation with God, and if the purpose of it is to know God better, then this can happen best in community.

C. S. Lewis argues that it takes a community of people to get to know an individual person. Reflecting on his own friendships, he observed that some aspects of one of his friend's personality were brought out only through interaction with a second friend. That meant if he lost the second friend, he lost the part of his first friend that was otherwise invisible. 'By myself I am not large enough to call the whole man into activity; I want other lights than my own to show all his facets.'[77] If it takes a community to know an ordinary human being, how much more necessary would it be to get to know Jesus alongside others? By praying with friends, you will be able to hear and see facets of Jesus that you have not yet perceived.

That is why, Lewis thinks, that the angels in Isaiah 6 are crying, 'Holy, Holy, Holy' *to one another.* Each angel is communicating to all the rest the part of the glory it sees. Knowing the Lord is communal and cumulative, we must pray and praise together. That way 'the more we share the Heavenly Bread between us, the more we shall all have.'[78]

Prayer

Let the message of Christ dwell among you richly

'"In the last days, God says, I will pour out my Spirit on all people. Your sons and daughters will prophesy, your young men will see visions, your old men will dream dreams."'

Acts 2:17

Australian theologian Peter Adam argues that what we call preaching, the formal public address to the gathered congregation on a Sunday, is only one form of what the Bible describes as the 'ministry of the Word' (Acts 6:2, 6:4).[79]

On the day of Pentecost Peter cited the words of the prophet Joel, who said that God would pour out his Spirit on all his people, and as a result 'your sons and daughters will prophesy' (Acts 2:17). Gerhard Friedrich, in the *Theological Dictionary of the New Testament,* says that there are at least thirty-three Greek words in the New Testament usually translated as 'preaching' or 'proclaiming.' Adam observes that these words describe activities that could not all be public speaking.[80] For example, Acts 8:4 says that all the Christians except the apostles went from place to place 'proclaiming the Messiah.' This cannot mean that every believer was standing up and preaching sermons to audiences. Priscilla and Aquila, for example, explained the Word of Christ to Apollos in their home (Acts 18:26). [...]

Paul calls all believers to 'let the message of Christ dwell among you richly' and to 'teach and admonish one another with all wisdom' (Col. 3:16). Every Christian should be able to give both teaching (*didaskalia,* the ordinary word for instruction) and admonition (*noutheo*—a common word for strong, life-changing counsel) that convey to others the teachings of the Bible. This must be done carefully, though informally, in conversations that are usually one on one. That is the most fundamental form of the ministry of the Word.

Preaching

The Lord opens hearts

On the Sabbath we went outside the city gate to the river, where we expected to find a place of prayer. We sat down and began to speak to the women who had gathered there. One of those listening was a woman from the city of Thyatira named Lydia, a dealer in purple cloth. She was a worshipper of God. The Lord opened her heart to respond to Paul's message.

Acts 16:13–14

One day I was reading Acts 16, the account of Paul's planting of the church in Philippi. On this occasion Paul presented the gospel to a group of women and one, Lydia, put her faith in Christ because 'the Lord opened her heart to respond to Paul's message' (Acts 16:14). While all the listeners heard the same address, only Lydia seems to have been permanently changed by it. We should not overread this to imply that God works only through a message at the moment of delivery or that he did not also help Paul as he formulated the message earlier. Nevertheless, it was clear to me from the text that the sermon's differing impact on individuals was due to the work of God's Spirit. Maybe Paul had Lydia in mind when he described the act of preaching as the gospel coming to listeners 'not simply with words but also with power, with the Holy Spirit and deep conviction' (1 Thess. 1:5).

I concluded that the difference between a bad sermon and a good sermon is largely located in the preachers—in their gifts and skills and in their preparation for any particular message. [. . .]

However, while the difference between a bad sermon and a good sermon is mainly the responsibility of the preacher, the difference between good preaching and *great* preaching lies mainly in the work of the Holy Spirit in the heart of the listener as well as the preacher. The message in Philippi came from Paul, but the effect of the sermon on hearts came from the Spirit.

Preaching

225

Nothing except Christ crucified

When I came to you, I did not come with eloquence or human wisdom as I proclaimed to you the testimony about God. For I resolved to know nothing while I was with you except Jesus Christ and him crucified.

1 Corinthians 2:1–2

At the time Paul was writing, the only Scripture to preach from was what we now call the Old Testament. Yet even when preaching from these texts Paul 'knew nothing' but Jesus—who did not appear by name in any of those texts. How could this be? Paul understood that all Scripture ultimately pointed to Jesus and his salvation; that every prophet, priest, and king was shedding light on the ultimate Prophet, Priest, and King. To present the Bible 'in its fullness' was to preach Christ as the main theme and substance of the Bible's message.

Classical rhetoric allowed the speaker *inventio*—the choice of a topic and the division of the topic into constituent parts, along with elaborate arguments and devices to support the speaker's thesis. For Paul, however, there is always one topic: Jesus. Wherever we go in the Bible, Jesus is the main subject. And even the breakdown of our topic is not completely left up to us—we are to lay out the topics and points about Jesus that the biblical text itself gives us. We must 'confine ourselves' to Jesus. Yet I can speak from forty years of experience as a preacher to tell you that the story of this one individual never needs to become repetitious—it contains the whole history of the universe and of humankind alike and is the only resolution of the plotlines of every one of our lives.

So Paul hasn't preached a text unless he has preached about Jesus, not merely as an example to follow but as a savior: 'Christ Jesus, who has become for us ... our righteousness, holiness and redemption' (1 Cor. 1:30).

Preaching

Preaching to the cultural heart

For since in the wisdom of God the world through its wisdom did not know him, God was pleased through the foolishness of what was preached to save those who believe. Jews demand signs and Greeks look for wisdom, but we preach Christ crucified: a stumbling block to Jews and foolishness to Gentiles, but to those whom God has called, both Jews and Greeks, Christ the power of God and the wisdom of God.

1 Corinthians 1:21–4

Paul here deftly summarizes the differences between Greek and Jewish cultural narratives. Each society has a worldview or 'world story' or 'cultural narrative' that shapes the identities and assumptions of those in that society. In general, the Greeks valued philosophy, the arts, and intellectual attainments, while the Jews valued power and practical skill over discursive thought. Paul challenges both cultural narratives with the cross of Jesus. To the Greeks, a salvation that came not through elevated thought and philosophy but through a crucified Savior was the opposite of wisdom—it was foolishness. To the Jews, a salvation that came not through power, through a deliverer who overthrew the Romans, but through a crucified Savior was the opposite of strength—it was weakness. Paul uses the gospel to confront each culture with the idolatrous nature of its trusts and values.

And yet after challenging each culture, he also discerns and affirms its core aspiration. You want wisdom, says Paul to Greek listeners, but look at the cross. Didn't it make it possible for God to be both just *and* justifier of those who believe? Isn't this the ultimate wisdom? You want power, says Paul to his Jewish listeners, but look at the cross. Doesn't it make it possible for God to defeat our most powerful enemies—sin, guilt, and death itself—without destroying us? Isn't this the ultimate strength? [. . .]

Like Paul, we must invite and attract people through their culture's aspirations—calling them to come to Christ, the true wisdom and the true righteousness, the true power, the true beauty.

Preaching

Preaching Christ by the Spirit's power

My message and my preaching were not with wise and persuasive words, but with a demonstration of the Spirit's power, so that your faith might not rest on human wisdom, but on God's power.

1 Corinthians 2:4–5

The famous nineteenth-century British preacher Charles Spurgeon was bold in his insistence that every sermon lift up Jesus for all listeners to behold. He complained that he often heard sermons that were 'very learned . . . fine and magnificent,' yet all about moral truth and ethical practice and inspiring concepts and 'not a word about Christ.' Here is what he says about such preaching, evoking the words of Mary Magdalene: 'They have taken away my Lord, and I know not where they have laid him. I heard nothing about Christ!'[81] He is right. Unless we preach Jesus rather than a set of 'morals of the story' or timeless principles or good advice, people will never truly understand, love, or obey the Word of God. What Spurgeon calls for is harder than it sounds and rarer than you would think.

So there are two things we must do. As we preach, we are to serve and love the truth of God's Word and also to serve and love the people before us. We serve the Word by preaching the text clearly and preaching the gospel every time. We reach the people by preaching to the culture and to the heart.

Then there is what God must do. He brings the Word home to our hearers through the 'demonstration of the Spirit and of power' (1 Cor. 2:4). [. . .]

How do all these things happen? They all happen as we preach Christ. To preach the text truly and the gospel every time, to engage the culture and reach the heart, to cooperate with the Spirit's mission in the world—we must preach Christ from all of Scripture.

Preaching

Confidence in God's Word

Then the LORD reached out his hand and touched my mouth and said to me, 'I have put my words in your mouth. See, today I appoint you over nations and kingdoms to uproot and tear down, to destroy and overthrow, to build and to plant.'

Jeremiah 1:9–10

One way to develop an appropriate confidence in the Scripture is by seeing what the Bible says about itself. Start with a thorough study and analysis of Psalm 119, and distill all it says about the character of the Scripture and its role and use in our lives. [...] It is important to know not only in general that the Bible is true but also that in the Bible God's words are identical to his actions. When he says, 'Let there be light,' there is light (Gen. 1:3). When God renames someone, it automatically remakes him (Gen. 17:5). The Bible does not say that God speaks and then proceeds to act, that he names and then proceeds to shape—but that God's speaking and acting are the same thing. His word *is* his action, his divine power.[82]

So how do we hear God's active Word today if we are not prophets or apostles who actually sat at Jesus' feet? God's words in the mouths of the prophets (Jer. 1:9–10), written down, are *still* God's words to us when we read them today (Jer. 36:1–32). Ward says that it is crucial for the preacher to recognize this. 'God's ongoing dynamic action through the Spirit' is 'supremely related to the language and meanings of Scripture.'[83] In other words, as we unfold the meaning of the language of Scripture, God becomes powerfully active in our lives. The Bible is not merely information, not even just completely true information. It is 'alive and active' (Heb. 4:12)—God's power in verbal form.

Preaching

Christ in all of scripture

He said to them, 'How foolish you are, and how slow to believe all that the prophets have spoken! Did not the Messiah have to suffer these things and then enter his glory?' And beginning with Moses and all the Prophets, he explained to them what was said in all the Scriptures concerning himself.

Luke 24:25–7

O nly if we preach Christ every time can we show how the whole Bible fits together.

When Jesus met the two disciples on the road to Emmaus, he discovered that they were in despair because their Messiah had been crucified. [...] Later he appeared to the apostles and other disciples in the upper room and explained the same thing to them, namely, that he is the key to understanding 'the Law of Moses, the Prophets and the Psalms' (Luke 24:44). Jesus blamed the confusion of the disciples on their inability to see that the Old Testament is all about him and his salvation.

The apostolic writers are famously 'Christ centered' in their interpretation of the Hebrew Scriptures. They continually quote psalms as the words of Christ—and not just 'messianic' or 'royal' psalms where the speaker is clearly a messianic figure. For example, Hebrews 10:5–6 quotes Psalm 40:6–8 as something Christ said when 'he came into the world.'

Sacrifice and offering you did not desire, but my ears you have opened—burnt offerings and sin offerings you did not require. Then I said, 'Here I am, I have come—it is written about me in the scroll—I desire to do your will, my God . . .'

But when we readers look at Psalm 40, we see absolutely nothing that would indicate that the speaker is Jesus or some messianic figure. Why would the Hebrews author assume that Psalm 40 was about Jesus? He does so because he knows what Jesus told his disciples in Luke 24, that all the Scripture is really about him. The Bible is in the end a single, great story that comes to a climax in Jesus Christ.

Preaching

The fulfilment of covenant history

I will take you as my own people, and I will be your God. Then you will know that I am the LORD your God, who brought you out from under the yoke of the Egyptians.

Exodus 6:7

Each genre and part of the Old Testament looks toward Christ and informs us about who he is in some way that the others do not. [...] one of the main questions constantly raised by the historical books, from Judges through 2 Chronicles, has to do with the nature of the covenant. [...] The question is this: In light of the constant failures of the people to live up to their covenant promises to serve God, is the covenant conditional or unconditional? Will God say that it is conditional? ('Because you broke the covenant, I will cut you off, curse you, and abandon you forever.') Or will he say it is unconditional? ('Though you have rejected me, I will never wholly abandon you, but I will remain with you.') Which is it? [...] This mystery is one of the main tensions that drive the dramatic action. Since his people have forsaken him, will he forsake them?

There seems to be no simple answer that will not compromise something we know of God. Will his holiness give way to his love, so that he overlooks sin? Or will his love be overwhelmed by his holiness and justice, so that the divine hammer falls? Either way it seems he is not as truly loving or as truly holy as he otherwise reveals himself to be. See the plot tension in the story?

And then Jesus comes, and as we see him crying, 'My God, my God, why have you forsaken me?' we realize the answer. Is the covenant between God and his people conditional or unconditional? Yes. Yes. Jesus came and fulfilled the conditions so God could love us unconditionally.

Preaching

The true and better leader

'Moses was faithful as a servant in all God's house,' bearing witness to what would be spoken by God in the future. But Christ is faithful as the Son over God's house.

Hebrews 3:5–6

All the major figures and leaders of the Scriptures point us to Christ, the ultimate leader who calls out and forms a people for God. [...]

Jesus is the true and better Adam, who *passed* the test in the garden and whose obedience is imputed to us (1 Corinthians 15). [...]

Jesus is the true and better Abraham, who answered the call of God to leave the comfortable and familiar and go out into the void 'not knowing whither he went' to create a new people of God.

Jesus is the true and better Isaac, who was not just offered up by his father on the mount but was truly sacrificed for us all. God said to Abraham, 'Now I know you love me, because you did not withhold your son, your only son whom you love, from me.' Now we can say to God, 'Now *we* know that you love us, because you did not withhold your son, your only son whom you love, from us.'

Jesus is the true and far better Jacob, who wrestled with God and took the blow of justice we deserved so that we, like Jacob, receive only the wounds of grace to wake us up and discipline us.

Jesus is the true and better Joseph, who at the right hand of the King forgives those who betrayed and sold him and uses his new power to save them.

Jesus is the true and better Moses, who stands in the gap between the people and the Lord and who mediates a new covenant (Hebrews 3).

Jesus is the true and better rock of Moses, who, struck with the rod of God's justice, now gives us water in the desert.

Preaching

The true and better Jonah

For as Jonah was three days and three nights in the belly of a huge fish, so the Son of Man will be three days and three nights in the heart of the earth.

Matthew 12:40

At the end of Mark 4 we see Jesus stilling the storm, and his rebuke: 'Do you still have no faith?' (Mark 4:40). It would be easy to preach this in an inadvertently moralistic way. We could just draw out the lesson that we need to work on our faith and trust God when things get bad. That would ultimately be merely a how-to sermon—how to have faith and hold on in storms. It wouldn't show us the gospel very clearly.

But Mark is intentionally recapping the Jonah episode in Mark 4. [. . .] As Jesus says in Matthew 12:40, he is the ultimate Jonah, who was thrown into the ultimate deeps—of eternal justice—for us. [. . .] Jonah died for his own sin, but Jesus is thrown into the ultimate storm for *our* sin. Jesus was able to save the disciples from the storm because he was thrown into the ultimate storm. [. . .]

Are you in something like a storm in your life? Have you prayed and felt like God must be asleep? He is not. How do you know? Because he turned his prow into that ultimate storm and endured it for you—so you can know he will not abandon you in your infinitely smaller storms. Why not trust the one who did that for you?

Preaching

The true and better Tree of Life

The fruit of the righteous is a tree of life, and the one who is wise saves lives.

Proverbs 11:30

The Bible begins and ends with the tree of life—in Genesis and Revelation. In the beginning we lost the tree of life; we lost paradise. In the end, through the work of Jesus we regain the tree of life, which now stands prominently in the middle of the city of God. So this tree represents eternal life and vitality, as opposed to decay and death working in us.

Now, this tree shows up in only one other place in the Bible, in the book of Proverbs. There, wisdom itself is the tree of life. Growth in wisdom is understood as growth in knowing God, in knowing ourselves, and in godly character and relationships— what we would call spiritual growth in the 'fruit' of the Spirit. So Proverbs is saying that it is possible, in a sense, to eat from this tree now in an experience of spiritual growth. The New Testament shows us how. The Spirit unites us with Christ by faith, and now 'life works within us' even as we still have death working in our bodies. But how is this all possible?

Galatians 3:13 reminds us that when Jesus was crucified, he was cursed because he was 'hanged on a tree' (ESV). George Herbert puts it so vividly in 'The Sacrifice' when he depicts Jesus speaking from the cross. He says, 'All ye who pass by, behold and see; Man stole the fruit, now I must climb the tree; A tree of life for all, but only me. Was ever grief like mine?' What is Jesus saying? Because Jesus got the tree of death, we can have the tree of life. Herbert is even more poignantly saying that Jesus turned the cross into a tree of life for us, at infinite cost to himself.

Preaching

The true and better David

David said to the Philistine, 'You come against me with sword and spear and javelin, but I come against you in the name of the LORD Almighty, the God of the armies of Israel, whom you have defied.'

1 Samuel 17:45

Look at the story of David and Goliath. What is the meaning of that narrative for us? [. . .] If I read the story of David and Goliath as basically giving me an example, then it is really about me. *I* must summon up the faith and courage to fight the giants in my life. But if I think of the Bible as being about the Lord and his salvation, and if I read the David and Goliath text in that light, it throws many things into relief. The very point of the passage was that the Israelites could *not* face the giant themselves. They needed a substitute, who turned out to be not a strong person but a weak one. And God uses the deliverer's weakness as the very means to bring about the destruction of Goliath. David triumphs through weakness and his victory is imputed to his people. In his triumph, they triumphed.

How can one not recognize Jesus in this story? Jesus faced the ultimate giants (sin and death) not at the risk of his life but at the cost of his life. But he triumphed through his weakness and now his triumph is ours—his victory is imputed to us. Until I see that Jesus fought the real giants *for* me, I will never have the courage to be able to fight ordinary giants in life (suffering, disappointment, failure, criticism, hardship). How *can* I ever fight the 'giant' of failure, unless I have a deep security that God will not abandon me? [. . .] I am no longer petrified by failure, because I triumph in Jesus, our true David. Unless I first believe in the one to whom David *points,* I'll never become like David at all.

Preaching

The true and better Israel

'When Israel was a child, I loved him, and out of Egypt I called my son.'
Hosea 11:1

It is not simply the stories of individuals that point us to Christ. The redemptive purpose of God is to redeem a *people* and renew *creation*. Therefore, all the major events in the history of the formation of the people of God also point us to Christ.

Jesus is the one through whom all people are created (John 1). Thus the creation story itself points forward to the new creation in Christ. Jesus is the one who went through temptation and probation in the wilderness. Thus the story of the fall points forward to the successful probation and active obedience of Christ. The exodus story points forward to the true exodus Jesus led for his people through his death (Luke 9:31). He led them not just out of economic and political bondage but out of bondage to sin and death itself through his death and resurrection. The wandering in the wilderness and the exile to Babylon points forward to Jesus' 'homelessness' and wandering and wilderness temptation, culminating in his suffering as the scapegoat outside the gate. He underwent the ultimate exile that fulfilled the righteousness of God fully.

Jesus is very literally the true Israel, the seed (Gal. 3:16–17). He is the only one who is faithful to the covenant. He is a remnant of one. He fulfills all the obligations of the covenant and earns the blessings of the covenant for all who believe. When Hosea talks about the exodus of Israel from Egypt, he [...] calls all of Israel 'my son.' But Matthew quotes this verse referring to Jesus (Matt. 2:15) because Jesus is the true Israel.

Preaching

The true and better Blessed One

'Blessed are the poor in spirit, for theirs is the kingdom of heaven.
Blessed are those who mourn, for they will be comforted.'

Matthew 5:3–4

L ook at the beatitudes in the Sermon on the Mount [. . .] if we are preaching just on the beatitudes, Matthew 5:1–10, it would be easy to fall into mere moral exhortation. 'Be like this—try quite hard—and you will be Jesus' disciples.'

But [. . .] they also describe Jesus himself. And when we think of that we see how what he did gives us what each beatitude promises.

Why can you and I be as rich as kings? Because *he* became spiritually and utterly poor. Why can you and I be comforted? Only because he mourned; because he wept inconsolably and died in the dark. [. . .] Why is it that someday you and I are going to be able to see God? Because Jesus Christ set his face like a flint to go up to Jerusalem and die for us (Luke 9:51). You and I can see God because, on the cross, Jesus could not.

When you see Jesus Christ being poor in spirit *for you,* that helps you become poor in spirit before God and say, 'I need your grace.' And once you get it and you are filled, then you are merciful, you become a peacemaker, you find God in prayer and wait someday for the beatific vision, to see God as he is (1 John 3:1–3). The beatitudes, like nearly everything else in Scripture, point us to Jesus far more than we think.

Preaching

Actions shape the heart

Do not set foot on the path of the wicked or walk in the way of evil-doers. Avoid it, do not travel on it; turn from it and go on your way. For they cannot rest until they do evil; they are robbed of sleep till they make someone stumble.

Proverbs 4:14–16

Walking on a *path* always takes you somewhere. Life is likened to a path because every action takes you somewhere. That is, the act changes you, making it easier for you to do it again. Eventually it becomes so natural to be cruel and selfish that you *cannot rest* unless you are doing it. 'Sow a thought, reap an action; sow an action, reap a habit; sow a habit, reap a character; sow a character, reap a destiny.'[84]

Modern people think feelings determine what we do and that it is hypocritical to act loving if they don't feel loving. Proverbs, however, tells us that our actions shape our feelings. So if you don't feel love for someone, don't let that stop you. Do the actions of love, and often the feelings follow. When Jesus tells us to love our opponents (Matt. 5:43–8), he does not mean to work up warm feelings. He is telling us to seek our opponents' good, even at a sacrifice. So start doing the actions of love—take that path—and you will see your heart changing.

Think of one hard-to-love person in your life. What practical things could you do to begin to love them better?

The Way of Wisdom

Actions open the eyes

The path of the righteous is like the morning sun, shining ever brighter till the full light of day. But the way of the wicked is like deep darkness; they do not know what makes them stumble.

Proverbs 4:18–19

The paths of love and of selfishness lead to two different end points. But they also differ along the way. One path brightens gradually and the other darkens. The darkness represents increasing self-deception. We say, 'I'm not proud, just confident. I'm not abrasive, just direct. I'm not greedy, just sharp in business.' The more we follow the path of self, the more we live in denial until, when life breaks down, we do not know what makes us stumble. Self-deception is not the worst thing you can do, but it's the means by which we do the very worst things. The sin that is most distorting your life right now is the one you can't see.

On the other hand, those growing in grace (2 Pet. 3:18) take the path *shining ever brighter.* They see more and more things about God and themselves that they were denying. Why? The gospel so assures us of God's love that we are finally capable of admitting the worst about ourselves. In his love, based on Christ's work, not ours, it is finally safe to do so.

Ask two or three good friends, 'What is a character flaw of mine that others can see but I can't see as clearly?'

The Way of Wisdom

The heart shapes the actions

Above all else, guard your heart, for everything you do flows from it.
Keep your mouth free of perversity; keep corrupt talk far from your lips.
Let your eyes look straight ahead; fix your gaze directly before you.
Give careful thought to the paths for your feet and be steadfast in all
your ways.

Proverbs 4:23–6

In the Bible the heart is not primarily the seat of the emotions in contrast to the head as the seat of reason. Rather, the heart is the seat of your deepest trusts, commitments, and loves, from which *everything . . . flows*. What the heart most loves and trusts, the mind finds reasonable, the emotions find desirable, and the will finds doable.

How do you guard your heart? The passage hints that, though ultimately the heart is the central control, our words, eyes, and feet can influence the heart. If we gaze longingly enough at an object, it may capture our heart through the imagination (as when Achan looked, desired, and finally stole the treasure in Joshua 7). If we speak bitterly against someone, we can sour our heart toward them. The best way to *guard your heart* for wisdom is worship, in which the mouth, the mind, the imagination, and even the body are all oriented to God.

Is there some way in which you are failing to guard your heart right now? Are there things you are seeing or doing that may be moving your heart away from God?

The Way of Wisdom

God and the heart

All a person's ways seem pure to them, but motives are weighed by the LORD.

Proverbs 16:2

Y ou don't know yourself unless you know that your motives are never *pure*, and that they always seem better to you than they do to the Lord, who *weighs* them. This has huge implications for decision-making and relationships. If you are always sure of your sincerity and purity, you will make impulsive snap judgments. You will be too dismissive of some options and ideas and too doggedly committed to others.

Not trusting your heart prevents two opposite errors. On the one hand, our consciences can be too easy on us. 'My conscience is clear, but that does not make me innocent' (1 Cor. 4:4). Follow God's Word instead of your feelings. If the Scripture says it is wrong, it is. On the other hand, our hearts can be too hard on us. 'If our hearts condemn us, ... God is greater than our hearts' (1 John 3:20). Follow the gospel instead of your feelings. You are loved for Christ's sake, not because your heart and life are perfect. Without God's word of grace to build us up (Acts 20:32), we will fall into false guilt or false innocence.

Into which of these two mistakes are you more likely to fall? What can you do about it?

The Way of Wisdom

Not even one

Who can say, 'I have kept my heart pure; I am clean and without sin'?
Proverbs 20:9

Proverbs may appear to imply that we can make ourselves good through our efforts. Yet at key places the book reminds us that wisdom is a gift of grace, and here is one of them. No one can make themselves good. Similarly, 'there is no one righteous, not even one' (Rom. 3:10), and 'if you, LORD, kept a record of sins ... who could stand?' (Ps. 130:3). How does this truth make us wise?

First, it means that everyone is lost. To be *clean* and *pure* is to be acceptable before God, but no one is. Psalm 130:3 says no one can 'stand' before God. So the wise do not divide the world into the 'good guys' and the 'bad guys.' Both moral and immoral are alienated from God, though in different ways. Second, it means God must save by grace. So the wise fuel their efforts for right living out of joy and gratitude for the free salvation they have in Christ. They escape the drudgery and crushing motive of seeking righteousness in order to deserve it.

Do you tend to divide the world into the 'good' types and 'bad' types? How does that contradict a sound doctrine of sin?

The Way of Wisdom

Confession

Whoever conceals their sins does not prosper, but the one who confesses and renounces them finds mercy.

Proverbs 28:13

If we try to cover up our sin, God will expose us. If we expose our sin, God will cover it with his *mercy*. How do we *conceal* sins from others? We lie. We blame-shift and make excuses. We tell people to mind their own business and point to the good things we have done. We rationalize that our motives were good or that our action wasn't technically wrong.

But we also hide our sins from ourselves. We find ways to justify them, as we give lip service and admit a sin but we don't renounce it. Despite the subterfuge, deep down we know we are sinners, that there is something seriously wrong with us. This produces severe imbalances in our psychological life, from which flow many ills: eating disorders, anxiety, substance abuse, overwork, anger. We may find ourselves so needy for affirmation that we stay in the wrong, or even abusive, relationships. The solution? 'If we confess our sins ... we have an advocate with the Father—Jesus Christ, the Righteous One. He is the atoning sacrifice for our sins' (1 John 1:9, 2:1–2).

What is your most typical strategy for concealing your sin—from others or from yourself?

The Way of Wisdom

The discerning heart

The discerning heart seeks knowledge, but the mouth of a fool feeds on folly.

Proverbs 15:14

Fools can be said to be all mouth, always spouting foolishness. The wise, however, are all heart—and every new experience is a way for their hearts to become more *discerning*.

In a TV episode, based on an Agatha Christie story, a retired Scotland Yard inspector explains to an incredulous friend that Miss Marple is the greatest criminologist in England. 'There she sits,' he says, 'an elderly spinster. Sweet, placid, or so you'd think. Yet her mind has plumbed the depths of human iniquity and taken it all in a day's work. She has lived all her life in a little rural village of St. Mary Mead. It's extraordinary! She knows the world only through the prism of that village and its daily life, but by knowing the village so thoroughly, she seems to know the world.' Like Jesus, the ultimate wise one, she loves people but she doesn't trust human nature (John 2:23–5). The secrets of wisdom are locked in your ordinary experience if you know how to learn from it. Ask God to help you develop a *discerning heart*.[85]

In what area or way has God enabled you to grow in discernment during the past year?

The Way of Wisdom

The importance of the heart

For where your treasure is, there your heart will be also.

Matthew 6:21

Modern readers of the Bible will almost always misunderstand the term 'heart.' They run it through their contemporary grid and conclude that it means the emotions. But the Bible often talks about *thinking* with the heart or *acting* with the heart, which does not fit with our modern concept at all. Nor did the ancient Greeks have a biblical understanding of the heart. Virtue was to them a matter of spirit over body, and that meant reason and will triumphing over unruly bodily passions. Today, we continue to pit the mind and the feelings against each other, but we have radically reversed the ancient order. Emotions are the 'true' self, not the rational thoughts.

The biblical view of the heart is 'none of the above.' In the Bible the heart is the seat of the mind, will, *and* emotions, all together. Genesis 6:5 says about the human race that 'every inclination of the thoughts of the human heart was only evil all the time.' One commentator writes: '*Leb* 'heart' is the center of the human personality in biblical anthropology, where will and thought originate; it is not merely the source of emotions as in English.'[86] [...]

No wonder the Bible says that God ignores outward matters and looks supremely at the heart (1 Sam. 16:7; 1 Cor. 4:5; Jer. 17:10).

Preaching

Changing minds and hearts

Above all else, guard your heart, for everything you do flows from it.

Proverbs 4:23

Whatever captures the heart's trust and love also controls the feelings and behavior. What the heart most wants the mind finds reasonable, the emotions find valuable, and the will finds doable. It is all-important, then, that preaching move the heart to stop trusting and loving other things more than God. What makes people into what they are is the order of their loves—what they love most, more, less, and least. That is more fundamental to who you are than even the beliefs to which you mentally subscribe. Your loves show what you actually believe in, not what you say you do. People, therefore, change not by merely changing their thinking but by changing what they love most. Such a shift requires nothing *less* than changing your thinking, but it entails much more.

So the goal of the sermon cannot be merely to make the truth clear and understandable to the mind, but must also be to make it gripping and real to the heart. Change happens not just by giving the mind new arguments but also by feeding the imagination new beauties.

Preaching

Capturing the imagination

I pray that you, being rooted and established in love, may have power, together with all the Lord's holy people, to grasp how wide and long and high and deep is the love of Christ, and to know this love that surpasses knowledge—that you may be filled to the measure of all the fullness of God.

Ephesians 3:17–19

Many years ago, in my first pastorate, I met with a teenage girl in our congregation. She was about sixteen at the time, and she was discouraged and becoming depressed. I tried to encourage her, but there was a revelatory moment when she said, 'Yes, I know Jesus loves me, he saved me, he's going to take me to heaven—but what good is it when no boy at school will even look at you?'

She said she 'knew' all these truths about being a Christian, but they were of no comfort to her. The attention (or the lack of it) of a cute boy at school was far more consoling, energizing, and foundational for her joy and self-worth than the love of Christ. Of course this was a perfectly normal response for a teenage girl. Nevertheless it was revealing of how our hearts work. [...] Christ's love was an abstract concept while the love of these others was real to her heart. That was the reality that had captured her imagination.

In Ephesians 3, Paul prays for his readers and asks that 'Christ may dwell in your hearts through faith ... and ... know this love that surpasses knowledge ... [and] be filled [with] ... all the fullness of God' (Eph. 3:17–19). [...] There are many things Christians know but they don't really know. They know these things in part, but they haven't grasped them with the heart and had the imagination so captured that it has changed them thoroughly from the inside out.

Preaching

Imagination and empathy

The LORD sent Nathan to David. When he came to him, he said, 'There were two men in a certain town, one rich and the other poor. The rich man had a very large number of sheep and cattle, but the poor man had nothing except one little ewe lamb that he had bought.'

2 Samuel 12:1–3

In 2 Samuel 11 David has an affair with Bathsheba, then arranges for her husband, Uriah, to be killed in battle, and finally marries her. Though doubtless having some pangs of conscience, David justifies his behavior to himself in some way. [...] In the next chapter Nathan the prophet comes to challenge the king over his sin. But he does not do so immediately. [...]

Nathan tells the king a story of a rich man with many possessions and a poor man who owned only one little lamb. 'He raised it, and it grew up with him and his children. It shared his food, drank from his cup and even slept in his arms. It was like a daughter to him' (2 Samuel 12:3). Nathan then explains that the rich man throws a feast but refuses to supply his guests with food out of his own abundant herds of livestock and instead steals the poor man's lamb and prepares it as the main course for the dinner. What should be done about this rich man, Nathan asks the king? David 'burns with anger' at this story and says that the man who did this should die, 'because he did such a thing and had no pity.' Nathan immediately responds, 'You are the man!' (2 Samuel 12:5–7).

David is filled with rationalizations that blind him to the injustice in his own life story. So Nathan takes him (through his imagination) into someone else's life experience, where he can see injustice in its true colors and be outraged. [...] He is cut to the heart—and repents.

Preaching

The hidden truth of fantasy

He has also set eternity in the human heart; yet no one can fathom what God has done from beginning to end.

Ecclesiastes 3:11

If we are going to preach to the heart, we need also to evoke wonder. Tolkien's famous essay 'On Fairy Stories' argues that there are indelible, deep longings in the human heart that realistic fiction cannot satisfy. Fantasy fiction—fairy tales and science fiction and similar literature—depict characters who:

- get outside of time altogether;
- escape death;
- hold communion with nonhuman beings;
- find a perfect love from which they never part;
- triumph finally over evil.

[...] The enduring appeal of stories that represent these conditions is unquestionable. But why? As a Christian, Tolkien believed that these stories resonate so deeply because they bear witness to an underlying reality. Even if we do not intellectually believe that there is a God or life after death, our hearts (in the Christian view) sense somehow that these things characterize life as it was and should be and eventually will be again. We are so deeply interested in these stories because we have intuitions of the creation/fall/redemption/restoration plotline of the Bible. Even if we repress the knowledge of that plotline intellectually, we can't not know it imaginatively, and our hearts are stirred by any stories that evoke it.

Preaching

The good spell of the gospel

This grace was given us in Christ Jesus before the beginning of time, but it has now been revealed through the appearing of our Saviour, Christ Jesus, who has destroyed death and has brought life and immortality to light through the gospel.

2 Timothy 1:9b–10

The English word 'gospel' comes from the Middle English word *Godspell* which derives from two Old English words: *good* and *spell* (story). In Old English 'to tell a story' was 'to cast a spell.' Stories capture the heart and imagination and give us deep joy. The Gospel of Jesus Christ is *the Goodspell*. It is *the* story that all other joy-bringing, spell-casting, heart-shaping stories only point to. What's special about this one? It is the one story that satisfies all these longings—yet is historically *true*.

If Jesus Christ was really raised from the dead—if he is really the Son of God and you believe in him—all those things that you long for most desperately are real and will come true. We *will* escape time and death. We will know love without parting, we will even communicate with nonhuman beings, and we will see evil defeated forever. In fairy stories, especially the best and most well-told ones, we get a temporary reprieve from a life in which our deepest desires are all violently rebuffed. However, if the gospel is true—and it is—all those longings will be fulfilled.

Preaching

A subtext of worship

One thing I ask from the LORD, this only do I seek: that I may dwell in the house of the LORD all the days of my life, to gaze on the beauty of the LORD and to seek him in his temple.

Psalm 27:4

The subtext is the message under your message. It is the real, intended meaning (conscious or unconscious) of a message, which is deeper than the surface meanings of the words.

One kind of subtext [in preaching] is 'Aren't we great?' [...] its main goal is to furnish a sense of self-reinforcement to a group. [...] A second kind of subtext is 'Aren't I great?' The speaker is seeking to exhibit his or her skills and promote the products of the church. [...] A third kind of subtext is 'Isn't this truth great?' The goal is to increase the knowledge of the receivers, so that they can live in a desired way. [...]

A last kind of subtext is 'Isn't Christ great?' This is the most complex and complete of all, and it takes the most skill. It aims beyond information, beyond capturing the imagination, and even beyond behavior change to the goal of changing what our heart most sets its affections on. The message: 'Look at how Christ is so much grander and more wonderful than you thought! Don't you see that all your problems stem from failing to see this?'

There is no way to convey this right and true subtext through technique; it comes down to your spiritual life as a preacher [...] the temptation will be to let the pulpit drive you to the Word, but instead you must let the Word drive you to the pulpit. Prepare the preacher more than you prepare the sermon.

Preaching

251

Introvert or extrovert?

As water reflects the face, so one's life reflects the heart.

Proverbs 27:19

As water shows us our face, *so one's life reflects the heart*. But whose heart and whose life are being referred to? Is it saying that we should explore our life history to understand what is in our hearts—as did Augustine in his *Confessions*? Or does it mean that by getting to know others, you can learn about your own heart? For example, there is no better way to see what you are doing wrong in your own marriage than to try to counsel and help friends whose marriage is troubled.

There's good reason to think that the ambiguity of the proverb is deliberate. To truly come to wise self-knowledge you must use both methods. Introverts are more naturally inclined to explore their own lives and extroverts to get involved in the lives of others. But both methods for self-knowledge are needed. Introverts should get out more, and extroverts should spend more time in solitary thought.

Are you more of an introvert or extrovert? How can you begin to use the way of wisdom that you are not naturally inclined to use?

The Way of Wisdom

Inside and outside

Like a coating of silver dross on earthenware are fervent lips with an evil heart. Enemies disguise themselves with their lips, but in their hearts they harbour deceit. Though their speech is charming, do not believe them, for seven abominations fill their hearts.

Proverbs 26:23–5

Proverbs 26:23 introduces the image of a vessel that looks like pure silver but is just valueless clay with a thin *coating of silver dross*. This distinction between the inside and outside is crucial to biblical wisdom. In the fairy tale *The Princess and Curdie*, by George MacDonald, the hero is given a magical ability. He can touch the hand of someone and discern their true inward character. So he might shake the hand of a beautiful woman or man and perceive the claw of a vulture, or he might take the hand of a monster and feel the fingers of a loving child. This ability, of course, enables him to triumph.

The more you grow in godly wisdom, the more you get this same world-beating ability. 'Wise folk see through the façade of hypocrisy, withhold trust, and do not take liars at face value.'[87] In order to live wisely in our present culture of self-promotion, fake news, alternative facts, and the overthrow of reason, the ability to discern evil disguised as good could not be more important.

Recall a time when you seriously misread someone's character and intentions, perhaps because of attractive superficialities. How likely are you to make the same mistake again?

The Way of Wisdom

Deep waters

The purposes of a person's heart are deep waters, but one who has insight draws them out.

Proverbs 20:5

If you want to hide something, a good way is to throw it into deep waters. So too our heart motives seem out of sight. However, 'wise persons can bring to the surface what others have in mind, even when there are attempts at concealment.'[88] This tells us the wise are able to discern motives—both their own and those of others. While we want to think we are telling the truth for noble motives, are we really being driven by insecurity or resentment? While this person assures us he is on our side, is he really just using us for his own purposes?

We must remember it is possible to become overly suspicious or paranoid (28:1), or just uncharitable (1 Cor. 13:7), which can lead to as many wrong decisions as naïveté. As *insight* is a gift of God (2:6, 9:10), it is better to think of this ability to discern hearts not as a technique but as a spiritual gift from the only one who can see every heart to the very bottom (16:2). Don't look for little signs by which you can 'spy the lie.' Insight comes through growth in grace and its accompanying self-knowledge. 'My own heart'— we need no other—'showeth me the wickedness of the ungodly' (Psalm 36:1).[89]

How gullible are you?

The Way of Wisdom

Trapped by desire

What the wicked dread will overtake them; what the righteous desire will be granted . . . The righteousness of the upright delivers them, but the unfaithful are trapped by evil desires . . . Desire without knowledge is not good—how much more will hasty feet miss the way!

Proverbs 10:24, 11:6, 19:2

The 'heart' is not mere feeling but rather the seat of our deepest trusts and loves. Today's society, however, identifies our strongest feelings as the 'true self' and insists we express them. But wisdom recognizes that our desires can trap us (11:6). They can also be influenced from outside. Modern consumer capitalism creates the desire to accumulate material goods that, we think, will give us status and identity. Poor parenting can train children to so desire approval and love that they remain in abusive relationships or become workaholics.

Wise people do not simply accept their desires as they are, nor with hasty feet run to fulfill them. Rather, as Augustine counseled, they reorder their desires with the knowledge of the truth. The problem of the workaholic, for example, is not that we love work too much, but that we love God too little, relative to our career. What the righteous desire is ultimately God himself, seeing his face. 'I . . . will see your face . . . I will be satisfied with seeing your likeness' (Ps. 17:15). Only if we cultivate our relationship to God and grow the desire for him will our other desires not entrap us.

What loves or desires do you have that are 'inordinate,' that push God out of the top spot?

The Way of Wisdom

255

Ordering desire

*A longing fulfilled is sweet to the soul, but fools detest turning from
evil . . . Do not let your heart envy sinners, but always be zealous for
the fear of the LORD. There is surely a future hope for you, and your
hope will not be cut off.*

Proverbs 13:19, 23:17–18

The soul has an appetite. We are drawn to good things that are
satisfying, but nothing besides God himself should be a
nonnegotiable necessity for life. Every other enjoyment comes
with the danger that we make it such. 'To set your heart on [any
good] thing is to weaken the power to assess it. It must be had, at
all costs, not now because of its worth but because you have
promised it to yourself.'[90]

How, then, can we desire God above all other things? Plato said
actions flow from thinking and Aristotle taught that our thinking
is shaped by our actions. Proverbs says they are both right.
Contemplate 23:17–18. Use the mind to think—what are the only
things that finally last? (*There is . . . a future hope.*) Set the heart on
God in prayer and worship until you don't just believe but experience awe and wonder (*be zealous . . . fear*) before him. And set the
will on obedience. Don't *envy* (or imitate) *sinners*. These things
will reorder your desires.

How specifically will you implement any of these strategies
this week? See the prayer below for one.

The Way of Wisdom

The sociology of desire

Do not envy the wicked, do not desire their company; for their hearts plot violence, and their lips talk about making trouble.

Proverbs 24:1–2

Sociologists know that we tend to find most plausible the ideas of the people with whom we spend the most time and to whom our admiration is most directed. If we 'sit in the company of mockers' (Ps. 1:1) or of the cruel and violent (verse 2), we will become like them. It is easy to *envy* mockers and cruel people because they are often successful through their ruthlessness.

Today we believe that we can create our own identity through our own free choices. We may think we are being 'true to ourselves' when we shed the constraints of traditional values and morality, but in reality we are simply allowing a new community to tell us who we are. 'The question of individual identity is always also a question of community, from family and church, school and business, all the way up to nation and state. Communities create the paths we walk.'[91]

Why do you hang out with the people you do? Have your choices been influenced by a desire to be like the people you spend time with the most?

The Way of Wisdom

Approval

Fear of man will prove to be a snare, but whoever trusts in the Lord is kept safe.

Proverbs 29:25

The only way to reorder our desires toward God is to identify where our hearts are already committed instead. For the next four days we will look at four typical God substitutes. The first is human approval. The *fear of man* is a *snare*. If we look to human beings more than to God for our worth and value, we will be trapped by anxiety, by an over-need to please, by the inability to withdraw from exploitative relationships, by the inability to take criticism, and by a cowardice that makes us unable to confront others. Our feelings will be easily hurt and we will tend to over-commit out of a desire for acceptance.

The devastation that comes from the fear of man has many forms. It includes parents who are afraid to discipline their children and employees who are unable to call out corruption in their companies. But we must obey God rather than men (Acts 5:29). The only thing that casts out the fear of man is a deep love relationship with God (1 John 4:18). Then we can say, 'The Lord is my helper; I will not be afraid. What can mere mortals do to me?' (Heb, 13:6)

Whose approval is functionally more important to you than God's?

The Way of Wisdom

A puzzling story?

The word of the LORD came to Jonah son of Amittai . . .

Jonah 1:1

Like most people raised in a churchgoing home, I have been aware of the story of Jonah since childhood. As a minister who teaches the Bible, however, I have gone through several stages of puzzlement and wonder at this short book. [. . .]

The narrative of Jonah seduces the reader into thinking of it as a simple fable, with the account of the great fish as the dramatic, if implausible, high point. Careful readers, however, find it to be an ingenious and artfully crafted work of literature. Its four chapters recount two incidents. In chapters 1 and 2 Jonah is given a command from God but fails to obey it; and in chapters 3 and 4 he is given the command again and this time carries it out. The two accounts are laid out in almost completely parallel patterns. [. . .]

The careful structure of the book reveals nuances of the author's message. Both episodes show how Jonah, a staunch religious believer, regards and relates to people who are racially and religiously different from him. The book of Jonah yields many insights about God's love for societies and people beyond the community of believers; about his opposition to toxic nationalism and disdain for other races; and about how to be 'in mission' in the world despite the subtle and unavoidable power of idolatry in our own lives and hearts. Grasping these insights can make us bridge builders, peacemakers, and agents of reconciliation in the world. Such people are the need of the hour.

The Prodigal Prophet

Prodigal prophet

'Go to the great city of Nineveh and preach against it, because its wickedness has come up before me.'

Jonah 1:2

Jonah wants a God of his own making, a God who simply smites the bad people, for instance, the wicked Ninevites and blesses the good people, for instance, Jonah and his countrymen. When the real God—not Jonah's counterfeit—keeps showing up, Jonah is thrown into fury or despair. Jonah finds the real God to be an enigma because he cannot reconcile the mercy of God with his justice. How, Jonah asks, can God be merciful and forgiving to people who have done such violence and evil? How can God be *both* merciful and just?

That question is not answered in the book of Jonah. As part of the entire Bible, however, the book of Jonah is like a chapter that drives the Scripture's overall plotline forward. It teaches us to look ahead to how God saved the world through the one who called himself the ultimate Jonah (Matt. 12:41) so that he could be both just and the justifier of those who believe (Rom. 3:26). Only when we readers fully grasp this gospel will we be neither cruel exploiters like the Ninevites nor Pharisaical believers like Jonah, but rather Spirit-changed, Christ-like women and men.

Many students of the book have noticed that in the first half Jonah plays the 'prodigal son' of Jesus' famous parable (Luke 15:11–24), who ran from his father. In the second half of the book, however, Jonah is like the 'older brother' (Luke 15:25–32), who obeys his father but berates him for his graciousness to repentant sinners. The parable ends with a question from the father to the Pharisaical son, just as the book of Jonah ends with a question to the Pharisaical prophet.

The Prodigal Prophet

Running from God

But Jonah ran away from the LORD and headed for Tarshish. He went down to Joppa, where he found a ship bound for that port. After paying the fare, he went aboard and sailed for Tarshish to flee from the LORD.

Jonah 1:3

Jonah did the exact opposite of what God told him to do. Called to go east, he went west. Directed to travel overland, he went to sea. Sent to the big city, he bought a one-way ticket to the end of the world.

Why did he refuse? [. . .] God describes Nineveh both here and later as that 'great' city, and indeed it was. It was both a military and a cultural powerhouse. Why would the populace listen to someone like Jonah? How long, for example, would a Jewish rabbi have lasted in 1941 if he had stood on the streets of Berlin and called on Nazi Germany to repent? At the most practical level, the prospects of success were none, and the chances of death were high.

Jonah would not have been able to see any theological justification for this mission either. [. . .] Wasn't Israel God's chosen, loved people through whom he was fulfilling his purposes in the world? Wasn't Nineveh an evil society on a collision course with the Lord? Wasn't Assyria unusually violent and oppressive, even for its time? [. . .]

So Jonah had a problem with the job he was given. But he had a bigger problem with the One who gave it to him. Jonah concluded that because he could not see any good reasons for God's command, there couldn't be any. Jonah doubted the goodness, wisdom, and justice of God.

We have all had that experience. [. . .] When this happens we have to decide—does God know what's best, or do we?

The Prodigal Prophet

Two ways of running

You rely on the law and boast ... in God ... You know his will and approve of what is superior because you are instructed by the law.

Romans 2:17–18

Jonah runs away from God. But if we for a moment stand back and look at the entirety of the book, Jonah will teach us that there are two different strategies for escaping from God. Paul outlines these in Romans 1–3. [...] We all know that we can run from God by becoming immoral and irreligious. But Paul is saying it is also possible to avoid God by becoming *very* religious and moral.

The classic example in the gospels of these two ways to run from God is in Luke 15, the parable of the two sons. [...] Jonah takes turns acting as both the 'younger brother' and the 'older brother.' In the first two chapters of the book, Jonah disobeys and runs away from the Lord and yet ultimately repents and asks for God's grace, just as the younger brother leaves home but returns repentant.

In the last two chapters, however, Jonah obeys God's command to go and preach to Nineveh. In both cases, however, he's trying to get control of the agenda. When God accepts the repentance of the Ninevites, just like the older brother in Luke 15, Jonah bristles with self-righteous anger at God's graciousness and mercy to sinners.

And that is the problem facing Jonah, namely, the mystery of God's mercy. It is a theological problem, but it is at the same time a heart problem. Unless Jonah can see his own sin, and see himself as living wholly by the mercy of God, he will never understand how God can be merciful to evil people and still be just and faithful.

The Prodigal Prophet

The world's storms

Then the LORD sent a great wind on the sea, and such a violent storm arose that the ship threatened to break up.

Jonah 1:4

The dismaying news is that every act of disobedience to God has a storm attached to it. This is one of the great themes of the Old Testament wisdom literature, especially the book of Proverbs. We must be careful here. This is not to say that every difficult thing that comes into our lives is the punishment for some particular sin. The entire book of Job contradicts the common belief that good people will have lives that go well, and that if your life is going badly, it must be your fault. The Bible does not say that every difficulty is the result of sin—but it does teach that every sin will bring you into difficulty.

We cannot treat our bodies indifferently and still expect to have good health. We cannot treat people indifferently and expect to maintain their friendship. We cannot all put our own selfish interests ahead of the common good and still have a functioning society. If we violate the design and purpose of things—if we sin against our bodies, our relationships, or society—they strike back. There are consequences. If we violate the laws of God, we are violating our own design, since God built us to know, serve, and love him. The Bible speaks sometimes about God punishing sin ('The Lord detests all the proud of heart ... They will not go unpunished,' Proverbs 16:5) but some other times of the sin itself punishing us ('The violence of the wicked will drag them away, for they refuse to do what is right,' Proverbs 21:7). Both are true at once. All sin has a storm attached to it.

The Prodigal Prophet

God turns storms to good

No discipline seems pleasant at the time, but painful. Later on, however, it produces a harvest of righteousness and peace for those who have been trained by it.

Hebrews 12:11

The dismaying news is that sin always has a storm attached to it, but there is comforting news too. For Jonah the storm was the consequence of his sin, yet the sailors were caught in it too. Most often the storms of life come upon us not as the consequence of a particular sin but as the unavoidable consequence of living in a fallen, troubled world. It has been said that 'man is born to trouble as surely as sparks fly upward' (Job 5:7), and therefore the world is filled with destructive storms. Yet as we will see, this storm leads the sailors to genuine faith in the true God even though it was not their fault. Jonah himself begins his journey to understand the grace of God in a new way. When storms come into our lives, whether as a consequence of our wrongdoing or not, Christians have the promise that God will use them for their good (Romans 8:28). [. . .]

The Bible does not say that every difficulty is the result of our sin—but it does teach that, for Christians, every difficulty can help reduce the power of sin over our hearts. Storms can wake us up to truths we would otherwise never see. Storms can develop faith, hope, love, patience, humility, and self-control in us that nothing else can. And innumerable people have testified that they found faith in Christ and eternal life only because some great storm drove them toward God.

The Prodigal Prophet

God of all people

All the sailors were afraid and each cried out to his own god. And they threw the cargo into the sea to lighten the ship. But Jonah had gone below deck, where he lay down and fell into a deep sleep. The captain went to him and said, 'How can you sleep? Get up and call on your god! Maybe he will take notice of us so that we will not perish.'

Jonah 1:5–6

The sailors are in peril. They have used what technology and religious resources they have, but these are not enough. They sense that they cannot be saved without help from Jonah, but he is doing nothing to help. And so we have this memorable picture of the heathen captain reprimanding God's holy prophet. [. . .]

We are all—believers and nonbelievers—'in the same boat.' (Never was that old saying truer than it was for Jonah!) If crime plagues a community, or poor health, or a water shortage, or the loss of jobs, if an economy and social order is broken, we are all in the same boat. For a moment, Jonah lives in the same 'neighborhood' with these sailors, and the storm that threatens one person threatens the entire community. Jonah fled because he did *not* want to work for the good of the pagans—he wanted to serve exclusively the interests of believers. But God shows him here that he is the God of all people and Jonah needs to see himself as being part of the whole human community, not only a member of a faith community.

This is not a merely pragmatic argument: 'Believers had better help nonbelievers or things will not go well with them.' The Bible tells us we are co-humans with all people—made in God's image and therefore infinitely precious to him (Gen. 9:6; James 3:9). [. . .]

In Jesus' Sermon on the Mount he said that the world would see the good deeds of believers and glorify God (Matt. 5:16). The world will not see who our Lord is if we do not live as we ought. In the words of one book we are *The Church Before the Watching World*.[92]

The Prodigal Prophet

Recognizing common grace

*Every good and perfect gift is from above, coming down from the
Father of the heavenly lights, who does not change like shifting
shadows.*

James 1:17

The pagan sailors provide a graphic portrayal of what theologians have called 'common grace.' [...] The doctrine of common grace is the teaching that God bestows gifts of wisdom, moral insight, goodness, and beauty across humanity, regardless of race or religious belief. [...]

That means that all good and great artistic expressions, skillful farming, effective governments, and scientific advances are God's gifts to the human race. They are undeserved, gifts of God's mercy and grace. They are also 'common.' That is, they are distributed to any and all. [...]

Certainly common grace was staring Jonah right in the face. Jonah himself was a recipient of what has been called 'special grace.' He had received the Word of God, a revelation of his will not available to human reason or wisdom, however great. Jonah was a follower of the Lord, the true God. So how was it possible that the pagans were outshining Jonah? Common grace means that nonbelievers often act more righteously than believers despite their lack of faith; whereas believers, filled with remaining sin, often act far worse than their right belief in God would lead us to expect. All this means Christians should be humble and respectful toward those who do not share their faith. They should be appreciative of the work of all people, knowing that nonbelievers have many things to teach them. Jonah is learning this the hard way.

The Prodigal Prophet

Whose are you?

Then the sailors said to each other, 'Come, let us cast lots to find out who is responsible for this calamity.' They cast lots and the lot fell on Jonah. So they asked him, 'Tell us, who is responsible for making all this trouble for us? What kind of work do you do? Where do you come from? What is your country? From what people are you?'

Jonah 1:7–8

These questions of the sailors show a good understanding of how we constitute our identity. To ask about purpose, place, and people is an insightful way of asking, 'Who are you?' [. . .]

The sailors, however, are not asking these questions simply to let Jonah express himself, as we do in modern Western culture. Their urgent goal is to understand the God who has been angered so they can determine what they should do. In ancient times, every racial group, every place, and even every profession had its own god or gods. To find out which deity Jonah had offended, they did not need to ask, 'What is your god's name?' All they had to ask was who he was. In their minds, human identity factors were inextricably linked to what you worshipped. Who you were and what you worshipped were just two sides of the same coin. It was the most foundational layer of your identity. [. . .]

The sailors knew that identity is always rooted in the things we look toward to save us, the things to which we give ultimate allegiance. To ask, 'Who are you?' is to ask, 'Whose are you?' To know who you are is to know what you have given yourself to, what controls you, what you most fundamentally trust.

The Prodigal Prophet

Embracing the other

He answered, 'I am a Hebrew and I worship the LORD, the God of heaven, who made the sea and the dry land.' This terrified them and they asked, 'What have you done?' (They knew he was running away from the LORD, because he had already told them so.)

Jonah 1:9–10

Though the question about race comes last in the list, Jonah answers it first. 'I am a Hebrew,' he says before anything else. In a text so sparing with words, it is significant that he reverses the order and puts his race out front as the most significant part of his identity. [...]

If his race was more foundational to his self-image than his faith, it begins to explain why Jonah was so opposed to calling Nineveh to repentance. The prospect of calling people of other nations to faith in God would not be appealing under any circumstances to someone with this spiritually shallow identity. Jonah's relationship with God was not as basic to his significance as his race. That is why, when loyalty to his people and loyalty to the Word of God seemed to be in conflict, he chose to support his nation over taking God's love and message to a new society. [...]

What Jonah is doing is what some have called *othering*. To categorize people as *the Other* is to focus on the ways they are different from oneself, to focus on their strangeness and to reduce them to these characteristics until they are dehumanized. We then can say, 'You know how *they* are,' so we don't need to engage with them. This makes it possible to exclude them in various ways—by simply ignoring them, or by forcing them to conform to our beliefs and practices, or by requiring them to live in certain poor neighborhoods, or by just driving them out.

[...] Jonah is in desperate need of the very mercy of God that he finds so troubling. Under the power of God's grace his identity will have to change, as will ours.

The Prodigal Prophet

The pattern of love

The sea was getting rougher and rougher. So they asked him, 'What should we do to you to make the sea calm down for us?' 'Pick me up and throw me into the sea,' he replied, 'and it will become calm. I know that it is my fault that this great storm has come upon you.'

Jonah 1:11–12

Why does he say this? Is he repenting, and simply saying something like 'I deserve death for my sin against God—kill me'? Or are his motives the very opposite? Is he saying something like 'I would rather die than obey God and go to Nineveh—kill me'? Is he submitting to God or rebelling against God? [. . .]

The answer is likely somewhere in the middle. There is no reason to think that Jonah's motives and intentions would be any more orderly and coherent than ours would be in such a moment of peril and crisis. [. . .] Notice that he says nothing about God. His concern is elsewhere. He says that if they throw him into the water, 'the sea will become quiet *for you*, for I declare it is on my account that this great storm has come *upon you*.' Jonah starts to take responsibility for the situation not because he's looking at God but because he's looking at them. And this is significant. [. . .]

Often the first step in coming to one's senses spiritually is when we finally start thinking of somebody—anybody—other than ourselves. So he is saying something like this: 'You are dying for me, but I should be dying for you. I'm the one with whom God is angry. Throw me in.'

Jonah's pity arouses in him one of the most primordial of human intuitions, namely, that the truest pattern of love is substitutionary. [. . .] True love meets the needs of the loved one no matter the cost to oneself. All life-changing love is some kind of substitutionary sacrifice.

The Prodigal Prophet

'The sea ceased from its raging'

Then they cried out to the LORD, 'Please, LORD, do not let us die for taking this man's life. Do not hold us accountable for killing an inno-cent man, for you, LORD, have done as you pleased.' Then they took Jonah and threw him overboard, and the raging sea grew calm. At this the men greatly feared the LORD, and they offered a sacrifice to the LORD and made vows to him.

Jonah 1:14–16

The moment Jonah went under the water, the storm switched off as suddenly as a light being turned off. We are told that the sea 'ceased from its raging' (verse 15). Some might see this as poetic personification, a mere rhetorical flourish, but is that all it is? The 'anger' of the storm was a real expression of the anger of God toward his rebellious prophet, which was turned aside when Jonah was cast into the waves. In the same way, Jesus' sacrifice is called a 'propitiation' (Rom. 3:25; Heb. 2:17; 1 John 2:2, 4:10), an old word that means Christ dealt with the wrath of God on sin and evil by standing in our place and bearing the punishment we deserve.

Many today find the idea of an angry God to be distasteful, even though modern people agree widely that to be passionate for justice does entail rightful anger. [. . .] If we read the book of Jonah as a stand-alone text, we could get the impression by this point that the biblical God was ill-tempered and vengeful. But even within the horizon of the entire story, we see that God refrains from giving Jonah all he deserves. Since Jesus is not merely a man but God come to earth, then far from depicting a vindictive deity, the whole Bible shows us a God who comes and bears his own penalty, so great is his mercy.

The Prodigal Prophet

Running from grace

Now the LORD provided a huge fish to swallow Jonah, and Jonah was in the belly of the fish three days and three nights. From inside the fish Jonah prayed to the LORD his God.

Jonah 1:17–2:1

With 20/20 hindsight, we can see that the most important lessons we have learned in life are the result of God's severe mercies. They are events that were difficult or even excruciating at the time but later came to yield more good in our lives than we could have foreseen.

The great fish is a perfect example of such a severe mercy. Obviously, the fish saved Jonah's life by swallowing him. On the other hand, he was still in a watery prison. He was still sinking to the bottom of the world, to 'the roots of the mountains,' far from help and hope. He was still alive, but for how long? It was only a temporary respite unless God provided another act of deliverance. [...]

If Jonah was to begin finally to ascend, both in the water and in faith, he had to be brought to the very end of himself. The way up was, first of all, down. The usual place to learn the greatest secrets of God's grace is at the bottom.

But it is not simply *being* at the bottom that begins to change Jonah but *prayer* at the bottom. [...] Jonah begins to pray, and at the climax of the prayer, he speaks of *chesdh* (Jonah 2:9). It is a key biblical word often translated as 'steadfast love' or 'grace.' It refers to the covenant love of God. It takes the whole prayer for Jonah to get there—to a declaration about God's grace—but when he does, he is released back into the land of the living.

The Prodigal Prophet

Amazing grace

'I said, "I have been banished from your sight; yet I will look again toward your holy temple."'

Jonah 2:4

[... What w]e must grasp, if we are to understand God's grace in a way that transforms, is how *costly* the salvation is that God provides. Not once but twice in his prayer, Jonah looks not merely toward heaven but 'toward your holy temple' (verse 4) and 'to the temple of your holiness' (verse 7). Why? Jonah knew that it was over the mercy seat in the temple that God promised to speak to us (Exod. 25:22). The mercy seat was a slab of gold over the top of the Ark of the Covenant, in which resided the tablets of the Ten Commandments. On the Day of Atonement, a priest sprinkled the blood of the atoning sacrifice for the sins of the people on the mercy seat (Lev. 16:14–15).

What a picture! The temple was the residence of the holy God, his perfect moral righteousness represented by the Ten Commandments, which no human being ever has or ever can keep. How shall we approach God? Won't the law of God condemn us? Yes it would, except for the blood of the atoning sacrifice on the mercy seat, over the Ten Commandments, shielding us from its condemnation. It is only when the death of another secures our forgiveness that we can speak with God.

Neither Jonah nor any other Israelite at that time understood all that this meant, but a better picture of the gospel of Jesus could hardly be imagined. [...] Not until centuries later would it be revealed that atonement could not be effected by the blood of bulls and goats but only by the once-for-all sacrifice of Jesus Christ (Heb. 10:4–10).

The Prodigal Prophet

Doing justice, preaching wrath

Jonah obeyed the word of the LORD and went to Nineveh. Now Nineveh was a very large city; it took three days to go through it. Jonah began by going a day's journey into the city, proclaiming, 'Forty more days and Nineveh will be overthrown.'

Jonah 3:3–4

Some commentators jump to the conclusion that Jonah preached salvation through faith [... but] there is no evidence of conversion to faith in the Lord. Others conclude that modern-day readers should emulate Jonah by providing social services in cities rather than doing evangelism. However, Jonah did not go to Nineveh just to quietly do social work. He preached the threat of divine judgment loudly in God's name. [...] Usually those who are most concerned about working for social justice do not also stand up and speak clearly about the God of the Bible's judgment on those who do not do his will. On the other hand, those who publicly preach repentance most forcefully are not usually known for demanding justice for the oppressed.

Nevertheless, this text encourages us to do both. In this instance, God seeks social reform through his prophet, a change in the Ninevites' exploitative and violent behavior. Yet he also directs that the city should be told about a God of wrath who will punish sin. [...]

To work against social injustice and to call people to repentance before God interlock theologically. [...] In his great 'I Have a Dream' speech, Dr King did not appeal to modern, secular individualism. He did not say, 'All should be free to define their own meaning in life and moral truth.' Rather he quoted Scripture and called his society to 'Let [God's] justice roll on like a river, righteousness like a never-failing stream' (Amos 5:24).

The Prodigal Prophet

Why do people repent?

The Ninevites believed God. A fast was proclaimed, and all of them, from the greatest to the least, put on sackcloth. When Jonah's warning reached the king of Nineveh, he rose from his throne, took off his royal robes, covered himself with sackcloth and sat down in the dust.

Jonah 3:5–6

To Jonah's shock, the people neither laughed nor laid hands on him. Instead, the entire city responded. [. . .] Against all expectations, the powerful, violent city of Nineveh put on sackcloth—a sign of mass repentance. And they did so 'from the greatest of them to the least' (verse 5), from the top to the bottom of the social spectrum. How could this have happened? [. . .]

Many argue that while the reported summary of Jonah's message to Nineveh was a bare threat (verse 4), it is reasonable to infer that he gave them more information about God than is mentioned in the text. That is almost certainly true. They did, for example, turn to God in the hope that he would hear them. This makes it likely that at least they questioned Jonah to find out if there was any hope of God's forgiveness.

Nevertheless, the biblical text does not tell us that God sent Jonah with the purpose of converting the populace into a saving, covenant relationship with him. He was warning them about their evil, violent behavior and the inevitable consequences if they did not relent and change.

And while we know from the rest of the Bible that changing social behavior is not sufficient for salvation, and that God cannot give final forgiveness without faith and an atoning sacrifice (cf. Num. 14:18; Heb. 9:22), nevertheless, God's response is instructive. Though the people of Nineveh do not forsake their idols and sacrifice to him, God in his mercy relents from his threat to destroy the city. For the time being, he expresses favor in response to the city's intention and effort at social reform.

The Prodigal Prophet

Heart storms

But to Jonah this seemed very wrong, and he became angry. He prayed to the LORD, 'Isn't this what I said, LORD, when I was still at home? ... Now, LORD, take away my life, for it is better for me to die than to live.'

Jonah 4:1–3

[We might] expect that the book would end in chapter 3 on a note of triumph, with 'and Jonah returned to his own land rejoicing.' Instead, events take an unexpected turn. [...] Why [...] when Jonah has just preached to the toughest audience of his life—and they have responded positively down to the last person—would he melt down in furious rage?

As a missionary, Jonah should have been glad that the Ninevites had taken a first step. Coming to full faith in God does not usually happen overnight, as it did with the sailors in Jonah's boat. The people of the city showed their willingness to repent, and Jonah should have prepared to help them continue in their journey by teaching them the character of this new God, the Lord, and what it means to be in a covenant relationship with him. Instead he was furious that they had even begun to move toward God. Rather than going back into the city to teach and preach, he stayed outside it, in hopes that maybe God would still judge it (Jonah 4:5).

When Christian believers care more for their own interests and security than for the good and salvation of other races and ethnicities, they are sinning like Jonah. If they value the economic and military flourishing of their country over the good of the human race and the furtherance of God's work in the world, they are sinning like Jonah. Their identity is more rooted in their race and nationality than in being saved sinners and children of God. Jonah's rightful love for his country and people had become inordinate, too great, rivaling God.

The Prodigal Prophet

The problem of self-righteousness

But the LORD replied, 'Is it right for you to be angry?'

Jonah 4:1–4

As long as there is something more important than God to your heart, you will be, like Jonah, both fragile and self-righteous. Whatever it is, it will create pride and an inclination to look down upon those who do not have it. It will also create fear and insecurity. It is the basis for your happiness, and if anything threatens it, you will be overwhelmed with anger, anxiety, and despair.

To reach heart bedrock with God's grace is to recognize all the ways that we make good things into idols and ways of saving ourselves. It is to instead finally recognize that we live wholly by God's grace. Then we begin serving the Lord not in order to get things from him but just for *him*, for his own sake, just for who he is, for the joy of knowing him, delighting him, and becoming like him. When we've reached bedrock with God's grace, it begins to drain us, slowly but surely, of both self-righteousness and fear.

God quietly rebukes Jonah with [his] question [...] Anger is not wrong. If you love something and it is threatened or harmed, anger is the proper response. But 'such' anger—inordinate anger of self-righteousness and fear—is a sign that the thing Jonah loves is a counterfeit god. He is inordinately committed to his race and nation. God will have to deal with this idolatry if Jonah is ever to get the infinite peace of resting in God's grace alone.

The Prodigal Prophet

The God who is patient

The LORD God provided a leafy plant and made it grow up over Jonah to give shade for his head to ease his discomfort, and Jonah was very happy about the plant. But at dawn the next day God provided a worm, which chewed the plant so that it withered ... God said to Jonah, 'Is it right for you to be angry about the plant?'

Jonah 4:6–7, 9

Jonah seemingly had a conversion experience in the fish. He grasped God's grace and obeyed the command to preach God's Word fearlessly. [...] Now all that is forgotten. Jonah is like the ungrateful servant who, having been forgiven, refuses to forgive others (Matt. 18:21–35).

Despite all this, God is patient with him. Jonah returns to the same angry opposition to God he had at the outset. This time, however, God does not send a towering storm but instead begins to counsel Jonah gently.

This is both a lesson in humility and a strong consolation. Often we give people the impression that 'after conversion everything is rosy, there are no more problems, one is automatically in tune with God's will ... It is not hard but sweet to do what God demands.' On the contrary, 'Paul speaks of two men battling in him [the "old man" and the "new man"] Jonah shows it too ... We continue to be sinners' (cf. Gal. 5:17; Eph. 4:22–4). Of course, we cannot use this to justify bad behavior, but we can take the deepest comfort in seeing that 'God knows the totality of [the human heart] ... that this does not exhaust God's love and patience, that he continues to take this rebellious child by the hand.'[93]

The Prodigal Prophet

The God who weeps

'You have been concerned about this plant, though you did not tend it or make it grow. It sprang up overnight and died overnight. And should I not have concern for the great city of Nineveh, in which there are more than a hundred and twenty thousand people who cannot tell their right hand from their left—and also many animals?'

Jonah 4:10–11

The word used in verses 10 and 11 for ['concern'] is a word that means to grieve over someone or something, to have your heart broken, to weep for it.[94] [. . .] God says, in essence, 'You weep over plants, but my compassion is for people.'

For God to apply this word to himself is radical. This is the language of attachment. God weeps over the evil and lostness of Nineveh. When you put your love on someone, you can be happy only if they are happy, and their distress becomes your distress. The love of attachment makes you vulnerable to suffering, and yet that is what God says about himself—here and in other places (cf. Isa. 63:9). In Genesis 6:6 it says that when God looked down on the evil of the earth, 'his heart was filled with pain' (NCV). [. . .]

We need many things, and we get emotionally attached to things that meet those needs. God, however, needs nothing. He is utterly and perfectly happy in himself, and he doesn't need us. So how could he get attached to us?

The only answer is that an infinite, omnipotent, self-sufficient divine being loves only voluntarily. [. . .] Elsewhere we see God looking at Israel, sinking into evil and sin, and God speaks about his heart literally turning over within him. 'How can I give you up, O Ephraim? How can I hand you over, O Israel? . . . My heart recoils within me; my compassion grows warm and tender' (Hosea 11:8, ESV).

The Prodigal Prophet

The weeping God in human form

As he approached Jerusalem and saw the city, he wept over it and said, 'If you, even you, had only known on this day what would bring you peace—but now it is hidden from your eyes . . . because you did not recognize the time of God's coming to you.'

Luke 19:41–2, 44

If you are acquainted at all with the New Testament, it is impossible to read about this generous God without remembering Jesus. God is saying to Jonah, 'I am weeping and grieving over this city—why aren't you? If you are my prophet, why don't you have my compassion?' Jonah did not weep over the city, but Jesus, the true prophet, did.

Jesus was riding into Jerusalem on the last week of his life. He knew he would suffer at the hands of the leaders and the mob of this city, but instead of being full of wrath or absorbed with self-pity, like Jonah, [he wept over it . . .]

On the cross, Jesus cried out, 'Father, forgive them, for they do not know what they are doing' (Luke 23:34). Jesus is saying, 'Father, they are torturing and killing me. They are denying and betraying me. But none of them, not even the Pharisees, really completely understand what they are doing.' We can only look in wonder on such a heart. [. . .]

Jesus is the prophet Jonah should have been. Yet, of course, he is infinitely more than that. Jesus did not merely weep for us; he died for us. Jonah went outside the city, hoping to witness its condemnation, but Jesus Christ went outside the city to die on a cross to accomplish its salvation.

The Prodigal Prophet

Born into a living hope

Praise be to the God and Father of our Lord Jesus Christ! In his great mercy he has given us new birth into a living hope through the resurrection of Jesus Christ from the dead.

1 Peter 1:3

Life is a journey, and finding and knowing God is fundamental to that journey. [...] The most fundamental transition any human being can make is what the Bible refers to as the new birth (John 3:1–8), or becoming a 'new creation' (2 Cor. 5:17). This can happen at any time in a life, of course, but often the circumstances that lead us to vital faith in Christ occur during these tectonic shifts in life stages. Over forty-five years of ministry, my wife, Kathy, and I have seen that people are particularly open to exploring a relationship with God at times of major life transition.

The Christian faith teaches that every person should experience two births. In one's first birth you are born into the natural world. Then, in what Charles Wesley calls our 'second birth,' which Jesus himself describes as being 'born again' (John 3:3), we are born into the kingdom of God and receive new spiritual life. The first birth is ours because God is our Creator; the second birth can be ours because God is also our Redeemer. The Lord is the author of both.

In light of this, we want to consider the spiritual issues surrounding both births. What does it mean to receive a new human life from God? What are the responsibilities of the family and the church to newborns? How can we help our children who are with us through the first birth come to experience the second birth?

On Birth

Fearfully and wonderfully made

For you created my inmost being; you knit me together in my mother's womb. I praise you because I am fearfully and wonderfully made . . . Your eyes saw my unformed body; all the days ordained for me were written in your book.

Psalm 139:13–14, 16

The phrase we are 'fearfully and wonderfully made' is full of interest. Every baby born into the world is a wonderful creation, but at the same time a frightening one. Anyone who looks on a newborn—realizing this is a new human life in the image of the Creator, come into the world along with particular gifts and callings and a life planned by the Lord of history—must respond with a kind of fear and trembling. And no one should behold a child with more awe and fear than the child's parents.

When Kathy and I brought home our firstborn, I was surprised to see her cuddle him close and weep. Partly this was her hormones talking, she said, but partly it was a recognition of what we had let this tiny little person in for as a member of a fallen race. Yes, 'all the days ordained for him' were 'written in God's book,' but as an adult she knew that our son's book would contain disappointment, hurt, failure, pain, loss, and ultimately his own death. All this would happen no matter how hard we would try to shield him. So she literally trembled before the responsibility of being a parent to this wonder of the universe. And when I thought about it, so did I.

On Birth

The gift of baptism

On the eighth day, when it was time to circumcise the child, he was named Jesus, the name the angel had given him before he was conceived. When the time came for the purification rites required by the Law of Moses, Joseph and Mary took him to Jerusalem to present him to the Lord.

Luke 2:21–2

Children are a joy, but parents often sense a responsibility that can be overwhelming. The Christian church offers, in response, the sacrament of baptism. While not all Christians practice infant baptism, most have some way of publicly dedicating their children to God, which follows the Jewish practice. [. . .]

When we bring our children to God in baptism, it does not confer salvation automatically on the child. Just as God does not magically create new human beings but does it through the union of a man and a woman, so he normally brings about our second birth much like our first birth—through love relationships and, so often, through the family.

Sin tends to run in families. We see weaknesses in our parents and grandparents that show up in us even though we dislike the traits, even when we try with all our might to avoid them. But *grace* tends to run in families, too. Love and good models of faith and grace can lead a child to seek those things for himself or herself. [. . .]

And while baptism may not save the child, we believe real divine grace and strength from God comes down in response to these vows, as our God is a covenant God who honors promises (Ps. 56:12–13).

On Birth

Enduring the sword

This child is destined to cause the falling and rising of many in Israel, and to be a sign that will be spoken against, so that the thoughts of many hearts will be revealed. And a sword will pierce your own soul too.

Luke 2:34–5

Simeon is saying that for all the peace that Jesus will bring into the world, he will also bring conflict. His claim to be the Son of God will bring salvation and rest to many people, but others will reject it and so people will be divided over him. And Mary in particular, as Jesus' mother, will experience both the profoundest joy at seeing the greatness of her son *and* the deepest grief as she watches his arrest, torture, and death. Of course on the far side of Jesus' resurrection it would become clear to Mary that what her son endured was for the salvation of us all. But up until that moment, her experience was not very different from what mothers, and indeed all parents, experience. Amidst the joy—a sword.

In a sense every love relationship brings 'a sword in the heart,' because when you love someone truly you bind your heart to the other person with the result that your happiness is tied to his or her happiness. [. . .]

No wonder so many modern people have given parenting a pass. But just as Jesus could not bless the world without the suffering of his parents, so we cannot give the world the blessing of our children's new life without accepting the sword in our hearts. We should bear that sword with extraordinary prayer rather than self-pity and worry (Phil. 4:6), but also with the knowledge that Jesus himself gave us the blessing of his salvation at unimaginable cost—and with literal nails and thorns.

On Birth

Born of God

Yet to all who did receive him, to those who believed in his name, he gave the right to become children of God—children born not of natural descent, nor of human decision or a husband's will, but born of God.

John 1:12–13

To be 'born of God' is no longer to have a name or identity based on either 'natural descent'—the social status or family pedigree of the traditional culture—or 'human decision'—the achievement and performance of the modern meritocracy. Instead it is to have the 'rights' and privileges of being God's child. It's a new sense of self and worth based on God's fatherly love and his identification with us, all secured by Christ's work, not ours. That is what we are born into when we are born again. [. . .]

The gospel [. . .] gives us a unique, transformative new self-understanding. It tells us we are so lost and incapable of pleasing God that Jesus had to die for us, but we are so loved that he was glad to die for us. On the cross our sins were put on him—he was treated as our life record deserves—so that if we put our faith in him, we receive his righteousness; that is, we are treated as Jesus' life record deserves (2 Cor. 5:21). God now loves us 'in Christ,' as if we had done all he has done. He loves us 'even as' he loves his Son (John 17:23). That becomes the deepest foundation of our identity, meaning, and self-view, demoting but not removing all the other things that are true of us.

On Birth

The beauty of Jesus

A woman giving birth to a child has pain because her hour has come; but when her baby is born she forgets the anguish because of her joy that a child is born into the world.

John 16:21

[...T]he first thing we must do to be converted is to turn away from our self-salvation schemes in repentance. But then we must turn toward Jesus in faith, seeing the beauty of what Christ has done. It's not enough just to believe in the grace of God in general; you have to have faith in what Jesus Christ has done in particular. [...]

Why, when [Jesus] is talking about his death, does he suddenly bring up a woman in labor? And why does he speak of the painful moment of giving birth as her 'hour'? Students of the Gospel of John know that whenever Jesus talks about his death on the Cross he calls it his 'hour.'

See what Jesus is saying? 'Your first birth brings you physical life because someone risked her life, but your second birth brings you spiritual and eternal life because someone gave his life. That someone was me.' And if we stay with Jesus' metaphor in John 16 it gets even more wonderful. He says that, in spite of her incredible pain, a new mother is filled with joy at the sight of her child. So Jesus has the audacity to say, 'That's just a dim hint of the joy I sense when I look at you. All my suffering, torment, and death I have willingly borne, for the greater joy of saving and loving you.' Until you see that and believe and rest in that, you cannot be born again.

On Birth

Growing in grace

But grow in the grace and knowledge of our Lord and Saviour Jesus Christ. To him be glory both now and for ever! Amen.

2 Peter 3:18

When the Bible calls you to grow in grace, it is very different than saying, 'Be virtuous.' Many have thought that the New Testament is simply calling everybody in general to base their lives on the ethical model of Jesus. Jesus was a man who did love and mercy and justice, they say. If we all lived like him, the world would be a better place.

With all due respect to the sentiment, the biblical authors are not that naïve and foolish. To call people to live like Christ, to adopt a way of life that goes utterly against our nature through an act of the will, is to ask for the impossible. The Bible's calls to Christians to become like Christ assume they've been born again and they are a partaker of the divine nature. When New Testament writers say, 'Love your neighbor as yourself,' they're saying, 'Nurture that new nature inside you so you can love your neighbor as yourself.' You have to be born in order to grow. If you're going to grow physically, you have to be born physically. If you're going to grow spiritually, you have to be born spiritually.

There is no excuse for not having a radically changed life if you're a Christian. Have you given up on change in certain areas? Learned to live with bad habits and patterns in your life? Have you silently made peace with wrong attitudes, fears, and resentments in your heart? You have 'everything you need' for a godly life (verse 3). Growth in grace is now a powerful possibility.

On Birth

Marriage was made for us

'Haven't you read,' he replied, 'that at the beginning the Creator "made them male and female," and said, "For this reason a man will leave his father and mother and be united to his wife, and the two will become one flesh"?'

Matthew 19:4–5

The book of Genesis tells us that God established marriage even as he created the human race. This should not be understood to teach that every individual adult must be married. Jesus himself was single, and since he stands as the great exemplar of what a human being should be, we cannot insist—as some cultures have—that you must be married to be a fully realized person. But neither can we see marriage, as our own culture does, as merely a development to guard property rights during the Neolithic Age that today can be altered or discarded as we please.

Wendell Berry famously addressed the modern idea that whether we have sex inside marriage or outside is 'a completely private decision.' He disagreed, saying, 'Sex is not and cannot be any individual's "own business," nor is it merely the private concern of any couple. Sex, like any other necessary, precious, and volatile power that is commonly held, is everybody's business.'[95] Sex outside of marriage creates babies outside of marriages, it often spreads disease, and it habituates us to treat others as pleasure objects rather than persons. All of these have a major impact on social conditions, conditions that affect everyone.

We know this line of thinking is deeply counterintuitive to modern people in the West, but it has been quite natural to most human beings in most places and times. Your choice regarding marriage is not ultimately a private decision. It affects everyone around you.

Marriage was made for us, and the human race was made for marriage.

On Marriage

Mutual self-giving

Flee from sexual immorality . . . Do you not know that your bodies are temples of the Holy Spirit, who is in you, whom you have received from God? You are not your own; you were bought at a price. Therefore honour God with your bodies.

1 Corinthians 6:18–20

From its very beginning, Christianity brought a revolutionary new understanding of sex into the world. It was seen as just one part—one uniquely joyful, powerful, and inseparable part—of mutual self-giving. To be loved and admired but not truly known is only mildly satisfying. To be known but rejected and not loved is our greatest nightmare. But to become vulnerable and so fully known and yet accepted and fully loved by someone we admire— that is the greatest possible satisfaction. In marriage, spouses lose their independence and so become vulnerable and interdependent. They do not hold themselves back so that they only relate temporarily, provisionally, and transactionally. They give their entire selves to each other—emotionally, physically, legally, economically.

The startling sex ethic of the early Christians was that sex is both a sign and a means for that total self-giving, and that it must not be used for any other purpose. To engage in sex for any other reason was to misunderstand it. Granting access to our physical bodies must be accompanied by the opening of our whole lives to each other through a lifelong marriage covenant. Only in that situation, the early Christians taught, does sex become the unitive and fulfilling act it was meant to be.

On Marriage

Avoiding idolatry in marriage

'This is now bone of my bones
and flesh of my flesh;
she shall be called "woman",
for she was taken out of man.'

Genesis 2:23

[. . . W]hen Adam sees Eve, he speaks poetry, the first recorded in the Bible. In most Bibles it is printed on the page indented and in verse form. The man explodes into song at the sight of his wife. [. . .]

Remember that Adam is speaking from paradise, where he has a perfect relationship with God. Yet finding a spouse and partner speaks to something so profound in us that Adam erupts in adoration through artistic expression. This points to an important fact that we must understand if we are going to have a successful marriage over the long term.

[. . . G]ood marriages run the great risk of turning your heart from God to your spouse as a greater source of love, safety, and joy. [. . .] This is easy to do because marriage is such a great thing. And it is easy to turn a great thing into the ultimate thing in your life.

You must not try to lessen your love for your spouse or the person you think you're going to marry. Rather, you have to increase your love for God. C. S. Lewis says it is probably impossible to love any human being too much. You may love him too much in comparison to your love for God, but it is the smallness of your love for God, not the greatness of your love for the person, that constitutes the inordinacy. Marriage will ruin us unless we have a true and existential love relationship with God.[96]

On Marriage

God our bridegroom

As a young man marries a young woman, so will your Builder marry you; as a bridegroom rejoices over his bride, so will your God rejoice over you.

Isaiah 62:5

Genesis 2:18 says, 'The LORD God said, "It is not good for the man to be alone."' That is a surprising statement. Why would Adam be lonely and unhappy in paradise, before there was any sin in the world? He had a perfect relationship with God; how could he be lonely? There's only one possible answer, really. God deliberately made it so that Adam would need someone besides God. That doesn't mean, of course, that our heart's *supreme* need for love isn't God. It is. What it does mean is that God designed us so that we also needed human love.

Consider what a humble, unself-centered act this is on God's part. God made human beings to need not just him, but other relationships, other selves, other hearts. The belief that God made people so he wouldn't be lonely, or so that he'd have someone to love (like having a child), or because he needed worshippers, is patently false. Yet it is nothing compared to the humility and sacrificial love God shows us later in the Bible when he says repeatedly through prophets such as Isaiah, Jeremiah, and Hosea, 'I am the bridegroom, and you, my people, are the bride.'

The 'bridegroom' language means that solely in God do you have the lover and spouse that will satisfy you supremely. He's the ultimate 'helpmeet.'

On Marriage

The most patient spouse ever

The Lord said to me, 'Go, show your love to your wife again, though she is loved by another man and is an adulteress. Love her as the Lord loves the Israelites, though they turn to other gods and love the sacred raisin cakes.'

Hosea 3:1

The imagery of 'bridegroom' also means that in God you have the most patient and long-suffering spouse who ever existed.

The theme of God as the bridegroom of his people runs all through the Bible. In the Old Testament, of course, God calls himself the husband of Israel. But Israel constantly turned to worship other gods and in so doing she is spoken of as being guilty of spiritual adultery. Jeremiah 2–3 and Ezekiel 16 are vivid depictions of this 'bad marriage,' but the most famous exposition of this theme is in the book of Hosea. There God tells his prophet to marry Gomer, a woman who will be unfaithful to Hosea, 'for like an adulterous wife this land [Israel] is guilty of unfaithfulness to the Lord' (Hosea 1:2). And this is what happens. She goes after other lovers. [. . .]

What the book of Hosea was hinting at we see writ large in the New Testament. God is the lover and spouse of his people. But we have given him the marriage from hell. God is in the longest-lived, worst marriage in the history of the world. We have turned to idols in our hearts, we have turned away from him, we have been absolutely terrible spouses. But God did not abandon us.

In Jesus Christ, God entered the world and paid the price to buy us away from our sin and enslavements by dying on the cross.

On Marriage

The signpost of sex

So, my brothers and sisters, you also died to the law through the body of Christ, that you might belong to another, to him who was raised from the dead, in order that we might bear fruit for God.

Romans 7:4

In Romans 7 the apostle Paul likens Christians to a woman who has been married 'to the law.' That is, we have been trying to save ourselves by our performance—whether that means religious observance of God's moral law or the pursuit of wealth, career, or some cause. But when we believe in Christ we become married 'to him who was raised from the dead, that we might bear fruit to God' (Rom. 7:4). This is a daring image. As a wife puts herself into the arms of her husband, and children are born into the world through her body, so we put ourselves in the arms of Jesus and then we also bear fruit—of our own changed lives (Gal. 5:22–3) or of good works that change the lives of others (Col. 1:6, 10). [. . .]

The Bible tells us that we currently know our Spouse only by faith, not by sight (2 Cor. 5:7). The love we experience here can only ever be partial. But when we actually see him face to face, the transformation of his love and the fulfillment of our being will be complete (1 John 3:2–3).

What do all these passages about Jesus being our husband and bridegroom mean? It means at least this—that sex in marriage is both a pointer to and a foretaste of the joy of that perfect future world of love. In heaven when we know him directly, we enter into a union of love with him and all other people who love him. On that great day there's going to be deep delight, towering joy, and deep security of which the most rapturous sex between a man and a woman is just an echo.

On Marriage

The end of history

'Let us rejoice and be glad and give him glory! For the wedding of the Lamb has come, and his bride has made herself ready.'

Revelation 19:7

As Luther says, in keeping with Saint Paul's views, we are in one sense already married to Christ. But there is another sense in which we are not yet married—we are more like engaged to him. Revelation tells us 'the marriage supper of the Lamb' is a future day in which we will be married to Jesus (Rev. 19:7). The great wedding day in which we fall into his arms is the only wedding day that will really make everything right in our lives.

It is significant that the Bible begins in Genesis with a wedding, and that wedding's original purpose was to fill the world with children of God. But Adam and Eve turned from God and the first wedding failed to fulfill its purpose.

When we come to the end of the Bible we see the church 'coming down out of heaven from God, prepared as a bride beautifully dressed for her husband.' The echoes of Genesis 2 are unmistakable. Again we see God bringing a bride to her husband, only this time the husband is Jesus and we are the bride. In that first marriage Adam failed to step in and help his wife when she needed him. But at the end of time there will be another wedding, the marriage supper of the Lamb, and *its* purpose is also to fill the world with children of God. *It* will succeed where the first marriage failed because, while the first husband in history failed, the Second Husband does not. The true Adam, Jesus Christ, will never fail his spouse, the Second Eve, his church.

On Marriage

The hope of the resurrection

Through him you believe in God, who raised him from the dead and glorified him, and so your faith and hope are in God.

1 Peter 1:21

One of the reasons for the remarkable rise of Christianity in its earliest centuries was that it offered resources for hope in the face of the numerous urban pandemics that were devastating the Roman world. [...]

And all this hope centers on one explosive event—the death and resurrection of Jesus Christ. That is what Christianity offers a world that has lost hope.

The Christians to whom Peter wrote had already 'suffered grief in all kinds of trials' (1 Pet. 1:6) and were now in the midst of a 'fiery ordeal' (1 Pet. 4:12). But Peter reminds them of this: 'He has given us new birth into a living hope through the resurrection of Jesus Christ from the dead ... so your faith and hope are in God' (1 Pet. 1:3,21). The fact of the resurrection means we have a hope for the future not based on scientific advance or social progress but on God himself (1 Pet. 1:21). And this is not simply an intellectual belief but, as Peter says, it is a 'living hope,' a vital part of the new spiritual life that comes into Christians by the Holy Spirit through what the New Testament calls 'the new birth.' Faith in the resurrection implants that hope into the root of our souls. It becomes such a part of who we are that we can face anything.

Hope in Times of Fear

Knowing the resurrection

I want to know Christ – yes, to know the power of his resurrection and participation in his sufferings, becoming like him in his death, and so, somehow, attaining to the resurrection from the dead.

Philippians 3:10–11

Many of us will have trouble thinking of any time that we heard an extensive treatment of the resurrection from the pulpit outside of Easter Sunday. In mainline Protestant pulpits the resurrection is usually seen as a general concept, a symbol that somehow good will triumph over evil. And when the resurrection is preached in evangelical church pulpits, the sermon often consists of a lengthy argument that it really happened. Yet it is one thing to know about the resurrection, and it is another thing, as Paul says, 'to *know the power* of his resurrection' (Phil. 3:10), to know it personally and experientially. Surprisingly, the church has not given us much guidance in that. [. . .]

Sam Allberry writes that many Christians, while believing in the resurrection and rehearsing that belief every Easter Sunday, 'then effectively stick it back in a drawer for the rest of the year' because they are 'at a loss to know what to do with it.'[97] Verses like Romans 4:25— 'he ... was raised for our justification'—show us that it is not just the death of Jesus but also his resurrection that saves us. Yet when most Christians give a 'gospel' presentation to explain how we can be saved, they talk exclusively about the cross and make the resurrection an afterthought or leave it out altogether.

Hope in Times of Fear

The good invasion

But Christ has indeed been raised from the dead, the firstfruits of those who have fallen asleep.

1 Corinthians 15:20

The resurrection is not a stupendous magic trick but an invasion. And the event that saved us—the movement from cross to resurrection—now remakes the lives of Christians from the inside out, by the power of the Spirit.

The cross and the resurrection together—and only together—bring the future new creation, the omnipotent power through which God renews and heals the entire world, *into our present.* When Christ paid the debt of sin on the cross, the veil in the temple was ripped from top to bottom (Matt. 27:51). That veil represented the separation of humanity from the holy presence of God. That presence had once made the earth a paradise and now, because of the death of Christ, that presence *can* come to us, and because of the resurrection of Christ, it *does* come to us. The risen Christ sends us the Holy Spirit, and both Christ and the Spirit are the 'firstfruits' (Rom. 8:23; 1 Cor. 15:20-3), the 'earnest' (Eph. 1:13-14; 2 Cor. 1:22,23, 5:5 KJV), a first installment, a down payment on the future triumph over death and of a new, remade material world. This renewing power from the future is only here partially, but it is actual and substantial—and has entered the present world.

Hope in Times of Fear

The power of the resurrection

His incomparably great power for us who believe . . . is the same as the mighty strength he exerted when he raised Christ from the dead and seated him at his right hand in the heavenly realms.

Ephesians 1:19–20

The 'incomparably great power' with which God raised Jesus from the dead is in us now (Rom. 8:23; Eph. 1:19–20). So we are to live in the 'light' of the future 'new creation' (Rom. 13:11–13; Gal. 6:15; cf. 1 Cor. 6:1–2). That is, we are to participate in that future resurrection life in the way we live now. If Jesus was raised from the dead, it changes everything: how we conduct relationships, our attitudes toward wealth and power, how we work in our vocations, our understanding and practice of sexuality, race relations, and justice.

Also, the cross and the resurrection together—and only together—give us the basic shape or pattern by which Christians now 'live in light of the new creation.' The cross and resurrection is the Great Reversal. Christ saves us through weakness, by giving up power and succumbing to a seeming defeat. But he triumphs—not despite the weakness and loss of power but *because of it* and *through it*. The Great Reversal becomes 'a dynamic' that 'opens out onto a rhythm of life, an ethic, and a way of looking at and living in the world' and every aspect of life.[98] By living this principle, death and resurrection, we renew human life here—only partially, but substantially. The 'already but not yet' presence of the new creation avoids both naïveté and cynicism, both utopianism and defeatism.

Hope in Times of Fear

The necessity of the resurrection

And if Christ has not been raised, our preaching is useless and so is your faith.

1 Corinthians 15:14

Because Jesus' death for sin and resurrection happened in history, everything has changed. *Everything.*

In 1 Corinthians 15:14 Paul says, 'If Christ has not been raised, our preaching is useless,' and the Greek word for *useless* is *kenos*, without power. Paul is saying that mere ethical exhortations—that 'we need to work against injustice' or 'we need to keep up hope in the face of anxiety'—as right as they are, are nonetheless *impotent* if Jesus hasn't been raised from the dead in history. If he was raised, we have not only every reason in the world to work for the good, but also the actual inward power to do so. But if he was not raised, then, both the ancient philosophers and modern scientists agree, the world will eventually burn up, and no one will be around to mourn for it, and nothing anyone does will in the end make any difference.

Liberal Christianity, though now in steep demographic decline among believers, is nonetheless highly popular with the modern media, which sees it as the only viable version of the faith. But a non-historical faith—a non-supernatural faith—simply won't do. It did not change lives and the world at the beginning, and it won't do so now.

Hope in Times of Fear

The evidence for the resurrection

'I am not insane, most excellent Festus,' Paul replied. 'What I am saying is true and reasonable. The king is familiar with these things, and I can speak freely to him. I am convinced that none of this has escaped his notice, because it was not done in a corner.'

Acts 26:25–6

In Acts 26 Paul spoke to King Agrippa and Festus, the Roman governor. He talked about Christ's death and resurrection. In the middle of his discussion, Festus cried, 'Paul, your great learning is driving you insane' (Acts 26:24). Paul's response was respectful but surprisingly confident.

Paul says that his faith in the resurrection is 'reasonable'—a word that refers to careful, rational thought. He is not making mere assertions but is offering arguments. Paul can also say confidently to Agrippa that he knew the facts of Jesus' death, of the empty tomb, and of the reports of the eyewitnesses to the resurrection, because these things were 'not done in a corner.' They were public knowledge and so there was substantial evidence for what he was saying [. . .] He provides two main arguments for the resurrection.

First, the tomb was empty. The gospel summary does not merely say that Jesus died but also 'that he was buried.' That would be redundant unless to make the point that this was not a 'spiritual' event, that the body was gone and the tomb empty. The fact of the empty tomb is accepted by most scholars, including those who don't accept the resurrection. [. . .]

The second main argument is that a large number of people, across a diversity of circumstances, testified that they had seen the risen Jesus. We are not talking about one single sighting, or several appearances in one remote location where they could be staged.

Hope in Times of Fear

The strangeness of the resurrection

Now that same day two of them were going to a village called
Emmaus . . . As they talked and discussed these things with each other,
Jesus himself came up and walked along with them; but they were kept
from recognising him.

Luke 24:13–16

In his Gifford Lectures, John Polkinghorne says that the inability of the first eyewitnesses to recognize the resurrected Christ was remarkable. He argues that if people of that time (or ours) were to make up a story about someone resurrected, they would have drawn from the two kinds of legends about people returning from the dead, depicting him as either 'a dazzling heavenly figure or a resuscitated corpse.'[99] N. T. Wright agrees. There were stories in the Jewish apocalyptic tradition of figures appearing 'in blinding light or dazzling radiance, or wreathed in clouds.' Daniel 12:2–3 describes the resurrected at the end of time as 'shining like the brightness of the heavens.' 1 Samuel 28 tells about King Saul speaking with the ghost of the dead prophet Samuel, who appears as 'a ghostly figure' (verse 13). Surely if Jewish gospel writers wanted to make up a story to teach that Jesus had risen from the dead, they could have drawn on those accounts and depicted him as too bright to look upon or as a frightening phantasm. Instead the risen Jesus appears to be completely ordinary—'as a human being among human beings.'[100]

[. . .] Jesus is neither a ghost nor a dazzling apparition, nor does he have a revived, normal human body. There simply was nothing like this in Jewish and Greco-Roman literature and legend for the gospel writers to draw on. These were wholly new conceptual categories, major departures from anything any religion or culture had ever imagined before. It was an entirely new way to think of body and spirit.

Hope in Times of Fear

Can we know that the resurrection happened?

With this in mind, since I myself have carefully investigated everything from the beginning, I too decided to write an orderly account for you, most excellent Theophilus, so that you may know the certainty of the things you have been taught.

Luke 1:3–4

Does all this *prove* beyond a shadow of rational doubt that the resurrection of Jesus Christ actually occurred? As Wright and others point out, no event in past history can be empirically proven the way something can be tested in a laboratory. We can't know that William the Conqueror invaded England in 1066 in exactly the same way we know that a compound liquefies at such and such temperature. However, once we make that distinction, we can still say we know that things in history happened if there is a great deal of historical evidence that they did. [. . .]

What this means is that, on the one hand, the use of human reason alone cannot force us to believe in the resurrection. There is room for intellectual doubt of almost any historical event. On the other hand, we can see that belief in the resurrection of Christ is *not* a blind leap of faith. It has left an enormous footprint, as it were, in history. [. . .]

Our moral values, our beliefs about human nature, our beliefs about whether the material universe was its own cause or was created by God—all of these fundamental assumptions about reality come through a combination of reasoning, evidence, and faith. Can we *know*, for example, that all human beings have equal dignity and human rights? Although there is much evidence for that belief, human rights cannot be scientifically proven so that any skeptic would be forced to accept them. And can we *know* that the resurrection happened? Even if you come to believe, on rational grounds, that the resurrection of Jesus probably happened, you still must exercise faith to become a Christian.

Hope in Times of Fear

A gracious faith

*For I am the least of the apostles and do not even deserve to be called
an apostle, because I persecuted the church of God. But by the grace
of God I am what I am, and his grace to me was not without effect. No,
I worked harder than all of them—yet not I, but the grace of God that
was with me.*

1 Corinthians 15:9–10

Belief or nonbelief in the resurrection is never merely an intellectual process. We are not computers. We are flesh-and-blood human beings, and when we confront the claim of the resurrection, we address it not only with logic but with a lifetime of hopes and fears and preexisting faith commitments. And we will never be able to accept it until we see our need for God's grace. [...]

What was it that made Paul into a completely different person? Three times he uses the word *grace*. The man formerly known as Saul in no way thought he needed mercy and forgiveness. He was, in his mind, far more zealous for the truth and for God than anyone he knew (Phil. 3:6). But when life humbled him and he saw his flaws and insufficiency and that he needed God's grace, that made him open to claims and truths to which he was previously closed.

Before we become Christians, most of us also think of ourselves as sincere seekers after the truth. We feel like we're pretty good people. But most Christians, like Paul, look back on their lives and see that they had never really been sincere seekers after truth at all. They had wanted a truth and a God that fitted their desire to be in charge of their own lives. And yet God came after them, found them, and graciously helped them see their own blindness and their unwarranted distrust of him.

Hope in Times of Fear

Hope from the future

'The time has come,' he said. 'The kingdom of God has come near. Repent and believe the good news!'

Mark 1:15

It has been common for Christians to believe that the cross alone saves us from our sins. Then the resurrection is viewed as a wonderful miracle that proved Jesus was the Son of God, but nothing more than that. I became a Christian during my undergraduate years and, looking back, I realized that I adopted that same attitude. I was glad to argue for the historical evidence for the resurrection, but I did not see it as something that affected how I lived my daily life now. [...]

It was not until I entered seminary in preparation for ministry that I learned something that I should have been taught as a new believer. The resurrection was indeed a miraculous display of God's power, but we should not see it as a *suspension* of the natural order of the world. Rather it was the beginning of the *restoration* of the natural order of the world, the world as God intended it to be. Since humanity turned away from God, both the human and natural worlds have been dominated by sin and evil, disorder and disease, suffering and death. But when Jesus rose from the dead, he inaugurated the first stage of the coming of God's kingdom power into the world to restore and heal all things.

The resurrection means not merely that Christians have a hope *for* the future but that they have hope that comes *from* the future.

Hope in Times of Fear

By faith alone

*For in the gospel the righteousness of God is revealed—a righteousness
that is by faith from first to last, just as it is written: 'The righteous will
live by faith.'*

Romans 1:17

If you believe that Jesus was a great teacher and you believe he
can help you and answer your prayers if you live according to
his ethical prescriptions, you are not yet a Christian. That's general
belief but not saving faith. Real Christian faith believes that Jesus
saves us through his death and resurrection so we can be accepted
by sheer grace. That is the gospel—the good news that we are
saved by the work of Christ through grace.

Martin Luther talks about his own conversion experience. He
was a monk, a student and teacher of Scripture, and yet this is how
he describes what happened:

*'In [the gospel] the righteousness of God is revealed [Romans 1:17] . . . I hated
that word "righteousness of God." . . . Though I lived as a monk without
reproach, I felt that I was a sinner before God with an extremely disturbed
conscience. I could not believe that he was placated by my satisfaction . . . There
I began to understand that the righteousness of God is that by which the righteous lives by a gift of God, namely by faith . . . Here I felt that I was altogether
born again and had entered paradise itself through open gates.'[101]*

[. . .] So faith is a gift of God. Built on thinking and evidence, acti-
vated by God's miraculous intervention, based on the radical discovery that Jesus has accomplished everything we need and we can be
adopted and accepted into God's family, and all of this by sheer grace.
Is that it? Do we simply sit down, content and transformed, with the
knowledge of this love? No—we are to spend the rest of our lives
tasting, experiencing, and being shaped by that gracious love.

Encounters with Jesus

Forgiveness without limit

Then Peter came to Jesus and asked, 'Lord, how many times shall I forgive my brother or sister who sins against me? Up to seven times?' Jesus answered, 'I tell you, not seven times, but seventy-seven times.'

Matthew 18:21–2

The Lord [gives] the issue of forgiveness great prominence in his teaching. Indeed, the only rider added to the Lord's Prayer itself is Matthew 6:14–15, in which he says emphatically that if we deny forgiveness to others, God will deny forgiveness to us.

The disciples were stunned by Jesus' claim that forgiveness by God and forgiveness of others were interdependent. Peter's question shows his concern that Jesus' command could be used by an unscrupulous perpetrator to sin against others without accountability. So Peter suggests a limit. 'Lord, how many times shall I forgive my brother or sister who sins against me? Up to seven times?' Peter's proposal would have seemed generous to him, for even the Talmud (b. Yoma 86b–87a) held that we have to forgive the same person only three times.[102]

Jesus refuses to grant that there is a limit to forgiveness. His startling declaration is that we must forgive 'not seven times, but seventy-seven times.' The term he uses is sometimes translated as meaning seventy *times* seven, or 490. But to focus on the precise number is to miss Jesus' meaning entirely. The number seven signified completeness. And that means

this [statement by Jesus is in] the language of hyperbole, not of calculation. Those who are concerned as to whether the figure should be 77 or 490 . . . have missed the point . . . [T]here is no limit, no place for keeping a tally of forgivenesses already used up. Peter's question was misconceived: if one is still counting . . . one is not forgiving.[103]

Forgive

The difficulty of forgiveness

'Therefore, the kingdom of heaven is like a king who wanted to settle accounts with his servants. As he began the settlement, a man who owed him ten thousand bags of gold was brought to him. Since he was not able to pay, the master ordered that he and his wife and his children and all that he had be sold to repay the debt.'

Matthew 18:23–5

A king had a servant who owed him a debt of ten thousand talents. All scholars point out the deliberately unrealistic nature of this sum. An ordinary working man could expect to earn perhaps a single talent in a year. Translated into today's terms, in which the average working-class job earns $40,000 a year, that makes the debt $400 billion—more than the gross national products of 80 percent of the countries of the world today. Granting that this is fiction, we still need to understand Jesus' intended meaning. Why did he introduce an inconceivable number? [...]

Forgiveness is difficult for us to receive. The enormous debt that the servant owes tells us that our debt to God is too large to ever make up. God's forgiveness cannot in any way be merited—it will have to be absolutely free. The servant's pathetic offer to pay the king back is as unrealistic as any effort to earn our way to heaven through good works. To say to God, 'If you forgive me, I'll go to church every week, I'll try harder to be a better person!' is as futile as saying, 'I'll pay back the 400 billion dollars by sending in five dollars a month.' It is also pointless to think, as the Unforgiving Servant thought, 'If I loathe and abase myself and grovel, then I will be worthy of forgiveness.' No amount of self-flagellation can undo the damage we've done. Our only hope is astounding, *free* grace and forgiveness from God himself.

Forgive

The request and the release

'At this the servant fell on his knees before him. "Be patient with me,"
he begged, "and I will pay back everything." The servant's master took
pity on him, cancelled the debt and let him go.'

Matthew 18:26–7

The servant asks that the king 'have patience with me, and I will pay you everything.' Falling on his knees signifies deep emotion, real sorrow for wrongdoing. The offer to 'pay back everything' is not just an expression of regret but an offer to make restitution. But even the most sincere effort on the part of the servant could never replace the money that the king and kingdom had lost. [. . .]

In response the king 'released him' and 'forgave him the debt,' freeing him from liability and obligation. The request by the servant for 'patience'—*makrothumeo*, a Greek word that literally means to be slow to boil or melt—hints at the cost of forgiveness. The older English translation for *makrothumeo* was 'long-suffering.' Patience is the ability to bear suffering rather than give in to it. To forgive someone's debt to you is to absorb the debt yourself. If a friend borrows your car, totals it through reckless driving, and hasn't any ability to remunerate you financially, you may say, 'I forgive you,' but the price of the wrong does not evaporate into the air. You either find the money to buy a new car or you go without one. Either way, forgiveness means the cost of the wrong moves from the perpetrator to you, and you bear it. [. . .]

Forgiveness is not merely difficult for us. While we have to speak carefully and reverently here, the parable points to what we will see in the rest of the Bible, namely, that God himself faces obstacles to forgiveness. The story hints at the extraordinary *costliness* of forgiveness to God.

Forgive

The new offence

'But when that servant went out, he found one of his fellow servants who owed him a hundred silver coins. He grabbed him and began to choke him. "Pay back what you owe me!" he demanded.

'His fellow servant fell to his knees and begged him, "Be patient with me, and I will pay it back."

'But he refused. Instead, he went off and had the man thrown into prison until he could pay the debt.'

Matthew 18:28–30

In the next scene we see the forgiven servant meeting a second servant. This second man owes the forgiven servant the modern equivalent of a few dollars. But the forgiven servant seizes him and starts choking him! The second servant responds in exactly the same way the forgiven servant responded to the king—making the very same request. But when his fellow servant cannot immediately produce the money, the forgiven servant throws him into prison. [...]

Forgiveness is also difficult for us to grant. Perhaps the most shocking part of the story is the callousness of the forgiven servant toward others. How could he fail to be softened and transformed by the king's mercy? As listeners to the story, we can see the incongruity clearly. Yet we who live only by the mercy of God every second of our lives fail to be kind, merciful, generous, gracious, and forgiving every day. This story, then, is an arrow pointed directly at our own hearts.

Forgive

The verdict

'When the other servants saw what had happened, they were outraged and went and told their master everything that had happened. Then the master called the servant in. "You wicked servant," he said, "I cancelled all that debt of yours because you begged me to. Shouldn't you have had mercy on your fellow servant just as I had on you?" In anger his master handed him over to the jailers to be tortured, until he should pay back all he owed.'

Matthew 18:31–4

The main idea here is found in the king's words of verse 33—'Shouldn't you have had mercy on your fellow servant just as I had on you?' Human forgiveness is dependent on divine forgiveness.

In other words, there are three basic dimensions to Christian forgiveness. First there is the vertical—God's forgiveness to us. Second there is the internal—our granting forgiveness to anyone who has wronged us. Third there is the horizontal—our offer to reconcile. The horizontal is based on the internal, and the internal is based on the vertical.

We must consciously base our forgiveness of others on God's forgiveness of us. The king's forgiveness should have made the servant a forgiver. Why didn't it? The answer, the missing link [. . .] is the lack of authentic repentance on the part of the servant. [. . .] The servant's expression of great emotion and sorrow turns out to have been self-pity rather than genuine contrition. And his failure to repent means there was no link between the vertical and the horizontal dimensions.

Forgive

(Our) failures of forgiveness

'This is how my heavenly Father will treat each of you unless you forgive your brother or sister from your heart.'

Matthew 18:35

Perhaps the most fundamental lesson of the parable is that human forgiveness must be based on an experience of divine forgiveness. A superficial reading of verse 35 ('this is how my heavenly Father will treat each of you unless you forgive . . .') has led some to interpret Jesus as saying that God's forgiveness of us depends on and is earned by our forgiveness of others. But the narrative of the story does not fit that interpretation at all. The king extends forgiveness first and then says specifically that the servant's forgiveness of his fellow servant should have been based on and motivated by the king's forgiveness of him. Jesus' final sentence means that divine mercy should change our *hearts* so that we are able to forgive as God forgave us. If we will not offer others forgiveness, it shows that we did not truly repent and receive God's. [. . .]

This parable is an account of forgiveness failure because *that is the usual human story*. The movement from divine forgiveness to human forgiveness is constantly being frustrated by human sin. Even in Jesus' other famous parable about forgiveness—the parable of the Prodigal Son—we see the Father's action causing offense and controversy instead of love and generosity. [. . .]

If we have truly grasped and received his salvation, it should change us as it did not change this man. God's mercy *must* and *will* make us merciful—if it doesn't, then we never understood or accepted God's mercy in truth.

Forgive

Paid in full

When you were dead in your sins and in the uncircumcision of your flesh, God made you alive with Christ. He forgave us all our sins, having cancelled the charge of our legal indebtedness, which stood against us and condemned us; he has taken it away, nailing it to the cross.

Colossians 2:13–14

If you are in a large department store, you may purchase an item at a cashier's station deep inside the store. What if you get to the exit and are stopped by a store employee who questions you about the merchandise you are carrying? You whip out your receipt and say, 'This proves that the price has been paid in full.' And with that you are free to go. In the resurrection God stamped 'Paid in full' across history and across your life. It is an assurance that the debt of sin has been paid.

Paul says, 'If Christ has not been raised, . . . you are still in your sins' (1 Cor. 15:17), which means that because Christ *is* raised, we are not 'in our sins.' Rather, as Paul says over one hundred times in his letters, you are in *him*, in Christ. Your sins are covered and the Father loves you 'even as' he loves Jesus (John 17:23). The Father looks at you and he sees a treasure. [. . .]

It doesn't matter who you have been or what you have done in your past. Think of Paul. What did he have in his past? He could remember the cries of innocent people and the looks on their faces as they died, like Stephen (Acts 7). Do you have anything like *that* in your past? Even if you did, it is no match for the grace of God. That is why, in the midst of describing the resurrection, Paul can jump quickly to the new truth that '[only] by the grace of God I am what I am' (1 Cor. 15:10).

Hope in Times of Fear

The temple to end all temples

Jesus answered them, 'Destroy this temple, and I will raise it again in three days.' They replied, 'It has taken forty-six years to build this temple, and you are going to raise it in three days?' But the temple he had spoken of was his body.

John 2:19–21

It was no surprise that even Jesus' disciples had no idea what he was talking about. He was saying that when he rose from the dead, he would *be* the new temple, the place where one could meet God. Indeed, he was declaring, the older tabernacle and temples were pointing to him all along.

When Jesus said that his resurrected body is the true temple, he was saying something like this: 'In all temples around the world, priests offer sacrifices and do rituals aiming to bridge the chasm you feel between yourself and God. But I am *the* sacrifice that ends all sacrifices. I am *the* priest who ends your need for priests. It was I who went under the sword (Gen. 3:24). I am the one who brings heaven to earth, because I am not just the bridge over the gap to God's glory. I *am* God's glory.' No one, of course, had ever said anything like this before. The founders of other religions built many temples. But Jesus *is* the temple to end all temples.

In Matthew 27:51 we are told that the moment Jesus died, the veil of the temple was torn in two from top to bottom as if by two mighty hands from above. At his death Jesus dismantled the old temple, and at his resurrection he established the new one. Now when we unite with the risen Christ by faith, through the Holy Spirit, the Shekinah glory presence of God that had dwelled behind the veil, inaccessibly, is now available to us.

Hope in Times of Fear

The upside down kingdom

'For even the Son of Man did not come to be served, but to serve, and to give his life as a ransom for many.'

Mark 10:45

The world's expectation was for a Messiah to come once. Instead Jesus announces a Messiah who comes twice, and that means something completely unlooked for—a Messiah who comes twice comes the first time in weakness, not strength. That is why the two-stage kingdom is, from the world's point of view, the 'upside-down' kingdom. This King comes in a way that reverses the values of the world. He comes in weakness and service, not strength and force, to die as a ransom for us.

There are three massive implications. First, it means that we enter the kingdom through this same upside-down pattern. Unlike in other religions, we do not achieve salvation by summoning up our strength to live a virtuous life. We receive salvation through the weakness of repentance. Second, it means that we also live and grow and serve in this kingdom not by taking power but, following Jesus, by giving up power in order to forgive, sacrifice, and serve. Finally, we see the whole world differently. We do not overly value the competent, confident, and successful. We do not bow and cater to the wealthy, brilliant, and able (James 2:1–7). Rather, we lift up those at the margins. [...]

In God's economy the high will be brought low and the low lifted up. As Hannah sings: 'The bows of the mighty are broken, but the feeble bind on strength' (1 Sam. 2:4 ESV). Those who seek to ascend to power will find they are only descending; those who descend in humility will find they have ascended, 'for all those who exalt themselves will be humbled, and those who humble themselves will be exalted' (Luke 14:11; cf. Luke 14:7–10).

Hope in Times of Fear

The once and future king

On his robe and on his thigh he has this name written: 'King of Kings and Lord of Lords.'

Revelation 19:16

On the tomb of King Arthur is written: 'Hic iacet Arthurus, rex quondam, rexque futurus' ('Here lies Arthur, the once and future king'). The promise is that this good king who had brought about the 'one, brief, shining moment' of Camelot would someday come back and make things right.

The odd thing about those legends is that the actual record of kings in history is abysmal. It is a record of tyranny and of slavery. Over the years almost all kingdoms have been toppled in favor of democracies. [...] And yet these legends of a true king still have enormous purchase, as we see from the blockbuster films, year after year, that are based on these older stories or narratives like them. [...]

There is evidence that deep in the human heart is a desire to crown a king. The Bible says we know, but suppress (Rom. 1:18–19), that we were created to serve and adore a king. The Bible tells us that there once was a King, and his beauty and his love and his compassion and his power and his wisdom were like the sun shining in full strength. [...]

This is the good news: This King will return and take his throne, and everything sad will come untrue. We will see him face to face finally. And yet 'the rightful king has landed, you may say landed in disguise, and is calling us to take part in a great campaign of sabotage' against the forces of darkness.[104] We are not only free but freedom fighters, in service of our once and future King.

Hope in Times of Fear

'So shall the Son of Man be lifted up'

Just as Moses lifted up the snake in the wilderness, so the Son of Man must be lifted up, that everyone who believes may have eternal life in him.

John 3:14–15

Why does God repeatedly choose the less powerful people and then work his deliverances through their powerlessness and suffering? The stories are moving because everyone loves to see a forgotten woman or belittled man come from behind and win. And these accounts of Jesus' love for the poor, outcasts, lepers, and tax collectors are encouraging, because we modern people care about justice. But it is a grave mistake to think that these biblical accounts are there to merely inspire us. Rather, they are written down to *convert* us, to convert us to Christ (1 Cor. 10:1–4,11). All these little reversals point us toward the Great Reversal, the death and resurrection of the Son of God.

Jesus Christ was a King who triumphantly entered his city (John 12:12–19), where his followers expected that he would be exalted and lifted up to the throne. Immediately after his triumphal entry, Jesus said that he would be 'lifted up from the earth,' but in order to die (John 12:32–3). Instead of a throne he would be lifted up on a cross. [...]

When Jesus said he would be lifted up on a cross *just as* the serpent was lifted up on a pole, he was referring to what Paul meant when he wrote in 2 Corinthians 5:21 that Jesus was 'made ... to be sin' and in Galatians 3:13 that Christ redeemed us 'by becoming a curse for us.' [...] On the cross God turned the curse of death on sin into a blessing for us.

Hope in Times of Fear

A living relationship

We proclaim to you what we have seen and heard, so that you also may have fellowship with us. And our fellowship is with the Father and with his Son, Jesus Christ.

1 John 1:3

Martin Luther famously says that when we put saving faith in Christ, our faith 'unites the soul to Christ just as a bride is united with her bridegroom.' A marriage is a relationship based on both law and love. [...] Christianity is a status and a union, like being adopted or being married, not a reward you get on the basis of your achievement. You are either married or you are not—you are either a Christian or you are not.

To understand the vital aspect of our relationship, consider the questions used by leaders during the Great Awakening in Britain, spearheaded by John and Charles Wesley. [...] In one of the manuals written for leaders of societies, the following kinds of questions were to be asked every week:[105]

How real has God been to your heart this week? How clear and vivid is your assurance and certainty of God's forgiveness and fatherly love?

Are you having any particular seasons of delight in God? Do you really sense his presence in your life, sense him giving you his love?

Have you been finding Scripture to be alive and active?

Are you finding certain biblical promises extremely precious and encouraging? Which ones?

Are you finding that God is challenging you or calling you to something through the Word? In what ways? [...]

The questions helped distinguish between believing in a remote God and having a living relationship with a living God. In such a relationship, based on Christ's grace, there is actual interchange of knowledge and love, and so God will challenge, comfort, summon, teach, and lead you.

Hope in Times of Fear

Seated with Christ in the heavenly realms

And God raised us up with Christ and seated us with him in the heavenly realms in Christ Jesus.

Ephesians 2:6

This statement shows how profound the changes are when anyone becomes a Christian. It is not a matter of turning over a new leaf and working harder at living a good life. It is not just membership in a new religious society. Rather, it is to be taken from one realm into another realm. It is to be united to him in the Holy Spirit and the powers of the age to come, such that 'by the new birth, by our regeneration, we are joined to the Lord Jesus Christ, and we become sharers and participators in His life and in all the blessings that come from him.'[106] [...]

This spiritual resurrection comes about when we believe that Jesus Christ died and rose for our salvation. But on the basis of that objective truth, a principle of future, heavenly life is put into us and that affects us subjectively. We begin to experience foretastes of our final future state—a freedom to change and be like Christ, a sense of God's reality, glory, and love in our hearts, and a new, loving solidarity with brothers and sisters in Christ.

Spiritual resurrection means that we are, in a sense, living in heaven while still on earth, living in the future while still being in the present.

Hope in Times of Fear

Forgiveness in the Books of Moses

' "This is what you are to say to Joseph: I ask you to forgive your broth-
ers the sins and the wrongs they committed in treating you so badly."
Now please forgive the sins of the servants of the God of your father.'
When their message came to him, Joseph wept.

Genesis 50:17

The first time forgiveness is explicitly mentioned in Genesis, and therefore in the Bible, is in the story of Joseph. Joseph's brothers ask him to forgive them for selling him into slavery (Gen. 50:17). The Hebrew word used is *nasah*, one with the sense of sending sin away so that the forgiver no longer counts it against the perpetrator. While Joseph does not say, literally, 'I forgive you,' he nevertheless responds by rejecting vengeance and pledges love to them—a crucial element in forgiveness.

Once we move out of Genesis, we see more frequent references to forgiveness. Moses prays for and receives God's forgiveness for the people (Exod. 32:32, 34:9; Num. 14:19–20). Most obvious is that the entire system of worship at the tabernacle is established to provide forgiveness. The animal sacrifices are for the forgiveness of sin (Lev. 4:20, 26, 31, 35, 5:10, 13, 16, 18; Num. 15:25, 26, 28). When Solomon builds the temple to replace the tabernacle, he prays that, through the temple, God will hear his people and forgive them. The theme of forgiveness dominates Solomon's prayers and understanding of the temple (1 Kings 8:30, 34, 36, 39, 50; 2 Chron. 6:21, 25, 27, 30, 39). At the heart of all the Old Testament worship, then, is forgiveness. Without it, there can be no relationship with God at all.

Forgive

Forgiveness in the Psalms

Out of the depths I cry to you, LORD; Lord, hear my voice. Let your ears be attentive to my cry for mercy. If you, LORD, kept a record of sins, Lord, who could stand? But with you there is forgiveness, so that we can, with reverence, serve you.

Psalm 130:1–4

The entire prayer teaches us several things about the Old Testament view of forgiveness.

It teaches us about the *universal need* for forgiveness. The psalmist poses a rhetorical question: If the Lord should 'mark iniquities'—i.e., keep a record of our sins and wrongdoings—'who could stand?' The answer is, obviously, no one. [. . .]

It teaches us about the *problem* of forgiveness. What makes forgiveness difficult is that sins create a 'record'—a residue of liability or obligation. [. . .] The psalmist, then, is saying that our sins create a record with God that will have to be 'paid up' on Judgment Day. We will all be lost and condemned. We will all perish in the 'payments due' of the record of our sins.

This psalm teaches us about the *fact* of God's forgiveness. The psalmist does not say, 'There *might* be forgiveness with you,' but rather 'There *is* forgiveness with you.' He is saying: 'Even though there is a record of sins that would condemn everyone, yet you find a way to forgive.' Yet he is astonished by this fact! He finds God's forgiveness shocking and inexplicable. How God accomplishes redemption is a complete mystery to the writer, even though it is not for us who know about Christ's death on the cross (cf. Romans 3:25–6).

Forgive

Forgiveness in the Prophets

'I, even I, am he who blots out your transgressions, for my own sake, and remembers your sins no more.'

Isaiah 43:25

The prophets' main burden was to tell the people that because of their faithlessness to the covenant, the consequences would be severe. [...] And yet God will remain a forgiving God and the punishment will only pave the way for a greater redemption, because he cannot forget his love for his people (Hosea 11:8). A remnant of his people will repent (Isa. 4:3, 6:13, 7:3ff.) and will live by faith (Hab. 2:4; Isa. 7:9, 28:16, 30:15). And he will make a new covenant with them, forgiving all their sins and giving them a new heart and spirit that will finally change them so they can walk with God in obedience and love (Jer. 24:7, 31:31ff., 32:37ff.; Ezek. 11:19ff., 36:24ff.). [...]

How will all this be accomplished? No prophet tells us more about this future than Isaiah. It will be through the Messiah, who is both a King (Isa. 11) and a suffering servant (Isa. 52:13–53:12). This servant not only will give salvation to Israel but will also bring in the Gentiles (Isa. 42:1). Our sins will not be remembered (Isa. 43:25). He will establish the new heavens and new earth, the new Jerusalem in which all peoples will be forgiven (Isa. 33:24).

There is nothing more astonishing than to realize that even the prophets, called by God to tell Israel about their sin and the coming judgments, could not avoid also speaking in the most moving way about God's grace and mercy. The message of the prophets, then, is that no amount of human evil and recalcitrance can ultimately stop God's forgiveness from finding its way to us.

Forgive

Forgiveness in the Gospels

'And you, my child, will be called a prophet of the Most High; for you will go on before the Lord to prepare the way for him, to give his people the knowledge of salvation through the forgiveness of their sins.'

Luke 1:76–7

At the beginning of the New Testament Gospels, the focus is already on forgiveness. The promise to Joseph in Matthew 1:21 was that the coming Messiah would save his people from their sins; the promise to Zechariah in Luke 1:77 was that Christ would give us 'the knowledge of salvation through the forgiveness of . . . sins.' Jesus' immediate forerunner, John the Baptist, preached 'a baptism of repentance for the forgiveness of sins' (Mark 1:4).

When Jesus himself came preaching and teaching, he declared repeatedly that we can know God's forgiveness and then, in turn, forgive those who wrong us. As we have seen, this is at the heart of the Lord's Prayer. 'Forgive us our debts, as we forgive our debtors' (Matthew 6:12, KJV).

Jesus adds: 'For if you forgive other people when they sin against you, your heavenly Father will also forgive you. But if you do not forgive others their sins, your Father will not forgive your sins' (Matt. 6:14–15). Despite the first impression, Jesus is not saying that God's forgiveness is based on or earned by our forgiveness of others. Not only do the Greek words for forgiveness not convey this, but the master parable of the Unforgiving Servant (Matt. 18:23–35) makes it clear that it is God's forgiveness of us that provides the basis—the motivation and the power—for our forgiveness of others. [. . .]

When Jesus forgives sins, he bears testimony not only to his deity but also to the life-transforming experience of forgiveness. When forgiving a woman, he says:

Therefore, I tell you, her many sins have been forgiven—as her great love has shown. But whoever has been forgiven little loves little. (Luke 7:47)

Forgive

321

The basis for forgiveness

'This is my blood of the covenant, which is poured out for many for the forgiveness of sins.'

Matthew 26:28

As the gospels begin with declarations of forgiveness of sins, so they end with them. [...]

At the end of his life Jesus gives the church the sacrament of the Lord's Supper [...] Here finally is an answer to all the questions raised in the Old Testament, especially since God revealed himself to Moses in Exodus 34:7 saying that he was the God who is both 'forgiving wickedness' and yet at the same time 'does not leave the guilty unpunished.' How is that possible? Doesn't forgiving people *mean* they go unpunished? How could he punish every sin and yet forgive us? [...]

The night before he died, Jesus gave us the answer to all the riddles. The basis—the objective means of forgiveness—is Jesus Christ's atoning death on the cross. His blood 'poured out,' signifying his death, is what makes it possible for us to be forgiven. Paul provides his own summary: 'He forgave us all our sins, having canceled the charge of our legal indebtedness, which stood against us and condemned us; he has taken it away, nailing it to the cross' (Col. 2:13–14). The writer of Hebrews speaks perhaps the most clearly of all: 'Day after day every priest stands and performs his religious duties; again and again he offers the same sacrifices, which can never take away sins. But when this priest had offered for all time one sacrifice for sins, he sat down at the right hand of God' (Heb. 10:11–12).

In short, on the cross Jesus satisfied both the justice and love of God in the most wise, wonderful, and glorious way.

Forgive

The God of fury and love

For God so loved the world that he gave his one and only Son, that whoever believes in him shall not perish but have eternal life. For God did not send his Son into the world to condemn the world, but to save the world through him. Whoever believes in him is not condemned, but whoever does not believe stands condemned already because they have not believed in the name of God's one and only Son.

John 3:16–18

Modern people struggle with the idea of a wrathful God who condemns, yet the Bible here puts condemnation in proximity to the most famous verse on love. In other words, the Bible never sees God's love and anger as being opposed to each other. Indeed, the Bible tells us that in God, not only are they not in tension but they are meaningless apart from each other and indeed they establish each other.

He's both love and fury. It's not that he's a split personality—being loving on alternate days and wrathful in between. The reason his wrath and love cohere is because they are not like ours—they are perfectly holy and good. [...]

When we see all the references to God's wrath in the Bible, we instinctively imagine God's anger must be like ours, and so we recoil. However, his anger is *not* wounded pride as ours is. God only gets angry at the evil destroying the things he loves—his creation and the human race he made for his own glory and for our happiness.

God is not just a God of love or a God of wrath. He is both, and if your concept of God can't include both, it will distort your view of reality in general and of forgiveness in particular.

Forgive

Where love and fury meet

God presented Christ as a sacrifice of atonement, through the shedding of his blood—to be received by faith. He did this to demonstrate his righteousness, because in his forbearance he had left the sins committed beforehand unpunished.

Romans 3:25

If the real God is a God of both love and fury, then God's reality is supremely revealed on the cross. That is where we must go to heal our understanding and receive an undivided heart. [. . .]

In many ways, it is this tension that drives the plot of the entire Bible. But the resolution is not merely the death of Christ but his voluntary death as the second person of the triune God, as a substitute in our place. The classic summary of the doctrine, in unsurpassed brevity and clarity, is by John Stott in *The Cross of Christ*:

The concept of substitution may be said, then, to lie at the heart of both sin and salvation. For the essence of sin is man substituting himself for God, while the essence of salvation is God substituting himself for man. Man asserts himself against God and puts himself where only God deserves to be; God sacrifices himself for man and puts himself where only man deserves to be. Man claims prerogatives which belong to God alone; God accepts penalties which belong to man alone.[107]

Paul himself says that the 'shedding of . . . blood' (Rom. 3:25) made it possible for God to be both 'just, and the justifier of' those who believe (Rom. 3:26, KJV). Just, yet forgiving.[. . .]

When Paul meditates on this, he often breaks into doxology: 'Oh, the . . . riches and wisdom and knowledge of God! How unsearchable are his judgments and how inscrutable his ways! . . . For from him and through him and to him are all things' (Rom. 11:33,36, ESV).

Forgive

Hope for relationships

'But when you give a banquet, invite the poor, the crippled, the lame, the blind, and you will be blessed. Although they cannot repay you, you will be repaid at the resurrection of the righteous.'

Luke 14:13–14

Here we see Jesus breaking completely free from the transactional, self-interested model for social relationships on which the world had been based for centuries, right down to the present day. Without this conclusion, Jesus' counsel to not seek the more honored seats could have been read as a subtle way to fit into the world's model. The idea would have been to 'Act very humble and never look like you are social climbing—and that is the very best way *to* social climb.'

But in verses 12–14 Jesus told Christians to actively befriend and serve people who could never open doors for you or invite you to their villas or bring you more clients and business. And the reason Christians live in such a radically different way is—the resurrection! 'Although they cannot repay you, you will be repaid at the resurrection of the righteous.' The glory and richness and bliss and love of the final resurrection and renewed world will infinitely, innumerable times over, more than recompense you for any sacrifices for righteousness in this life. [...]

Jesus adds, in verse 14, that those who provide uncalculating generosity toward those of low status will experience 'blessing' from God. But even here, Jesus does not tell people to give to others in order to get blessing. He is saying that only those who pour themselves out for others without any care for repayment—but merely as a joyful response to how God has already given them all things possible—will be blessed.

Hope in Times of Fear

325

Bearing witness on race

*So in Christ Jesus you are all children of God through faith, for all of
you who were baptised into Christ have clothed yourselves with Christ.
There is neither Jew nor Gentile, neither slave nor free, nor is there
male and female, for you are all one in Christ Jesus.*

Galatians 3:26–8

In Galatians Paul urges Christians to live in the light of the resurrection—not to mention the doctrine of justification—in such
a way that the world's high barriers and prejudices between races
and peoples are removed. [...]

Before the coming of Christianity, one was 'born to one's gods,'
because every people, city, place, craft guild, and large estate had its
own gods. Religion was a mere extension of culture. If you were
born in a particular place or into a particular people, worshipping
those gods was one of the ways you were part of that community.

But Christians believed that there was only one God and everyone should worship him regardless of their race, ethnicity, class,
nationality, or vocation, or of any other human status. The radical
implication was that your faith in God was not merely independent
of your ethnicity—it was more fundamental to who you were than
your ethnicity. It gave you a bond with all other Christians that was
deeper than any you had with your own race. This created the first
multiracial, multiethnic faith community. [...]

Modern-day Christians must admit that these extraordinary
resources for racial understanding, healing, and unity are largely
going untapped. The new self (Eph. 4:22–3) that is rooted in
Christ's love and work rather in than our race, culture, and achievements is something that must be *put on*. Only then can it overcome the natural 'hostility' between races (Eph. 2:14).

Hope in Times of Fear

Hope for justice

What other nation is so great as to have their gods near them the way the LORD our God is near us whenever we pray to him? And what other nation is so great as to have such righteous decrees and laws as this body of laws I am setting before you today?

Deuteronomy 4:7–8

One of God's purposes was that his people be a *corporate* witness to the nonbelieving world, to the 'nations' around Israel. A law-obedient people was not just a cadre of moral individuals. They constituted a counterculture, an alternate human society. [...]

The Bible says that if the people obey the law, the surrounding nations, despite their assumptions of cultural superiority, will conclude that Israel has found the wisdom and justice that they had sought in their own laws but had been unable to realize. They will see that Israel's society is wise and just because the Lord is nearer to Israel than their gods are to them. And so the impact of law keeping—if it is carried out as it should be—would ultimately be evangelistic. Jerusalem, in particular, was to be an urban community revealing the wisdom and justice of God to the nations. It was to be attractional—'the joy of the whole earth' (Psalm 48:2).

So the city of Jerusalem, if its citizens obeyed God, was to be an evangelistic witness. The earthly Jerusalem, in its communal life together, was to be a pointer to the perfect peace and justice of the New Jerusalem, the city of God to be established on earth at the end of time (Rev. 21–2). Was that merely an Old Testament idea? Not at all. Jesus said to his disciples that they were to be 'the light of the world' as a 'city set on a hill.'

Hope in Times of Fear

Things unseen

Therefore we do not lose heart. Though outwardly we are wasting away, yet inwardly we are being renewed day by day. For our light and momentary troubles are achieving for us an eternal glory that far outweighs them all. So we fix our eyes not on what is seen, but on what is unseen, since what is seen is temporary, but what is unseen is eternal.

2 Corinthians 4:16–18

Even though outwardly his body was aging and 'wasting away,' nevertheless inwardly Paul was being renewed and strengthened every day, and this is especially *through* afflictions. We know something of his 'light' troubles from his listing of them in 2 Corinthians 11:23–9. They include imprisonment, public floggings (at least five of them), and beatings. They were only 'momentary' and 'light' in comparison with the eternal and infinitely solid glory that he knew was in store for him.

However, there are two reasons he never lost heart in the face of his sufferings. One is that they were *renewing* him. They were making him more like Christ, finding his joy in God, his peace in God's love, his meaning in God's calling. More and more his heart was anchored in things that could not be shaken or taken away. He was growing in love, joy, peace, patience, humility, self-control, and the fruit of the Spirit (Gal. 5:22–3), and nothing was increasing those things in him more than his afflictions and the self-knowledge and God-reliance they brought. [. . .]

But in addition, they were *preparing* him for this future, eternal glory. [. . .] Paul is saying that his sufferings are not only inwardly strengthening him now but preparing him for an unimaginable joy and glory. How so? The next verse tells us. This renewal and preparation happen as we look not to the things that are seen but to 'the things that are unseen.'

Hope in Times of Fear

Effective hope

Now faith is confidence in what we hope for and assurance about what we do not see.

Hebrews 11:1

The New Testament uses the word *hope* in two ways. When it comes to hoping in human beings and ourselves, our *hope* is always relative, uncertain. If you lend to someone, you do so in the hope that they will pay you back (Luke 6:34); if we plow and thresh, we do so in the hope that there will be a harvest (1 Cor. 9:10).[108] We choose the best methods and wisest practices in order to secure the outcome we want. We insist to ourselves and others that 'we have it sorted' and under control. But we do not—we never do. This is relative, 'hope so' hope.

But when the object of hope is *not* any human agent but God, then hope means confidence, certainty, and full assurance (Heb. 11:1). To have hope in God is not to have an uncertain, anxious wish that he will affirm your plan but to recognize that he and he alone is trustworthy, that everything else will let you down (Ps. 42:5,11, 62:10), and that his plan is infinitely wise and good. If I believe in the resurrection of Jesus, that confirms that there is a God who is both good and powerful, who brings light out of darkness, and who is patiently working out a plan for his glory, our good, and the good of the world (Eph. 1:9–12; Rom. 8:28). Christian hope means that I stop betting my life and happiness on human agency and rest in him.

Hope in Times of Fear

Light and high beauty forever

Those who hope in the LORD will renew their strength. They will soar on wings like eagles; they will run and not grow weary, they will walk and not be faint.

Isaiah 40:31

J. R. R. Tolkien explains [the] difference between defiance and true hope in a passage in the last volume of his trilogy *The Lord of the Rings*. Sam Gamgee has been guarding his master, Frodo, during a harrowing journey through a deadly, evil country. At one point he rescued Frodo from a prison tower out of sheer force of will. Later he is falling asleep and sees a white star twinkling in the sky:

The beauty of it smote his heart, as he looked up out of the forsaken land, and hope returned to him. For like a shaft, clear and cold, the thought pierced him that in the end the Shadow was only a small and passing thing: there was light and high beauty forever beyond its reach. His song in the Tower had been defiance rather than hope; for then he was thinking of himself. Now, for a moment, his own fate, and even his master's, ceased to trouble him.[109]

This perfectly captures the difference between relative hope in human agency and infallible hope in God. In the tower, Sam had put his hope in his plan and his prowess. And certainly stoicism or powerful anger can get us through some crises, temporarily. But real courage comes with self-forgetfulness based on joy. It comes from a deep conviction that we here on earth are trapped temporarily in a little corner of darkness, but that the universe of God is an enormous place of light and high beauty and that is our certain, final destiny. It is so because of Jesus. He was so committed to bringing us into that light and beauty that he lost all glory and gladness and was plunged into the depths so that we can know that 'weeping may stay for the night, but rejoicing comes in the morning' (Psalm 30:5).

Hope in Times of Fear

When darkness seems your closest friend

Why, LORD, do you reject me and hide your face from me? [. . .] You have taken from me friend and neighbour—darkness is my closest friend.

Psalm 88:14, 18

M ost psalms that are laments and cries of pain end on at least some note of hope. But Psalm 88 recounts all the writer's griefs and his imminent death and ends by saying that God has abandoned him and that 'darkness is my closest friend' (verse 18). In fact, in the middle of the psalm he actually asks bitterly, 'Do their [the dead's] spirits rise up and praise you? Is your love declared in the grave?' (verses 10–11). He is in despair. But the New Testament answers with the Great Reversal. Do the dead rise up to praise? Yes! Is your love declared in the grave? Oh yes!

Here's your hope.

Jesus was truly abandoned so that you only feel abandoned but you're not. When Jesus Christ was in the Garden of Gethsemane and the ultimate darkness was coming down on him and he knew it was coming, he didn't abandon you; he died for you. If Jesus Christ didn't abandon you in *his* darkness, the ultimate darkness, why would he abandon you now, in yours?

Because it can be said truly of Jesus Christ that, on the cross, darkness was his only friend, and so he paid for your sins—then you can know that in your darkness God is still there as your friend. He hasn't abandoned you. He's not going to take two payments for the same debt. Jesus paid for your sins, and now he loves you.

If you know—and keep on remembering—that resurrection is coming, then you won't be in utter darkness.

Hope in Times of Fear

Neither death nor life

For I am convinced that neither death nor life, neither angels nor demons, neither the present nor the future, nor any powers, neither height nor depth, nor anything else in all creation, will be able to separate us from the love of God that is in Christ Jesus our Lord.

Romans 8:38–9

Death is the Great Interruption, tearing loved ones away from us, or us from them.

Death is the Great Schism, ripping apart the material and immaterial parts of our being and sundering a whole person, who was never meant to be disembodied, even for a moment. [. . .]

Death is hideous and frightening and cruel and unusual. It is not the way life is supposed to be, and our grief in the face of death acknowledges that.

Death is our Great Enemy, more than anything. It makes a claim on each and every one of us, pursuing us relentlessly through all our days. Modern people write and talk endlessly about love, especially romantic love, which eludes many. But no one can avoid death. [. . .]

Rather than living in fear of death, we should see it as spiritual smelling salts that will awaken us out of our false belief that we will live forever. When you are at a funeral, especially one for a friend or a loved one, listen to God speaking to you, telling you that everything in life is temporary except for His love. This is reality.

Everything in this life is going to be taken away from us, except one thing: God's love, which can go into death with us and take us through it and into his arms. It's the one thing you can't lose.

On Death

Our champion

*In bringing many sons and daughters to glory, it was fitting that God,
for whom and through whom everything exists, should make the
pioneer of their salvation perfect through what he suffered . . . He too
shared in their humanity so that by his death he might break the power
of him who holds the power of death—that is, the devil—and free
those who all their lives were held in slavery by their fear of death.*

Hebrews 2:10, 14–15

In order to save us, Jesus became the 'pioneer' of our salvation
through suffering and death. The Greek word here is *archēgos*.
Bible scholar William Lane says it really ought to be translated as
'our champion.'[110]

A champion was somebody who engaged in representative
combat. When David fought Goliath, they both fought as cham-
pions for their respective armies. They fought as substitutes. If
your champion won, the whole army won the battle, even though
none of them lifted a finger. That is what Jesus did. He took on
our greatest enemies—sin and death. Unlike David, he didn't just
risk his life, he gave his life, but in doing so he defeated them. He
took the penalty we deserve for our sins—the punishment of
death—in our place, as our substitute. But because he himself was
a man of perfect, sinless love for God and neighbor, death could
not hold him (Acts 2:24). He rose from the dead.

That's why in Hebrews 2:14, the writer says he destroyed the
power of death because he died for us, taking away our penalty
and guaranteeing the future resurrection of all who unite with
him by faith. Jesus Christ, our great captain and champion, has
killed death.

On Death

Where, O death, is your sting?

'Where, O death, is your victory? Where, O death, is your sting?'

1 Corinthians 15:55

Paul is not facing death stoically. He's *taunting* it. How can anyone in his right mind look at humanity's most powerful enemy *and taunt it*? Paul immediately gives the answer: 'The sting of death is sin, and the power of sin is the law. But thanks be to God! He gives us the victory through our Lord Jesus Christ' (1 Cor. 15:56–7). Paul says that the 'sting of death' [...] is our conscience, our sense of sin and judgment before the moral law. But Christ has taken it away—or more accurately, taken it upon himself for all who believe.

Donald Grey Barnhouse was the minister of Tenth Presbyterian Church in Philadelphia when his wife, only in her late thirties, died of cancer, leaving him with four children under the age of twelve. When driving with his children to the funeral, a large truck pulled past them in the left lane, casting its shadow over them. Barnhouse asked all in the car, 'Would you rather be run over by the truck or the shadow of the truck?' His eleven-year-old answered, 'Shadow, of course.' Their father concluded, 'Well, that's what has happened to your mother ... Only the shadow of death has passed over her, because death itself ran over Jesus.'[III]

The sting of death is sin, and the poison went into Jesus.

On Death

Weep with those who weep

Rejoice with those who rejoice; mourn with those who mourn.

Romans 12:15

Death was not in God's original design for the world and human life. Look at the first three chapters of Genesis. We were not meant to die; we were meant to last. We were meant to get more and more beautiful as time goes on, not more and more enfeebled. We were meant to get stronger, not to weaken and die. Paul explains elsewhere, in Romans 8:18–23, that when we turned from God to be our own Lords and Saviors, everything broke. Our bodies, the natural order, our hearts, our relationships—nothing works the way it was originally designed. It is all marred, distorted, broken, and death is part of that (Gen. 3:7–19). So Jesus weeps and is angry at the monstrosity of death. It is a deep distortion of the creation he loves.

Therefore, the stoic, 'keep a stiff upper lip' reaction to death and grief is wrong. There are many versions of this. One goes like this: 'Now, now. He is with the Lord. The Lord works all things together for good. There's no need to weep too much. Of course you will miss him, but he's in heaven now. And everything happens for a reason.' Technically there may be nothing wrong with any of these statements. They may be true. But Jesus knew all of them as well [in John 11]. He knew Lazarus was going to be raised. He knew that this was part of the Father's plan for his ministry. And he was still grieving with sorrow and anger. Why? Because that is the right response to the evil and unnaturalness of death.

On Death

Grieving with hope

Brothers and sisters, we do not want you to . . . grieve like the rest of mankind, who have no hope.

1 Thessalonians 4:13

However, though we are definitely right to grieve, Saint Paul says we must grieve with hope. As we have seen, to suppress grief and outrage at death is not only bad for us psychologically, it's actually bad for our humanity. Yet anger can dehumanize us, too, making us bitter and hard. Which means that we cannot *only* 'rage against the dying of the light.' We also need a hope that influences how we grieve.

But what is there to hope for? Look at Jesus Christ at the tomb of his friend Lazarus. He's grieving, he's weeping, and he's angry, even though he knows that in a few minutes he will raise his friend from the dead.

But he knows something that no one else could even imagine. At the end of chapter 11 of John, after he raised his friend Lazarus from the dead, all of his opponents said, 'Well, that's the last straw. We've got to kill him now. We've got to kill Jesus.'

Jesus knew that to raise Lazarus from the dead would push his enemies toward extreme measures. So he knew that the only way he could get Lazarus out of the tomb was if he put himself into it. Indeed, if he is to guarantee resurrection for all who believe in him, he must put himself into the grave. On the cross that's what he did. [. . .]

Jesus conquered death, and we will share in his resurrection. That's our hope.

On Death

Personal hope

For the Lord himself will come down from heaven, with a loud command, with the voice of the archangel and with the trumpet call of God, and the dead in Christ will rise first. After that, we who are still alive and are left will be caught up together with them in the clouds to meet the Lord in the air. And so we will be with the Lord for ever.

1 Thessalonians 4:16–17

Notice all the references that we will be *with* one another. You will be with people you've lost. And do you see the word 'together'? We will be with the Lord together forever. These are words that mean personal relationships—perfect relationships of love that go on forever.

Jonathan Edward's famous sermon 'Heaven Is a World of Love' begins by arguing that the greatest happiness we can know is to be loved by another person, and yet, he adds, on earth the greatest love relationships are like a pipe so clogged that only a little water (or love) actually gets through. In heaven, however, all these 'clogs' are removed and the love we will experience will be infinitely, inexpressibly greater than anything we have known here.[112] On earth we hide behind facades for fear of being rejected, but that means we never experience the transforming power of being fully known yet truly loved at the same time. In addition, we love selfishly and enviously, which disrupts, weakens, and even ends love relationships. [...]

Edwards concludes by declaring that all of these things that reduce love in this world to a trickle at the bottom of a riverbed are removed when we get to heaven, where love is an endless deluge and fountain of delight and bliss flowing in and out of us infinitely and eternally.

The Christian hope is for a personal future of love relationships.

On Death

Material hope

For since death came through a man, the resurrection of the dead comes also through a man. For as in Adam all die, so in Christ all will be made alive.

1 Corinthians 15:21–2

Our hope is also material. Notice that Paul does not say merely that we will go to heaven. He says that the 'dead in Christ will rise' (1 Thess. 4:16). Yes, we believe our souls go to heaven when we die, but that isn't the climactic end of our salvation. At the end of all things, we will get new bodies. We will be raised like Jesus was raised. Remember that when the risen Jesus met his disciples he insisted that he had 'flesh and bones,' that he was not a spirit. He ate in front of them to prove the point (Luke 24:37–43). He taught them that, unlike all other major religions, Christianity promises not a spirit-only future, but a renewed heavens and earth, a perfected material world from which all suffering and tears, disease, evil, injustice, and death have been eliminated.

Our future is not an immaterial one. We are not going to float in the kingdom of God like ghosts. We're going to walk, eat, hug, and be hugged. We're going to love. We're going to sing, because we're going to have vocal cords. And we will do all this in degrees of joy, excellence, satisfaction, beauty, and power we cannot now imagine. We're going to eat and drink with the Son of Man.

And this is the final defeat of death. This is not merely a consolation in heaven for the material life we lost. This is a restoration of that life. It's getting the love, the body, the mind, the being we've always longed for.

On Death

Beatific hope

For God, who said, 'Let light shine out of darkness,' made his light shine in our hearts to give us the light of the knowledge of God's glory displayed in the face of Christ.

2 Corinthians 4:6

Along with personal hope and material hope, there is beatific hope. Paul does not say we will simply be together with others. Nor does he talk so much about how lovely the world will be when it's healed. That's not the main thing in his mind. Here's the final note, the biggest emphasis—that we will be 'with *the Lord* forever' (1 Thess. 4:17). It means we will be in perfect communion with him, we will see the Lord face to face. This is what has been historically called the 'beatific vision.'

Paul talks about it in 1 Corinthians 13:12 when he says, 'For now we see only a reflection as in a mirror; then we shall see face to face. Now I know in part; then I shall know fully, even as I am fully known.' John speaks of it in 1 John 3:2 when he says, 'We know that when Christ appears, we shall be like him, for we shall see him as he is.' When we look into the face of Christ it will completely transform us because, as Paul says, we will finally be fully known yet fully loved. [. . .]

When at last you see the God of the universe looking at you with love, all of the potentialities of your soul will be released and you will experience the glorious freedom of the children of God.

On Death

Assured hope

We believe that Jesus died and rose again, and so we believe that God
will bring with Jesus those who have fallen asleep in him.

1 Thessalonians 4:14

What is Paul talking about? The wages of sin is death (Rom. 6:23)—that is what we deserve. When a prisoner has fully paid his debt he is released; the law no longer has any claim on him. So when Jesus fully paid the debt of sin with his death, he was resurrected. The law and death had no more claim on him. Nor does it have any claim on us if we believe in him. 'There is now no condemnation for those who are in Christ Jesus' (Rom. 8:1). When we put our faith in him we are as free from condemnation as if we had paid the penalty ourselves—as if we had died. 'Now if we died with Christ, we believe that we will also live with him' (Rom. 6:8). That's what Paul is saying here in 1 Thessalonians 4. We not only know about the future world of love, the vision of God, and a renewed universe. We are assured that these astounding things are ours. We do not anxiously wonder if we have been good enough to be with God when we die. We live with deep assurance of all of these things. This, too, is part of our unequaled Christian hope.

What more could we ask for?

On Death

The mountains and the trees will sing for joy

Sing for joy, you heavens, for the LORD has done this; shout aloud, you earth beneath. Burst into song, you mountains, you forests and all your trees; for the LORD has redeemed Jacob, he displays his glory in Israel.

Isaiah 44:23

In our culture one of the few places where it is acceptable to talk about death is at a funeral. [. . .] At a funeral service (as opposed to a memorial service) we are literally in the presence of death. There is a dead body in that coffin. While people have many reactions to being in the presence of death, there are two opposite mistakes we can make: One is to despair too much; the other is to shrug it off and not learn what we should from it.

Neither will be of much benefit to you, so we must do as the Bible tells us to do: We should grieve, yet we should have hope; we should wake up from our denial and discover a source of peace that will not leave us; and finally, we should laugh and sing.

The Bible says that when the Son of God returns, the mountains and the woods will sing for joy. When the Son of God rises with healing in his wings, when Jesus Christ comes back, the Bible says the mountains and the trees will sing for joy, because in his hands we finally become everything God intended us to be.

And if it's true that the mountains and the trees will sing for joy, what will we be able to do?

On Death

Light in the darkness

The people walking in darkness have seen a great light; on those living in the land of deep darkness a light has dawned.

Isaiah 9:2

No matter what you want to do in a room, you have to first turn on the light, or you can't see to do anything else. Christmas contains many spiritual truths, but it will be hard to grasp the others unless we grasp this one first. That is, that the world is a dark place, and we will never find our way or see reality unless Jesus is our Light. [. . .]

How is the world 'dark'? In the Bible the word 'darkness' refers to both evil and ignorance. It means first that the world is filled with evil and untold suffering. Look at what was happening at the time of the birth of Jesus—violence, injustice, abuse of power, homelessness, refugees fleeing oppression, families ripped apart, and bottomless grief. Sounds exactly like today.

The message of Christianity is [. . .] 'Things really are this bad, and we can't heal or save ourselves. Things really are this dark—*nevertheless*, there is hope.' The Christmas message is that 'on those living in the land of deep darkness a light has dawned.' Notice that it doesn't say from the world a light has sprung, but upon the world a light has dawned. It has come from outside. There is light outside of this world, and Jesus has brought that light to save us; indeed, he *is* the Light (John 8:12).

Hidden Christmas

The meaning of light

*'I am the light of the world. Whoever follows me will never walk in
darkness, but will have the light of life.'*

John 8:12

When Isaiah speaks of God's light 'dawning' on a dark world,
he is using the sun as a symbol. Sunlight brings *life*, *truth*,
and *beauty*.

The sun gives us life. If the sun went out, we would freeze. The
sun is the source of all life. So too the Bible says that only in God
do we 'live and move and have our being' (Acts 17:28). We exist
only because he is upholding us, keeping us together every
moment. You are borrowing your being from him. This is true not
only of your physical body but also of your spirit, your soul. [...]

The sun shows us the truth. If you drive a car at night without
your headlights on, you will probably crash. Why? Light reveals
the truth of things, how they really are, and you will not have
enough truth to steer the car safely. So too the Bible says God is
the source of all truth (1 John 1:5–6). [...]

The sun is beautiful. Light is dazzling and gives joy. That is true
literally. In places where there are only a few hours of daylight at
certain times of the year, many suffer from depression. We need
light for joy. God is the source of all beauty and joy. St. Augustine
famously said, 'Our hearts are restless until they find their rest in
thee' (*Confessions* 1.1.1). [...] All joy is really found in God, and
anything you do enjoy is derivative, because what you are really
looking for is *him*, whether you know it or not.

Hidden Christmas

The dawning of the light

For to us a child is born, to us a son is given, and the government will be on his shoulders. And he will be called Wonderful Counsellor, Mighty God, Everlasting Father, Prince of Peace.

Isaiah 9:6–7

God alone, then, has the life, truth, and joy that we lack and cannot generate ourselves. How can this divine light 'dawn' or, as Isaiah 9 says, literally '*flash*' upon us? Verses 6 and 7, the most well-known verses of the chapter, answer with stunning directness. The text tells us the light has come '*for* to us a child is born.' This child brings it, because he is 'Wonderful Counselor, Mighty God, Everlasting Father, Prince of Peace.' It is remarkable that the four titles applied to this child belong to God alone. He is the Mighty God. He is the Everlasting Father, which means he is the Creator, and yet he is *born*. There's nothing like this claim in any of the other major religions. He is a human being. However, he is not just some kind of avatar of the divine principle. He is God!

It's almost too limiting to say that we 'celebrate' this at Christmas. We stare dumbstruck, lost in wonder, love, and praise. [. . .]

If God has really been born in a manger, then we have something that no other religion even claims to have. It's a God who truly understands you, from the inside of your experience. There's no other religion that says God has suffered, that God had to be courageous, that he knows what it is like to be abandoned by friends, to be crushed by injustice, to be tortured and die. Christmas shows he knows what you're going through. When you talk to him, he understands.

Hidden Christmas

The light of grace

But you are a chosen people, a royal priesthood, a holy nation, God's special possession, that you may declare the praises of him who called you out of darkness into his wonderful light.

1 Peter 2:9

Christmas is about receiving presents, but consider how challenging it is to receive certain kinds of gifts. Some gifts by their very nature make you swallow your pride. Imagine opening a present on Christmas morning from a friend—and it's a dieting book. Then you take off another ribbon and wrapper and you find it is another book from another friend, *Overcoming Selfishness*. If you say to them, 'Thank you *so* much,' you are in a sense admitting, 'For indeed I am fat and obnoxious.' In other words, some gifts are hard to receive, because to do so is to admit you have flaws and weaknesses and you need help. [. . .]

There has never been a gift offered that makes you swallow your pride to the depths that the gift of Jesus Christ requires us to do. Christmas means that we are so lost, so unable to save ourselves, that nothing less than the death of the Son of God himself could save us. That means you are *not* somebody who can pull yourself together and live a moral and good life.

To accept the true Christmas gift, you have to admit you're a sinner. You need to be saved by grace. You need to give up control of your life. That is descending lower than any of us really wants to go. Yet Jesus Christ's greatness is seen in how far down he came to love us. Your spiritual regeneration and eventual greatness will be achieved by going down the same path. He descended into greatness, and the Bible says it's only through repentance that you come into his light.

Hidden Christmas

Good news, not good advice

This is the genealogy of Jesus the Messiah the son of David, the son of Abraham.

Matthew 1:1

Matthew does not begin his story of Jesus' birth by saying, 'Once upon a time.' That is the way fairy tales and legends and myths and *Star Wars* begin. 'Once upon a time' signals that this probably didn't happen or that we don't know if it happened, but it is a beautiful story that teaches us so much. But that is not the kind of account Matthew is giving us. He says, 'This is the genealogy of Jesus Christ.' That means he is grounding what Jesus Christ is and does in history. Jesus is not a metaphor. He is real. This all happened. [...]

The biblical Christmas texts are accounts of what actually happened in history. They are not *Aesop's Fables*, inspiring examples of how to live well. Many people believe the gospel to be just another moralizing story, but they could not be more mistaken. There is no 'moral of the story' to the nativity. The shepherds, the parents of Jesus, the wise men—are not being held up primarily as examples for us. These Gospel narratives are telling you not what you should do but what God has done. The birth of the Son of God into the world is a gospel, good news, an announcement. You don't save yourself. God has come to save you.

Hidden Christmas

More than a fairy story

Let the fields be jubilant, and everything in them; let all the trees of the forest sing for joy.

Psalm 96:12

Here is a story about someone from a different world who breaks into ours and has miraculous powers, and can calm the storm and heal people and raise people from the dead. Then his enemies turn on him, and he is put to death, and it seems like all hope is over, but finally he rises from the dead and saves everyone. We read that and we think, *Another great fairy tale!* [...]

But Matthew's Gospel refutes that by grounding Jesus in history, not 'once upon a time.' He says this is no fairy tale. Jesus Christ is not one more lovely story [...] Jesus *is* the underlying reality to which all the stories point.

Jesus Christ has come from that eternal, supernatural world that we sense is there, that our hearts know is there even though our heads say no. At Christmas he punched a hole between the ideal and the real, the eternal and the temporal, and came into our world. That means, if Matthew is right, that there *is* an evil sorcerer in this world, and we are under enchantment, and there *is* a noble prince who has broken the enchantment, and there is a love from which we will never be parted. And we will indeed fly someday, and we will defeat death, and in this world, now 'red in tooth and claw,' someday even the trees are going to dance and sing (Psalm 65:13, 96:11–13).

Hidden Christmas

Genealogy of grace

David was the father of Solomon, whose mother had been Uriah's wife . . .

Matthew 1:6

Perhaps the most interesting character and background story in [Jesus'] whole genealogy [. . .] is in verse 6. There it says that in Jesus' line is King David. You think, *Now there is somebody you want in your genealogy—royalty!* However, Matthew adds, in one of the great, ironic understatements of the Bible, that David was the father of Solomon, 'whose mother had been Uriah's wife.' If you knew nothing about the biblical history, you would find that strange. Why not just give her name? Her name was Bathsheba, but Matthew is summoning us to recall a tragic and terrible chapter of Israel's history.

[. . . A]fter David became king, he looked upon Uriah's wife, Bathsheba, and he wanted her. He slept with her. Then he arranged to have Uriah killed in order to marry her. He did, and one of their children was Solomon, from whom Jesus is descended. Do you know why Matthew leaves off the name 'Bathsheba'? It is not a slight of Bathsheba—it is a slam of David. It was out of that dysfunctional family, and out of that deeply flawed man, that the Messiah came. [. . .]

What does it mean? [. . .] It doesn't matter your pedigree, it doesn't matter what you have done, it doesn't matter whether you have killed people. If you repent and believe in him, the grace of Jesus Christ can cover your sin and unite you with him.

Hidden Christmas

Son of the Most High

The angel said to her, 'Do not be afraid, Mary, you have found favour with God. You will conceive and give birth to a son, and you are to call him Jesus. He will be great and will be called the Son of the Most High. The Lord God will give him the throne of his father David, and he will reign over Jacob's descendants for ever; his kingdom will never end.'

Luke 1:30–3

What do we learn from the angel about who Jesus is? The message calls him the Son of the Most High. Now, sometimes in ancient languages you could be called a son of someone if you resembled or believed strongly in that person. In John 8, Jesus has a highly charged argument with the religious leaders, who claimed to be children of Abraham and of God. Jesus countered that they were children of the devil because they lied like him! But this title means much more than that Jesus was simply a follower of God, because the angel adds, 'He will reign over the house of Jacob forever.' Forever? And then—perhaps because he knows that Mary can't believe her ears—he makes the same statement in another way: 'His kingdom will never end.' He is saying, 'I really do mean *forever*.' So there is a promise that this child who is about to be born will not just be a mere political king, but will have a kingdom that will last forever. Indeed, the strong implication is that he is more than a mortal human being.

Encounters with Jesus

The power of the Most High

The angel answered, 'The Holy Spirit will come on you, and the power of the Most High will overshadow you. So the holy one to be born will be called the Son of God.'

Luke 1:35

'The power of the Most High will overshadow you.' That is a fascinating, mysterious statement, is it not? '[It] will overshadow you, so the holy one'—literally the text just says 'the holy'—'to be born will be called the Son of God.'

Now we are being told that this supernatural, eternal being will come into the world through a miraculous birth. And he will be called the Son of God—not merely because his character will bear a strong resemblance to God's, but because the very divine nature of God is going to be implanted in Mary in physical form. And, therefore, the one to be born will be perfectly holy, absolutely sinless, and will live forever as a both divine and human person. It is an utterly astounding statement. And an elegant and concise summary of what has come to be called the doctrine of the incarnation—that God became incarnate when the Son of God assumed a human nature and was born, in the flesh, into the world.

Encounters with Jesus

The importance of honest doubts

'How will this be,' Mary asked the angel, 'since I am a virgin?'

Luke 1:34

Mary ... express[es] her doubts openly. She says to the angel, 'How will this be, since I am a virgin?' ... Mary is not credulous. She doesn't say, 'Well, you're an angel and this is all miraculous. So I'll just accept it.' No, she says something any rational person would say. How can she have a child if she isn't having sex? This is an openly expressed doubt—to an angel! That shows a willingness to be honest about her uncertainties and questions.

Now, I would say there are two kinds of doubts: dishonest doubts and honest doubts. Dishonest doubts are both proud and cowardly; they show disdain and laziness. A dishonest doubt is to say, 'What a crazy idea!' and then just walk away. 'That's impossible' (or its more contemporary version, 'That's stupid') is an assertion, not an argument. It's a way of getting out of the hard work of thinking. But by contrast, honest doubts are humble, because they lead you to ask questions, not just put up a wall. And when you ask a real question, it makes you somewhat vulnerable. Mary's question to the angel actually asks for information and leaves her open to the possibility of a good answer that would cause her to shift her views. Honest doubts, then, are open to belief. If you are really asking for information and good arguments, you might get some.

And here's what I find wonderful. If she had never expressed a doubt, the angel would never have spoken one of the great statements in the Bible: 'Nothing will be impossible with God' (Luke 1:37 ESV).

Encounters with Jesus

Be it unto me according to thy word

'I am the Lord's servant,' Mary answered. 'May your word to me be fulfilled.' Then the angel left her.

Luke 1:38

After [Mary] hears 'Nothing will be impossible with God,' she makes her move. Actually, 'Nothing will be impossible with God' is a good argument. Do you believe in God, Mary? Yes. Well, if there is a God who created the world, who delivered your people and protected them for centuries, why couldn't he do this? And that made sense to her. And so Mary says, 'I am the Lord's servant, may it be to me as you have said' (Luke 1:38). That is a modern translation, but I prefer the elegance of the old King James Version, which says, 'Behold the handmaid of the Lord; be it unto me according to thy word.' [. . .]

In some fashion you have to say what Mary said when you give your life to Christ. Your heart must say something like this: 'I do not know all that you are going to ask of me, Lord. But I'll do whatever you say in your Word, whether I like it or not, and I'll accept patiently whatever you send into my life, whether I understand it or not.' In other words, you simply cannot know ahead of time all the things God will be asking you to do.

For example, most know that the Bible says we should not lie or cheat. But we may come to a place where telling the truth will cost us our career and telling a lie will save it. And thus following Christ will cost you dearly. [. . .] So you must simply say, 'I do not know all that is going to come, but one thing I know—I give up the right to decide whether or not I will do God's will. I will do it unconditionally.'

Encounters with Jesus

Courage to be with him

Because Joseph her husband was faithful to the law, and yet did not want to expose her to public disgrace, he had in mind to divorce her quietly. But after he had considered this, an angel of the Lord appeared to him in a dream and said, 'Joseph son of David, do not be afraid to take Mary home as your wife, because what is conceived in her is from the Holy Spirit.

Matthew 1:19–20

Luke 1 gives us Mary's perspective on the annunciation, while Matthew 1 gives us Joseph's. When Joseph discovered Mary was pregnant, and he knew that he was not the father, he decided to break off the engagement. But an angel appeared and gave Joseph his own message from God—he was to marry her anyway. Now, Joseph knew that if he married her, then everybody in their small town, in their shame-and-honor society, would know that the child had been conceived out of wedlock. They knew how to read a calendar. In fact, most of Mary's friends would discern she was pregnant before the wedding. Sooner or later, everyone would know that either they had sex before marriage or she was unfaithful to him, and in either case they would have violated the moral and social norms of that culture. They would forever be second-class citizens within their society. They and their children would be shunned by some, always suspected by everyone else.

So what did it mean for Joseph and Mary to accept the Word of the Lord, to say, 'We embrace the call to receive this child. We will accept whatever comes with it'? What did it take for them to literally have 'God with us' in their midst (Matt. 1:23)? What does it take to be *with him*? This text's answer is *courage*. And a willingness to do his will, no matter what.

Encounters with Jesus

The virgin birth

'Joseph son of David, do not be afraid to take Mary home as your wife, because what is conceived in her is from the Holy Spirit.'

Matthew 1:20

There are several ways that Matthew drives home the core Christmas message that Jesus is not simply a great teacher or even some angelic being but the divine God himself. In verse 20 the angel tells Joseph that the human life growing inside Mary has come not from any human being but from the heavenly Father. So Joseph learns that he will be Jesus' father only in a secondary sense. Mary is pregnant by the Holy Spirit. God is the real father.

However, the most direct statement of Jesus' identity comes in verse 23. There Matthew quotes from Isaiah 7:14, 'The virgin will conceive and give birth to a son, and will call him Immanuel,' which means 'God with us.' For centuries Jewish religious leaders and scholars had known that prophecy, but they had not thought it should be taken literally. They believed it was predicting the coming of some great leader through whose work, figuratively speaking, God would be present with his people.

But Matthew is saying this promise is greater than anyone imagined. It came true not figuratively but literally. Jesus Christ is 'God with us' because the human life growing in the womb of Mary was a miracle performed by God himself. This child is literally God.

Hidden Christmas

Hear well

And there were shepherds living out in the fields nearby, keeping watch over their flocks at night. An angel of the Lord appeared to them, and the glory of the Lord shone around them, and they were terrified.

Luke 2:8–9

At Christmas pageants each year thousands of children put on bathrobes to act the part of shepherds. We are accustomed to associating shepherds with the birth of Christ, but what are they doing there? What role do they play? Unfortunately, the meaning of the shepherds has become merely sentimental. In our imaginations they evoke lovely pastoral scenes and fluffy little lambs. But that is not why Luke selected this event out of the many others that he could have given us about the birth of Christ. He was trying to teach us something. The shepherds, like Mary, were given an angelic message. In response they listened well, overcame their fears, and went out into the world carrying the joyful news to others. [...]

The shepherds heard about Jesus from the angels and went to see him for themselves (Luke 2:15). Then the shepherds 'spread the word' (verse 17). They conveyed to others what the angels had told them and added their own eyewitness testimony to the message (verse 17). The result was that people who heard the shepherds were 'amazed,' but we are not told that they were led to believe. The message had a more powerful effect on the shepherds, however, who 'returned, glorifying and praising God for all the things they had heard' (verse 20).

Hidden Christmas

Fear not

But the angel said to them, 'Do not be afraid. I bring you good news that will cause great joy for all the people. Today in the town of David a Saviour has been born to you; he is the Messiah, the Lord.'

Luke 2:10–11

The older translations say, 'Fear not, for behold, I bring you good tidings.' The modern translations usually skip the term 'behold,' considering it an English archaism, but there really is a corresponding Greek word there in the biblical text. The angel literally says, 'Do not be fearing. *Be perceiving*. For I am telling you the gospel.' This is the principle—behold and you won't be afraid. If you take time to comprehend (behold) what is in the gospel message, it will remove the fear that has dominated and darkened your life. To the degree you truly *behold*—gaze at, grasp, relish, internalize, rejoice in—the gospel, to that degree the fears of your life will be undermined.

What is this gospel, this good news, at which we must gaze? *A Savior is born*. If you want to get over your fear of rejection and failure and be filled with his love, if you want to be completely forgiven and lay down the melancholy burden of self-justification, you have to rest in him as your Savior. [. . .]

And what about the greatest fear we have—of surrendering control? How can we trust him with our lives? The answer is that the little baby in the manger is the mighty *Christ the Lord*. So think, perceive, ponder. If the omnipotent Son of God would radically lose control—all for you—then you can trust him. And that should undermine your fear. [. . .]

Look! Won't you trust somebody who did all that for you? The angel is saying: 'You want relief from all your fear? *Behold!* Look at Christmas. Look at what he did.' And to the degree you behold it, and grasp it, and treasure and ponder it in your heart, to that degree those fears will start to diminish. *Fear not! Behold!*

Hidden Christmas

Treasuring up in our hearts

But Mary treasured up all these things and pondered them in her heart.
Luke 2:19

[Mary] not only pondered but also 'treasured' what she heard. This expression has more to do with the emotions and the heart. It means to keep something alive or to savor. Mary doesn't just try to understand the Word of God cognitively. She takes it all the way inside, as it were, to relish and experience it. The treasuring is not so much a technique as an attitude.

The Bible elsewhere speaks of this: 'I have hidden your word in my heart' (Ps. 119:11). Taking the message into my heart means not just to interpret it but to let it affect me deeply. It means, in a sense, preaching to myself, reminding myself of the preciousness, the value, the wonder, and the power of the particular truth I am treasuring. It is to ask myself questions: 'How would my life be different if I *really* believed this from the bottom of my heart? How would it change my thinking, feelings, actions? How would it change my relationships? How would it change my prayer life, my feelings and attitude toward God?'

If you don't do both of these things—ponder and treasure the Word of God—you will not truly hear the message. Your ears will hear it but not your mind and heart. It won't sink in, comfort, convict, or change you.

Hidden Christmas

357

The greatest hope

'She will give birth to a son, and you are to give him the name Jesus, because he will save his people from their sins.'

Matthew 1:21

The claim that Jesus is God also gives us the greatest possible hope. This means that our world is not all there is, that there is life and love after death, and that evil and suffering will one day end. And it means not just hope for the world, despite all its unending problems, but hope for you and me, despite all our unending failings. A God who was *only* holy would not have come down to us in Jesus Christ. He would have simply demanded that we pull ourselves together, that we be moral and holy enough to merit a relationship with him. A deity that was an 'all-accepting God of love' would not have needed to come to Earth either. This God of the modern imagination would have just overlooked sin and evil and embraced us. Neither the God of moralism nor the God of relativism would have bothered with Christmas.

The biblical God, however, is infinitely holy, so our sin could not be shrugged off. It had to be dealt with. He is also infinitely loving. He knows we could never climb up to him, so he has come down to us. God had to come himself and do what we couldn't do. He doesn't send someone; he doesn't send a committee report or a preacher to tell you how to save yourself. He comes himself to fetch us.

Christmas means, then, that for you and me there is all the hope in the world.

Hidden Christmas

One of us

... he made himself nothing by taking the very nature of a servant, being made in human likeness.

Philippians 2:7

Jesus is also one of *us*—he is human. The doctrine of Christmas, of the incarnation, is that Jesus was truly and fully God *and* truly and fully human. [...] The incarnation is *the* universe-sundering, history-altering, life-transforming, paradigm-shattering event of history.

However, from such a lofty height of this truth we must ask—what difference does it make to the way we actually live that God has become fully human?

Christians have historically understood passages such as Philippians 2:5–11 as teaching that when the Son of God became human he did not lay aside his deity. He was still God, but he emptied himself of his *glory*—of his divine prerogatives. He became vulnerable and ordinary; he lost his power and his beauty. 'He had no beauty or majesty to attract us to him ... that we should desire him' (Isa. 53:2). David and Moses speak of the beauty and glory of God. Yet Isaiah indicates that the incarnate Messiah did not have even a human attractiveness or beauty.

What does that mean to Christians, whom Paul calls to imitate the incarnation in their own lives (Phil. 2:5)? It means that Christians should never be starry-eyed about glamour. [...]

The fact that God became human and emptied himself of his glory means you should not want to hang out only with the people with power and glitz, who are networked and can open doors for you. You need to be willing to go to the people without power, without beauty, without money. That is the Christmas spirit, because God became one of us.

Hidden Christmas

Forgive on the spot

'And when you stand praying, if you hold anything against anyone, forgive them, so that your Father in heaven may forgive you your sins.'

Mark 11:25

[This is the first of two directives] Jesus gives [...] regarding forgiveness that at first sight appear contradictory. Taken together they are crucial for understanding how forgiveness actually works. It was customary to pray standing up (1 Kings 8:14,22; Nehemiah 9:4; Psalm 134:1; Luke 18:11,13). If you are praying and you realize or remember that you are holding something against someone, you must forgive them on the spot. Scholars point out that 'forgive them' (*aphiete*) is in the present tense of the imperative for the strongest possible emphasis.[113]

Jesus adds, 'so that your Father in heaven may forgive you your sins' (Mark 11:25). Again we should remember that this cannot mean that God's forgiveness is merited by ours. Rather, it means that to be unforgiving reveals that you have failed to understand and accept God's unmerited grace yourself. Perhaps you thought that your contrition and reparations before God earned his favor. You may have made your remorse and shame into a kind of 'good work' that (you thought) put God in your debt. The telltale sign that you have done something like this, rather than actually receiving God's unmerited forgiveness and mercy, is the inability to forgive others. The humility that comes from admitting your lostness *and* the joy that comes from knowing your acceptance in Christ are simply absent.

Without the humility that sees yourself as equally deserving of condemnation, and without the joy of knowing your standing in Christ's love, it will be impossible to give up your desire for revenge. [...] Jesus' point: if you realize you have not forgiven someone, do it right away.

Forgive

Confront and forgive

'If your brother or sister sins against you, rebuke them; and if they repent, forgive them. Even if they sin against you seven times in a day and seven times come back to you saying "I repent," you must forgive them.'

Luke 17:3–4

[Yesterday's] text taken alone would support [a] 'cheap grace' model of forgiveness, which puts all the emphasis on the wronged person banishing their anger and with no provision for change in the perpetrator. But this call to forgive on the spot—as you are praying—seems to contradict [this] statement by Jesus in Luke.

There are two responsibilities set forth here. First, if someone sins *against you*—rebuke them. This does not say that we must correct any sin we see anyone doing. Galatians 6:1 and 1 Thessalonians 5:14 give some direction here (more about this later), but this verse is not speaking of sin in general. Jesus says if someone sins against *you*, you are to 'rebuke,' a word that means to confront. But if they repent, your second responsibility is to forgive.

From this text we learn, first, that the responsibilities to confront and to forgive are equally laid on us. The reality of human temperament is that few can sustain such a balance without the help of the Holy Spirit. People are prone to be either more ready to confront and challenge than to forgive or more ready to forgive and forget than to challenge. We also learn here that the repentance Jesus speaks of might happen 'seven times in a day.' We should not think that Jesus is saying that this is a likely scenario. But what he is saying is that we should not require the perpetrator's repentance to be a long, drawn-out, self-flagellating affair. We should not forgive slowly or begrudgingly.

Forgive

Two aspects of forgiveness

See to it that no one falls short of the grace of God and that no bitter root grows up to cause trouble and defile many.

Hebrews 12:15

How can these two directives both be true? The answer is that the word *forgiveness* is being used in two somewhat different ways. In Mark 11 'forgive them' means inwardly being willing to not avenge oneself. In Luke 17 'forgive them' means 'reconcile to them.' There is, then, a kind of forgiveness that ends up being inward only and another kind that issues outwardly toward a possible restored relationship (cf. Matthew 5:24—'be reconciled to your brother,' ESV; Matthew 18:15—'If your brother sins against you, go and tell him his fault, between you and him alone. If he listens to you, you have gained your brother,' ESV). The victim of the wrongdoing in either case must forgive inwardly, while reconciliation depends on whether the perpetrator recognizes his wrongdoing and repents or does not. Some have called one of these 'attitudinal forgiveness' and the other 'reconciled forgiveness.'[114]

These are not two kinds of forgiveness but two aspects or stages of it. One could say that the first must always happen, and the second may happen but is not always possible. Attitudinal forgiveness can occur without reconciliation, but reconciliation cannot happen unless attitudinal forgiveness has already occurred. If the victim in Luke 17 has not personally forgiven, why would they be open to reconciliation? For a victim to be open to reconciling, they must have already done some kind of forgiveness in their heart. An unwillingness to repent on the part of the perpetrator is no excuse for ongoing bitterness, something that the Bible says will inevitably poison the soul (Hebrews 12:15).

Forgive

Love your enemies

*But I tell you, love your enemies and pray for those who persecute you,
that you may be children of your Father in heaven. He causes his sun
to rise on the evil and the good, and sends rain on the righteous and
the unrighteous.*

Matthew 5:44–5

'Y ou have heard that it was said' that you should 'love your
neighbor' (a quote of Leviticus 19:18) 'and hate your enemy.'
People, of course, interpreted the word *neighbor* to mean only your
own people—your own nation and religion. Outsiders were not
covered—they were not considered neighbors. The directive to
love one's neighbor applied only to those of the same race and
religion in that thinking.

But now Jesus says that is *not* the way to read the command to
'love your neighbor.' Elsewhere, in the parable of the Good
Samaritan (Luke 10:25–37), he teaches that one's neighbor is anyone
at all. The 'good neighbor' of the parable gives costly and risky help
to a man of a different religion and different nationality. Here in the
Sermon on the Mount, however, Jesus makes this explicit.

He makes clear that Christians are to show love rather than
hate to all people, even those of other religions and races. He
explicitly tells his disciples not to only greet 'brothers,' their own
people. Since the traditional greeting was often an embrace and
the word *shalom*, a word that means full flourishing and peace,
Jesus is saying that we cannot confine our commitment to the
good of others to our own tribe and people, not even to the
community of Christian believers. We are to open our arms and
hearts to the 'Other'—those religiously, racially, morally, and polit-
ically different from us. And we are to will their *shalom*.

Forgive

Union with Christ

Don't you know that all of us who were baptised into Christ Jesus were baptised into his death? We were therefore buried with him through baptism into death in order that, just as Christ was raised from the dead through the glory of the Father, we too may live a new life.

Romans 6:3–4

[. . . E]ven if we initially accept the fact of God's forgiveness and acceptance, we need to spend the rest of our lives deepening our understanding of it and refreshing our experience of it.

One way [. . .] to grow in your experience of God's forgiveness is to continually go deeper in the study of the various doctrines that are the basis for it. [. . .]

Perhaps the single most comprehensive biblical theme that encompasses all these blessings is the idea that when we believe in him we are united with him, both legally and vitally, in his life and death (Rom. 6:1–4) and his ascension (Eph. 2:6). What can it mean that we died with him or that we are seated in the heavenly places *now* with him? As the hymn says, 'I scarce can take it in.'

We are so united in Christ in the Father's eyes that when he sees us, he sees Jesus. Christians are so one with Christ that we are as forgiven as if *we* had already died for our sins, as if we had already been raised. We are so one with Christ that when the Father sees us, he treats us as if we deserve all the glory and honor that Jesus deserves. Over 160 times in the New Testament, Paul speaks of our being 'in Christ' or 'in him.' He calls himself 'a man in Christ' (2 Cor. 12:2). It utterly dominated Paul's self-understanding and it must dominate ours.

Forgive

Forward in love

A woman in that town who lived a sinful life learned that Jesus was eating at the Pharisee's house, so she came there with an alabaster jar of perfume. As she stood behind him at his feet weeping, she began to wet his feet with her tears. Then she wiped them with her hair, kissed them and poured perfume on them.

Luke 7:37–8

In Luke 7 Jesus was eating in the courtyard of the home of Simon the Pharisee when 'a woman of the city' approached him. The term was a euphemism for a sex worker. She knelt at Jesus' feet weeping and anointing them in an act of devotion. Simon recognized her as a 'sinner' and was amazed that Jesus accepted her public expressions of love rather than recoiling from her. Jesus responded with a parable of two debtors—one who owed ten times more than the other—who were both forgiven their debts by their lender. 'Which of them will love him more?' Jesus asked Simon (Luke 7:40–2). He got the obvious answer—the one who was forgiven more. [...]

The prophet Micah says God will 'tread our sins underfoot' and 'hurl all our iniquities into the depths of the sea' (Micah 7:19). The famous Dutch writer Corrie ten Boom would often say that when God throws our sins into the deepest sea, he puts up a sign: 'No fishing!' God has dealt with your sins. Don't go back to them to feel guilty about them all over. Go forward in love.[115]

Forgive

Endnotes

1 Debra Rienstra, *So Much More: An Invitation to Christian Spirituality* (Jossey-Bass, 2005), p. 41.

2 Flannery O'Connor, *Wise Blood: Three by Flannery O'Connor* (Signet, 1962), p. 16.

3 Rienstra, *So Much More,* p. 38.

4 Rebecca Pippert, *Hope Has Its Reasons* (Harper, 1990), Chapter 4, 'What Kind of God Gets Angry?'

5 Martin Luther, *A Commentary on St. Paul's Epistle to the Galatians* (James Clarke, 1953), p. 101.

6 Bruce K. Walke, *A Commentary on Micah* (Grand Rapids, MI: Eerdmans, 2007), p. 394.

7 Howard Peskett and Vinoth Ramachandra, *The Message of Mission: The Glory of Christ in All Time and Space* (Downers Grove, Ill.: InterVarsity Press, 2003), p. 113.

8 See D. A. Carson, *The Gospel According to John* (Leicester, UK: InterVarsity Press, 1991), p. 227

9 Stanley Hauerwas, 'Sex and Politics: Betrand Russell and "Human Sexuality,"' *Christian Century*, April 19, 1978, 417-22.

10 A Latin term meaning 'to be curved inward on oneself', used by Martin Luther to describe sinful human nature.

11 *Love in the Western World* (New York: Harper and Row, 1956), 300. Quoted in Diogenes Allen, *Love: Christian Romance, Marriage, Friendship* (Eugene, OR, Wipf and Stock, 2006), p. 96.

12 P. T. O'Brien, *The Letter to the Ephesians* (Grand Rapids, MI: Eerdmans, 1999), pp. 109–10.

13 Moshe Halbertal and Avishai Margalit, in *Idolatry* (Cambridge, Mass.: Harvard University Press, 1992), p. 10.

14 C. S. Lewis, *The Problem of Pain* (Harper, 2001), p. 91.

15 'How Firm a Foundation,' hymn by John Rippon, p. 1787.

16 Max Scheler, 'The Meaning of Suffering,' in *On Feeling, Knowing, and Valuing: Selected Writings*, ed. H. J. Bershady (University of Chicago Press, 1992), p. 111.

17 Ibid.

18 Aleksandr Solzhenitsyn, *The Gulag Archipelago 1918–1956* (Harper & Row, 1974).

19 Luc Ferry, *A Brief History of Thought: A Philosophical Guide to Living* (Harper, 2010), p. 63.

20 Quoted in Ronald K. Rittgers, *The Reformation of Suffering: Pastoral*

Theology and Lay Piety in Late Medieval and Early Modern Germany (Oxford University Press, 2012), p. 46.

21 Ambrose of Milan, *On the Death of Satyrus.* Quoted in Rittgers, *Reformation of Suffering,* pp. 43–4.

22 Aleksandr Solzhenitsyn, *The Gulag Archipelago* (New York: HarperCollins, 2002) p. 312.

23 'It Is Finished!', hymn by James Proctor.

24 J. K. Rowling, *Harry Potter and the Philosopher's Stone* (London: Bloomsbury, 1997), p. 216.

25 J. R. R. Tolkien, *The Letters of J. R. R. Tolkien*, ed. Humphrey Carpenter (1981), letter #121. Quoted at http://tolkien.cro.net/rings/sauron.html.

26 J. R. R. Tolkien, *The Return of the King* (New York: HarperCollins, 2004), pp. 1148–9.

27 Alvin Plantinga, 'Supralapsarianism, or "O Felix Culpa,"' in *Christian Faith and the Problem of Evil,* ed. Peter van Inwagen (Grand Rapids, MI: Eerdmans, 2004), p. 18.

28 For a good short summary of why we are all 'believers', see Christian Smith, 'Believing Animals', *Moral Believing Animals: Human Personhood and Culture* (Oxford University Press, 2003).

29 Miroslav Volf, 'Soft Difference: Theological Reflections on the Relation Between Church and Culture in 1 Peter', *Ex Auditu* 10 (1994): pp. 15–30.

30 See C. S. Lewis's appendix, 'Illustrations of the Tao' in *The Abolition of Man* (Macmillan, 1947).

31 See 'Christ's Agony', *The Works of Jonathan Edwards*, vol. 2, E. Hickman, ed. (Banner of Truth, 1972).

32 J. R. R. Tolkien, 'The Field of Cormallen', *The Return of the King* (various editions).

33 See Derek Kidner, *Psalms 1–72: An Introduction and Commentary* (Downers Grove, Ill.: InterVarsity Press, 1973), p. 161.

34 C. S. Lewis, *The Problem of Pain* (HarperOne, 2001), p. 157. Lewis is quoting George MacDonald.

35 Paul Ramsey, ed., *Ethical Writings: The Works of Jonathan Edwards*, vol. 8 (New Haven, CT: Yale University Press, 1989), pp. 403–536.

36 William G. T. Shedd, 'Introductory Essay' to Augustine's *On the Trinity*, in *A Select Library of the Nicene and Post-Nicene Fathers of the Christian Church*, ed. Philip Schaff, vol. 3 (Grand Rapids, MI: Eerdmans, 1979), p. 14.

37 J. Gresham Machen, *God Transcendent* (Carlisle, PA: Banner of Truth, 1982), 187–8.

38 Edmund P. Clowney in 'A Biblical Theology of Prayer,' in *Teach Us to Pray: Prayer in the Bible and the World*, ed. D. A. Carson (Eugene, OR: Wipf and Stock, 2002), p. 170.

39 Graeme Goldsworthy, *Prayer and the Knowledge of God* (Downers Grove, IL: InterVarsity, 2003), pp. 169–70.

40 See Irene Howat and John Nicholls, *Streets Paved with Gold: The Story of London City Mission* (Fearn, Scotland: Christian Focus, 2003).

41 Mishnah (Sanhedrin 10.5), quoted in J. Daniel Hays, *From Every People and Nation: A Biblical Theology of Race* (Downers Grove, Ill.: InterVarsity Press, 2003), p. 50n.

42 Ben Witherington, *Work: A Kingdom Perspective on Labor* (Grand Rapids, MI: Eerdmans, 2011), p. 2.

43 Derek Kidner, *Genesis: An Introduction and Commentary* (Downers Grove, Ill.: Inter-Varsity Press, 1967), p. 61.

44 Alec Motyer, *Look to the Rock: An Old Testament Background to Our Understanding of Christ* (Kregel, 1996), p. 71.

45 Alec Motyer, *The Prophecy of Isaiah* (Downers Grove, Ill.: Inter-Varsity Press, 1993), p. 235.

46 Roy Clements, *Faithful Living in an Unfaithful World* (Downers Grove, Ill: InterVarsity Press, 1998), p. 153.

47 Reinhold Niebuhr, *The Nature and Destiny of Man: Volume I, Human Nature* (New York: Scribner, 1964), p. 189.

48 David Clarkson, 'Soul Idolatry Excludes Men from Heaven,' in *The Practical Works of David Clarkson*, Volume II (Edinburgh: James Nichol, 1865), pp. 299ff.

49 Clarkson, 'Soul Idolatry', p. 311.

50 Douglas J. Moo, *The Epistle to the Romans* (Grand Rapids, MI.: Eerdmans, 1996), p. 110.

51 Martin Luther, *Treatise Concerning Good Works* (1520), Parts X, XI.

52 W. R. Forrester, *Christian Vocation* (Scribner, 1953), p. 129, quoted in Albert C. Wolters, *Creation Regained: A Transforming View of the World* (Grand Rapids, MI: Eerdmans, 1985), p. 44.

53 Quote from Kuyper's inaugural address at the dedication of the Free University. Found in *Abraham Kuyper: A Centennial Reader*, ed. James D. Bratt (Grand Rapids, MI: Eerdmans, 1998), p. 488.

54 D. Martyn Lloyd-Jones, *The Sons of God: An Exposition of Chapter 8:5–17* (Romans series) (Peabody, MA: Zondervan, 1974), pp. 275–399.

55 William H. Goold, ed., *The Works of John Owen,* vol. 9 (Carlisle, PA: Banner of Truth, 1967), p. 237.

56 John Murray, *Redemption: Accomplished and Applied* (Grand Rapids, MI: Eerdmans, 1955), pp. 169–70. Roman for emphasis is mine.

57 Austin Phelps, *The Still Hour: Or Communion with God* (Carlisle, PA: Banner of Truth, 1974), p. 9.

58 J. I. Packer, *Knowing God* (Downers Grove, IL: InterVarsity, 1993), pp. 39–40.

59 D. A. Carson, *The Gospel According to John*, Pillar New Testament Commentary series (Grand Rapids, MI: Eerdmans, 1991), pp. 496–7.

60 McNeill, *Calvin: Institutes*, 3.20.36., p. 899.

61 Martin Luther, "Personal Prayer Book," in *Luther's Works: Devotional Writings II*, ed. Gustav K. Wiencke, vol. 43 (Minneapolis: Fortress Press, 1968), 29.

62 Martin Luther, *Luther's Large Catechism*, trans. F. Samuel Janzow (St. Louis: Concordia, 1978), 84.

63 Augustine, Letter 130, trans. S. D. F. Salmond in *Nicene and Post-Nicene Fathers*, ed. Philip Schaff, chapter 12. (Buffalo, NY: Christian Literature Publishing Co., 1887). Revised and edited for New Advent by Kevin Knight. <http://www.newadvent.org/fathers/1102130.htm>.

64 Augustine, 'Our Lord's Sermon on the Mount,' trans. S. D. F. Salmond, in *Nicene and Post-Nicene Fathers,* ed. Philip Schaff, vol. 6, 1886 (Electronic edition, Veritatis Splendor, 2012), 156.

65 Calvin, John. *Institutes of the Christian Religion*. Edited by John T. McNeill. Vol. 2. (Louisville, KY: Westminster John Knox Press, 1960), 3.20.42., p. 905.

66 Luther, 'Personal Prayer Book,' p. 32.

67 Luther, 'Personal Prayer Book,' p. 33.

68 Augustine, Letter 130, in Schaff, *Nicene and Post-Nicene Fathers*, chapter 12.

69 McNeill, *Calvin: Institutes*, 3.20.44., pp. 907–8.

70 *Luther's Large Catechism*, p. 92.

71 *Luther's Large Catechism*, p. 93.

72 Augustine, 'Our Lord's Sermon on the Mount,' in Schaff, *Nicene and Post-Nicene Fathers*, p. 167.

73 McNeill, *Calvin: Institutes*, 3.20.46., p. 913.

74 McNeill, *Calvin: Institutes*, 3.20.46., p. 913.

75 *Luther's Large Catechism*, p. 96–7.

76 Augustine, Letter 130, in Schaff, *Nicene and Post-Nicene Fathers*, chapter 12. See also his 'Our Lord's Sermon on the Mount,' p. 171.

77 C. S. Lewis, *The Four Loves* (New York: Harcourt, 1960), p. 61.

78 Ibid., p. 62.

79 Peter Adam, *Speaking God's Words: A Practical Theology of Preaching* (Vancouver, British Columbia: Regent College Publishing, 1996), p. 59.

80 Ibid., p. 75.

81 Charles Spurgeon, 'Christ Precious to Believers' (sermon no. 242, March 13, 1859), in *The New Park Street Pulpit,* vol. 5 (repr., Pasadena, TX: Pilgrim Publications, 1975), p. 140.

82 Timothy Ward, *Words of Life: Scripture as the Living and Active Word of God* (Downers Grove, Ill.: InterVarsity Press, 2009), p. 25.

83 Ibid., p. 156.

84 The original author of this well-known quote is uncertain.

85 *Agatha Christie's Miss Marple: The Body in the Library* (originally broadcast on B in 1984), available at: www.youtube.com/watch?v=crds2h4a 3rk(28:00–29:20).

86 Gordon Wenham, *Genesis 1–15,* vol. 1, Word Biblical Commentary (Waco, Tex.: Word Books, 1987), p. 144.

87 Raymond C. Van Leeuwen, 'The Book of Proverbs', in *The New Interpreter's Bible*, vol. 5 (Nashville: Abingdon, 1997), p. 81.

88 Ibid., p. 185.

89 This translation of Psalm 36:1 was used by C. S. Lewis in his preface to *The Screwtape Letters* and *Screwtape Proposes a Toast* (1961). There is no consensus about this rendering (see T. Longman, *Psalms: An Introduction and Commentary*, Tyndale Old Testament Commentaries, vols. 15–16 (Downers Grove, Ill.: InterVarsity Press, 2014), p. 175.

90 Derek Kidner, *The Proverbs: An Introduction and Commentary* (Downers Grove, Ill.: InterVarsity Press, 1972), p. 104.

91 Van Leeuwen, 'Book of Proverbs,' p. 145.

92 Francis Schaeffer, *The Church Before the Watching World* (Downers Grove, IL: InterVarsity Press, 1971).

93 Jacques Ellul, *The Judgment of Jonah* (Grand Rapids, MI: Eerdmans, 1971), pp. 72–3.

94 James Bruckner, *The NIV Application Commentary: Jonah, Nahum, Habakkuk, Zephaniah* (Grand Rapids, MI: Zondervan, 2004), pp. 116 and 7n.

95 Wendell Berry, 'Sex, Economy, Freedom, and Community,' *Sex, Economy, Freedom, and Community* (New York: Pantheon, 1993), 119.

96 C. S. Lewis, *The Four Loves* (New York: HarperCollins, 2017), p. 157.

97 Sam Allberry, *Lifted: Experiencing the Resurrection Life* (Phillipsburg, NJ: Presbyterian and Reformed, 2012), pp. 15–16.

98 Christopher Watkin, *Michel Foucault* (Phillipsburg, NJ: Presbyterian and Reformed, 2018), p. 81.

99 John Polkinghorne, *The Faith of a Physicist* (Princeton, NJ: Princeton University Press, 2016), p. 115.

100 N. T. Wright, *The Resurrection of the Son of God: Christian Origins and the Question of God,* vol. 3 (Minneapolis: Fortress Press, 2003), p. 605.

101 From 'Preface to the Complete Edition of Luther's Latin Writings (1595),' in Timothy F. Lull and William R. Russell, eds, *Martin Luther's Basic Theological Writings,* 3rd edition (Fortress Press, 2012), p. 497.

102 This portion of the Talmud can be found at www.sefaria.org/Yoma.86b?lang=bi.

103 R. T. France, *The Gospel of Matthew* (Grand Rapids, MI: Eerdmans, 2007), p. 705.

104 C. S. Lewis, 'The Invasion' in *Mere Christianity* (New York: MacMillan, 1958), p. 56.

105 I have modernized the language of these questions. The original questions can be found in William Williams, *The Experience Meeting* (Vancouver, BC: Regent College Publishing, 2003), pp. 34–6, 39–41.

106 D. Martyn Lloyd-Jones, *God's Ultimate Purpose: An Exposition of Ephesians 1:1 to 23* (Grand Rapids, MI: Baker Book House, 1978), p. 71.

107 John R. W. Stott, *The Cross of Christ* (Downers Grove, IL: InterVarsity Press, 1986), p. 160.

108 Gerhard Kittel, Gerhard Friedrich, and Geoffrey William Bromiley, *Theological Dictionary of the New Testament* (Grand Rapids, MI: Eerdmans, 1985), p. 231.

109 J. R. R. Tolkien, *The Return of the King* (1955; repr., New York: HarperCollins, 2004), pp. 1148–9.

110 William L. Lane, Word Biblical Commentary *Hebrews 1–8,* vol. 47 (Dallas, TX: Word Books, 1991), pp. 55–8.

111 Margaret N. Barnhouse, *That Man Barnhouse* (Carol Stream, IL: Tyndale House, 1983), p. 186.

112 See Jonathan Edwards, 'Sermon Fifteen: Heaven Is a World of Love,' in *The Works of Jonathan Edwards*, WJE Online, Jonathan Edwards Center, Yale University,

113 Robert H. Gundry, *Mark: A Commentary on His Apology for the Cross*, vol. 2 (Grand Rapids, MI: Eerdmans, 1993), 649.

114 I am here borrowing terms from two writers who make the same formulation of two aspects of forgiveness, David Powlison, *Good and Angry: Redeeming Anger, Irritation, Complaining, and Bitterness* (Greensboro, NC: New Growth Press, 2016), pp. 84–7, and D. A. Carson, *Love in Hard Places* (Wheaton, IL: Crossway Books, 2002), p. 82.

115 R. T. France, *The Gospel of Matthew*, The New International Commentary on the New Testament (Grand Rapids, MI: Eerdmans, 2007), p. 224.

HODDER &
STOUGHTON

Hodder & Stoughton is the UK's
leading Christian publisher,
with a wide range of books from
the bestselling authors in the UK
and around the world ranging from
Christian lifestyle and theology to
apologetics, testimony and fiction.
We also publish the world's
most popular Bible translation
in modern English, the New
International Version, renowned
for its accuracy and readability.

Hodderfaith.com   Hodderbibles.co.uk
@HodderFaith   /HodderFaith